"MONEY BEING MADE HAND OVER FIST, STOCKS, GREENMAILING, OR CORPORATE RAIDERS ARE NOT WHAT COMES TO MIND WHEN ONE THINKS OF *THE NEW YORKER* . . . BUT HERE'S A BOOK THAT ZEROES IN ON THE BUSINESS END WHILE TOUCHING ON THE EDITORIAL WORKINGS OF THIS EXALTED MAGAZINE . . . MAHON PRESENTS AN ABSORBING ACCOUNT OF THE EVENTS LEADING UP TO THE PURPORTED LAST DAYS."

—*Library Journal*

"FULL OF WELL-CHOSEN DETAILS AND REVEALING PORTRAITS, MAHON'S CHRONICLE IS ENTERTAINING THROUGHOUT."

—*Kirkus Reviews*

GIGI MAHON is the author of *The Company That Bought the Boardwalk: A Reporter's Story of Resorts International*. She writes regularly for *New York* Magazine and was formerly a senior editor at *Barron's*.

The Last Days Of

THE NEW YORKER

Gigi Mahon

A PLUME BOOK

NEW AMERICAN LIBRARY

A DIVISION OF PENGUIN BOOKS USA INC., NEW YORK
PUBLISHED IN CANADA BY
PENGUIN BOOKS CANADA LIMITED, MARKHAM, ONTARIO

Published by arrangement with McGraw-Hill Publishing Company.

 PLUME TRADEMARK REG. U.S. PAT. OFF. AND FOREIGN COUNTRIES
REGISTERED TRADEMARK—MARCA REGISTRADA
HECHO EN DRESDEN, TN, U.S.A.

SIGNET, SIGNET CLASSIC, MENTOR, ONYX, PLUME, MERIDIAN
and NAL BOOKS are published *in the United States* by
New American Library, a division of Penguin Books USA Inc.,
1633 Broadway, New York, New York 10019,
in Canada by Penguin Books Canada Limited,
2801 John Street, Markham, Ontario L3R 1B4

Library of Congress Cataloging-in-Publication Data

Mahon, Gigi.
  The last days of The New Yorker.

  Reprint. Originally published: New York : McGraw-Hill, c1988.
  Bibliography: p.
  Includes index.
  1. New Yorker (New York, N.Y. : 1925)—History. 2. Publishers and
publishing—New York (N.Y.) 3. Consolidation and merger of corporations—
New York (N.Y.) 4. New York (N.Y.)—Intellectual life—20th century.
I. Title.
[PN4900.N35M34   1988b]   051   89-12393
ISBN 0-452-26322-0

Original hardcover edition designed by Patrice Fodero

First Plume Printing, December, 1989

1 2 3 4 5 6 7 8 9

To my parents,
Monica and Jim Mahon

Acknowledgments

It has been an interesting experience writing about *The New Yorker*, and I intend a note of irony. It is a subject that many people, most of them inside the editorial department at the magazine, believe should not be touched. "I know what you're doing and I don't approve of it" one editor told me, echoing the sentiments of many. The reaction was predictable because the idea that *The New Yorker* is somehow holy and exempt from scrutiny has prevailed for decades.

New Yorker editors and writers fumed when *Fortune* carried a lengthy report on their weekly in 1934 and they fumed still more thirty years later when Tom Wolfe penned a stinging piece in an early incarnation of *New York* magazine. Then–*New Yorker* editor William Shawn tried to have the latter piece suppressed, and it still caused him to bristle with anger twenty years after the fact. Nor is it just the works of outsiders that elicit objections. Books by staff members are discouraged as well. Those that appeared anyway, such as James Thurber's *The Years with Ross*, published in 1957, and Brendan Gill's *Here at The New Yorker*,

ACKNOWLEDGMENTS

published in 1975, were roundly criticized internally. I will not try to delve here into the collective psyche of *New Yorker* editorial staff to search for reasons for their reticence. Anyway, it would be a futile effort, since the most frequently proferred one is: "It's the way Mr. Shawn wants it." I cannot help, though, but express my obviously unshared discontent with the notion that people who depend for their livelihood upon going out and interviewing and reporting on others can find it beneath their dignity to be the donors of information.

In a like vein, S. I. Newhouse, a publisher who figures in this book and whose company has made billions out of the research and reporting efforts of the newspaper and magazine writers he employs, himself habitually refuses to give interviews. "I'm going to let you struggle along on your own," he told me when I approached him for an interview. Not content to stop there, he cautioned others among his executives and lawyers to do the same. Luckily for me, many did not heed his caution. Obviously, Mr. Newhouse does not embrace the philosophy of the late Henry Luce who, when advised by an executive not to give an interview to, appropriately enough, a *New Yorker* writer, replied that it was his responsibility as a publisher to cooperate. He could not send his reporters out to interview others and then stonewall writers who came calling on him.

A theme that runs through this book regards the traditional conflict in publishing between business and editorial. In stereotype, writers are communicators while businessmen and businesswomen are dour and secretive withholders of facts. In this case, the vast majority of businesspeople I approached were extremely helpful and gave generously of their time and information. Many were almost compulsive in their desire to tell the whole story, even when parts of it reflected badly on them. They also provided me with letters, notes, tapes, minutes of meetings, and a wealth of other such information. They would just as soon not

viii

ACKNOWLEDGMENTS

be singled out for thanks, but they know who they are and I am grateful to them.

I am also grateful to the *New Yorker* editors and writers who, against "party" policy, spoke to me, often at great length and on repeated occasions. I have been very concerned throughout this endeavor that the editorial department's side of the story be fairly presented.

Thanks, too, to Gladys Justin Carr, vice president and publisher, and Tom Miller, senior editor, at McGraw-Hill. *Very* special thanks to the most supportive agents in publishing, Molly Friedrich and Aaron Priest.

Finally, a loving thank you to my husband, Tom Theobald, who may not have known what he was getting into when he married a writer, but who has been supportive, nurturing, flexible, and dear beyond all reasonable expectations!

The Last Days Of

THE NEW YORKER

Prologue

When you enter 25 West Forty-third Street, the building that houses the offices of *The New Yorker*, you do so with the confidence that comes from moving through the world knowing not just where you are in place, but where you are in time. When you ride the elevator and exit on the nineteenth floor, the confidence crumbles. The overwhelming impression there is one of ages gone by. You have stepped into another decade. Perhaps the year is 1930, or maybe 1955. It is *not* 1988.

A receptionist sits in a booth behind a sliding glass window such as one finds in some dentists' offices. The small waiting area she guards is neither welcoming nor fashionable (fashionable lobbies are for *mass* market magazines) but rather resembles the set of a Sam Spade mystery. It is barely functional. The suite of furniture consists of two aged but not antique brown wooden chairs, a round brass tray-type table, and a small end table on which perches a large nondescript lamp. The cord from the lamp runs upward to an outlet almost in the middle of the wall. The chairs are often not functional, since they are frequently piled high with envelopes and other assorted papers.

Beyond the lobby lie narrow corridors, the walls of which are painted a color that hasn't the conviction to be either green or white. They appear dirty, owing in part to the pencil tracks that run horizontally along them, the residues of generations of ruminating writers who have paced back and forth, back and forth, dragging their implements as they went. The halls open onto small, boxy offices, each one numbered, some misshapen, having been carved out of once larger spaces in an effort to squeeze in more writers. Most boast a single window. The desks look like the original standard issue, ordered in bulk, no doubt, from some office supply store that has long since ceased to exist. A couch is crammed into any space remotely roomy enough to accommodate it.

Raoul Fleischmann, who helped Harold Ross found *The New Yorker* in 1925, caused the couches to be placed there. Fleischmann was a believer in afternoon naps, indulged in them himself, and encouraged the practice among businessmen and writers alike.

The office doors are often closed, either because writers and editors are toiling in solitude or because they are not there, having chosen to go off and ply their trade in places like Cape Cod or Sag Harbor, Long Island, or the Adirondack Mountains, or even Brazil or Beirut. When they are there, it is not that congenial a place and never has been. Whistling in the halls is, by tradition, forbidden. There is no merry jawing around the water cooler, although there is a water cooler, not a water fountain. It is not unheard of for writers to work in ignorance of the name of the fellow in the next office. Perhaps they have never even laid eyes on the fellow in the next office. On a writer or editor's first day of work, no superefficient personnel employee leads him or her on a round of introductions. That is the way it is and always has been.

At a place where tradition is preserved for the sake of tradition, events that might seem natural or evolutionary elsewhere take on monumental proportions. At *The New Yorker*, the event is this: In a corner office, an editor in shirtsleeves toils. It seems commonplace, unexceptional in the extreme, yet much has been made of those shirtsleeves. Photographers capture them, newspapers interpret them, writers and artists fear them. At any other institution, they would represent little more than comfort, but this is *The New Yorker*, and here they represent change.

The man is Robert Gottlieb, and he is not supposed to be here. He has recently arrived from a book house—albeit the high-minded Knopf—and he and his sleeves and sweaters and sneakers weren't in the script that had been neatly unfolding at *The New Yorker* for half a century. Someone has lopped off the old ending and tacked on a new one. Once there was a magazine, this tale of literary Camelot begins, that had achieved what no other could—the supreme and sublime dominance of writers and artists over accountants and admen, the subordination of business to editorial. Then suddenly there was Gottlieb, and even though he is an editor, he is also emblematic of the victory of commerce. S. I. Newhouse, new owner and businessman, put him there.

Gottlieb is only the third editor in the long history. First the magazine was Harold Ross's *New Yorker*, and then it became William Shawn's, and for all of the speculation about who would come next, no one ever conjured up the phrase "Gottlieb's *New Yorker*." He was, after all, an outsider. Furthermore, it had not dawned on most people that S. I. Newhouse alone would make the decision, especially since he had promised otherwise. They forgot that now it was Newhouse's *New Yorker*.

There is danger in making too much of it. After all, we live in a world where takeovers occur daily. Steel companies, banks, and stores are sold to the highest bidder. Our society operates on the principle that the one who owns it, controls it. The sports pages provide ample proof that Yankee owner George Steinbrenner can hire and fire any manager he pleases as often as he pleases. Why should *The New Yorker* be different? Its writers and editors have a ready answer to the question: Because it *is* different, they declare. "This isn't a magazine!" Harold Ross once proclaimed to a writer. "It's a movement!"

"We know we're precious," says a current writer, using that word as in the third dictionary definition of "affectedly refined." "That's what made the magazine special. That's why everyone pays so much attention to what happens here. If we weren't different, *The New Yorker* would never have become the magazine it did."

He is certainly correct that attention was paid. *New Yorker* watching has been a favorite pastime throughout the six decades of the magazine's existence. The weekly has been the center focus of thousands of newspaper and magazine articles and scores of books. For twenty years, the literary world found few topics more riveting than that of who would succeed William Shawn. Even widely circulated magazines like *Newsweek* and *Time* deemed it of enough interest to their readers to provide regular updates. But all of that emphasis on editorial served as a kind of unconscious and unintended diversionary tactic, for the real drama in the last few years was played out on another front: in the executive offices and the boardrooms, where a battle for control was being waged. In their quest for independence, the editors built a wall, forgetting that walls obscure in both directions. The writers weren't just "precious," they were naive. The power always rested in the hands of businessmen. It was dormant, but it was there.

The New Yorker does not have an exclusive on such rude awakenings, and in fact, they seem to be cropping up with increasing frequency in today's "media" world. CBS comes to mind. In the fall of 1986, in the midst of an executive power struggle, the conglomerate's board convened. One director, Walter Cronkite, was in the minority among boardmembers in that he was a *news*man, not a *business*man. After the board meeting, according to the *New York Times*, Cronkite repaired to a party-in-progress honoring "60 Minutes" correspondent Mike Wallace and his new bride. The revelers gathered about Cronkite, eager to learn what had transpired at the directors' session.

"I was terribly impressed with the board," Cronkite told them, with what seemed to be amazement. "I didn't know that business-people were so good."

Just as businessmen often dismiss creative people as wacky or childish, so, too, is there a tendency among creative people to think that business executives are not altogether smart, and therefore to discount them, or at the very least, take them for granted. It is dangerous thinking. At CBS, there is an ongoing imbroglio between news and corporate. Corporate usually wins.

At *The New Yorker*, there was no declared war between the two sides, just a sudden abandonment of writers and artists by business executives—or so the former viewed it.

"The business side was supposed to protect us!" rails a *New Yorker* writer. "That's what they were *there* for." It was, of course, more complicated than that.

What follows is a saga of publishing, a story whose principal theme, the conflict between business and editorial, has long been with us. But more specifically, it is the story of a magazine that many readers regard as the best that ever was. It is the story of the last days of *The New Yorker*.

1

The stage was set for the sale of *The New Yorker* the day it was founded. From the start there were two magazines, the business one and the editorial one, divided and sometimes divisive to the point of corporate schizophrenia. They were represented by two men, Harold Ross and Raoul Fleischmann. It is Ross who gets the credit for founding the magazine, as well he should. It was his idea and his genius. But it was Fleischmann's money.

Upon first inspection, Ross's start in life seems an unlikely one for a man who was destined to found *The New Yorker*. He was born in 1892 in Aspen, Colorado, then not a posh ski resort but instead a small silver-mining town. His father was a mining technician, his mother a schoolteacher. His eventual career path seems less unlikely in light of the fact that his mother's most fervent wish was that her son would grow up to write for the *Saturday Evening Post*. Ross was never a student, but he inherited his mother's love of words.

The family moved to Salt Lake City, where Ross dropped out of high school after sophomore year to work full time for the *Salt*

Lake City Tribune. He later told a biographer: "I found high school too dull and newspapers glamorous, what with riding on the fire engines, the police patrol and all." He left Salt Lake to ride the rails as a tramp newspaperman, serving time at twenty-three newspapers in, among other places, Sacramento, Panama, Atlanta, and New Orleans before enlisting in the army in the spring of 1917, when the United States entered World War I. While in training in an engineers' corps in Europe, Ross learned that the army planned to start a newspaper for enlisted men, *Stars & Stripes.* He tried, through regular channels, to get himself assigned to the paper, but failing that, he climbed out the window of a barracks at the foot of the Vosges Mountains in France and went A.W.O.L. to Paris, where he inveigled a position at the new paper. Others already at the publication or soon to arrive included *New York Times* drama critic Alexander Woollcott and Franklin P. Adams, or F.P.A., who would later write the popular "Conning Tower" column in the *New York World.* The officer allegedly in control was Lieutenant Guy Viskniskki, who tried, with little success, to apply his old sergeant's tactics to his literary band. When, for instance, he would line them up for morning calisthenics, Adams would stand behind a pole and occasionally flop an arm into view. The commander had trouble controlling them on the page as well. He once placed Ross under arrest following an argument over the use of a comma. Viskniskki's nerves wore out long before those of his alleged subordinates, and Ross and the others had the last word—they managed to get the lieutenant reassigned.

Ross later described the adventure this way: "Our commanding officer had a nervous breakdown and the editorial department was left without authoritative direction. Six of us... held a meeting to decide what to do. My idea, which prevailed, was that we should elect an editor and that editor would have full authority to give instructions to the others and to run the paper but could be removed at any time by a meeting of the six of us. My candidate for editor was Winterich [John T., a newspaperman from Springfield, Massachusetts], but he backed out. Winterich was more the editor than anyone else, from start to finish, but he shied away from the personal contacts that went with the job. I was never fired by the staff and we finished the war that way. Winterich really did most of the editing, though. Woollcott used to say that after my election I sent the staff out on so many assignments and such distant ones that it never got to meet again." *Stars & Stripes*, with Ross in charge, was a rousing success.

While in Paris, Ross and the others hung out at Nini's, a tiny restaurant at the top of Montmartre where they ate, drank, and played craps and poker. Nini's was the first home of what would later be christened the Thanatopsis Literary and Inside Straight Poker Club. It was at Nini's that Woollcott introduced Ross to Jane Grant, a feminist reporter from New York who was to become Ross's first wife and crucial helpmate in the founding of *The New Yorker*. During the *Stars & Stripes* years, Ross began to dream aloud about starting a lofty magazine to be read by the kinds of people who would write it. It would not pander and it would not please everyone. Writers would be allowed to write what they wanted, for the pure love of the craft. The dream would not soon become reality.

Back home, Ross first edited *The Home Sector*, an unsuccessful attempt at a peacetime *Stars & Stripes*, then the *American Legion Weekly* (he left because, he quipped, the magazine had almost as many editors as the Legion had members), then *Judge*, the humor weekly. Woollcott shepherded him into a circle of acquaintances that met for lunch at the Algonquin Hotel and came to be known as the Algonquin Round Table, that now legendary collective of creativity that numbered among its members Franklin P. Adams, Robert Benchley, Dorothy Parker, George S. Kaufman, Marc Connelly, Edna Ferber, Ring Lardner, and

Robert Sherwood. They were as famous for their *bon mots* off the pages as they were for those on. The anecdotes have been repeated thousands of times. There is Robert Benchley's telegram from Venice: "STREETS HERE FULL OF WATER. ADVISE." And Dorothy Parker's comment upon hearing of the death of Calvin Coolidge: "How can they tell?" And Marc Connelly's retort to the verbal jouster who rubbed Connelly's head and exclaimed, "That feels like my wife's behind." Connelly ran his own hand across his bald pate. "Why, so it does!" he exclaimed.

Few of the great witticisms are attributed to Ross. When he was funny, it was often unintentional. But he had a great appreciation of humor, and the wit that sprang from the Round Table had a profound influence on Ross and eventually on his magazine. It was the kind of urbane funniness that would come to be known as "*New Yorker* humor." Many of the Round Tablers wound up writing for Ross. The Algonquin was also the setting for the peacetime revival of the Thanatopsis Literary and Inside Straight Poker Club, though eventually the Saturday night game moved to the players' homes. The players were mostly in the "literature" business, but Raoul Fleischmann, introduced to the game in 1921 by F.P.A., was not. He was, incongruously, a baking company executive.

Raoul Fleischmann was the son of Louis Fleischmann, one of five Viennese brothers who emigrated to New York around the turn of the century. Two of Raoul's uncles founded the Fleischmann's yeast company. They placed their brother Louis in charge of the bakery subsidiary. Here are two bits of Fleischmann trivia: A charitable gesture on the part of the brothers, distributing unsold bread to the poor, gave rise to the word "breadline." And a town in the New York Catskill Mountains where the brothers settled is called Fleischmann to this day; the family it was named after is long gone from the area.

Raoul Fleischmann, as is common in the second generation

of any endeavor, shared in the family wealth, but not in its enthusiasm for yeast and baking. While he did dutifully run the baking business when his time came, it seemed far too basic an undertaking for one so polished and sophisticated. Raoul was possessed of an old-world Viennese charm. He was a boulevardier, keenly intent on the kinds of pursuits one might expect of a young man of inherited wealth and good looks. He liked to travel, favored French food and English tailors, frequented racetracks, and was an educated student of horseflesh who had great success at the window. He also had a sense of humor. When a magazine later called him "portly," he wrote in reply: "I beg to report that I do not consider myself 'portly,' merely fat in the wrong parts of the body." Fleischmann had aspirations not to write but to be with writers. It was his prowess at poker that gained him a seat at the Thanatopsis table. They dubbed him Royal Flushmann.

Fleischmann's manner and appearance were in stark contrast to those of Ross. Fleischmann was calm and diplomatic, Ross was crude and obstreperous. Ross was a large, gangly man whose hair stood straight on end like the hacked-off brush of a broom. Ina Claire made an oft-quoted remark that she'd like to take off her shoes and run barefoot through those locks, and Ross promptly had them battened down. Marc Connelly described Ross's mouth as "imbecilically gaping." His lower lip drooped pendulously, as if unsupported by muscle. He was indifferent and sloppy in dress. If one tried to guess which was the baker and which the editor, one would likely have got it wrong.

Jane Grant took credit for first spotting Fleischmann's potential as a benefactor for the new magazine. She thought he was ideal, because he had plenty of money but didn't seem like a man who would meddle in editorial affairs. Ross did not want to be owned by a large organization, like Henry Luce's Time Incorporated, where corporate interference was inevitable. It was also Grant who first approached Fleischmann with the idea. At a party at the home Raoul shared with his wife, Ruth, and their toddler son, Peter, Grant told the businessman about the magazine-to-be. She said that Ross had assured her that it could be launched with only $50,000, half of which she and Ross would raise themselves. Might Raoul be interested in contributing the other $25,000? He was taken with the idea, and ventured that he might, in his word, "risk" such capital.

The next day, Ross visited Fleischmann at his office to discuss the venture, but much to Jane Grant's subsequent dismay, Ross launched into a discussion of another magazine altogether, a marine gazette. In contrary fashion, Raoul Fleischmann later recalled the occasion as a lunch, and the idea as a "comic paper." In any case, the outcome was the same. Fleischmann found that idea dreary and told Ross so. Ross left discouraged. It took Grant a week to persuade her husband to return to Fleischmann to carry out the original mission. Ross made another trip and this time was better received. According to Fleischmann, Ross said his magazine would be "built around New York, with humor as merely an adjunct of the publication, rather than its base." Ross described a magazine that would be both commercial and classy. He expected it to have a snob appeal based on its true intellectual superiority. And he believed that the snob appeal would attract advertisers.

Fleischmann was a shrewd businessman, and much as he liked Ross's editorial concept, he was also intrigued by the publication's financial prospects. The popular magazines of the day, like *Judge* and the *Saturday Evening Post*, were aimed at a broad audience—the larger, more diverse, and more geographically distributed the better. *Vanity Fair* was the only successful magazine targeted at an urban audience, but it was a *national* urban audience. Ross intended to direct his magazine at New York, which made for a major distinction where advertising was concerned. Ross wondered why a Fifth Avenue department store or an East Side restaurant should allocate advertising dollars to reach readers in Des Moines, which is whom they were reaching through the available publications. Why shouldn't there be a loftily written humor magazine aimed specifically at New Yorkers? And why, to complete the circle of thought, wouldn't retailers utilize such an advertising outlet? Ross's all-out war on businessmen was not yet declared, but he already didn't trust them. The irony is that he could be quite a canny one himself.

Fleischmann agreed to fund the project. He and Ross formed F-R Publishing Corp., for Fleischmann-Ross. According to Fleischmann's memoirs, he put up $25,000 while Ross and Grant contributed $20,000. F-R was a private company in which each of them held 10 percent of the stock, valued at $33.33 a share. The balance was held for future distribution among other principals. They took office space in a Fleischmann-owned building at 25 West Forty-fifth Street, just a short distance from the mangy space at 25 West Forty-third Street they would burrow into a few years later. The budget, and Ross, dictated that the surroundings be modest, the furnishings salvaged. Ross's sensibilities were those of a newspaperman. "I don't want to look like the editor of *Vanity Fair!*" he roared. There was little danger of that. Ross's architectural contribution was ordering walls to be constantly rearranged, which made for some unusual configurations. (To this day, for instance, in the offices at 25 West Forty-third, there is a door in editorial that opens on a brick wall.)

The initial staff was meager. The only seasoned magazine pro, aside from Ross, was Rea Irvin, then art editor of *Life*, who appeared once a week at the *New Yorker* offices to examine the attempted art. Irvin created a typeface for the magazine which still is known as Irvin type. Ross's literary poker buddies found great cause for merriment in Ross's undertaking, especially when informed by the editor that their contributions would be rewarded with stock, not cash. It was difficult to believe that stock in so risky a proposition could ever be of value. Nevertheless, Marc Connelly, George S. Kaufman, Dorothy Parker, and Alexander Woollcott were all loyal enough to Ross to sign on as "advisory editors."

The first issue was months into development before anyone hit on a name for the magazine, and then public relations man John Peter Toohey came up with the tag too simple to be obvious: *The New Yorker*. Ross put pen to paper and wrote a lengthy description of his future journal. It is worth quoting in its entirety, because it has come to be regarded as a model prospectus by sixty years' worth of publishers since, and because eventually, *The New Yorker* could boast the rarest of achievements: It became exactly what it set out to be.

Ross wrote:

The New Yorker will be a reflection in word and picture of metropolitan life. It will be human. Its general tenor will be one of gaiety, wit and satire, but it will be more than a jester. It will not be what is commonly called radical or highbrow; it will be what is commonly called sophisticated, in that it will assume a reasonable degree of enlightenment on the part of its readers. It will hate bunk.

As compared to the newspaper, The New Yorker will be interpretive rather than stenographic. It will print facts that it will have to go behind the scenes to get, but it will not deal in scandal for the sake of scandal nor sensation for the sake of sensation. Its integrity will be above suspicion. It hopes to be so entertaining and informative as to be a necessity for the person who knows his way about or wants to.

The New Yorker will devote several pages a week to a covering of contemporary events and people of interest. This will be done by writers capable of appreciating the elements of a situation and, in setting them down, of indicating their importance and significance. The New Yorker will present the truth and the whole truth without fear and without favor, but will not be iconoclastic.

Amusements and the arts will be thoroughly covered by departments which will present, in addition to criticism, the personality, the anecdote, the color and chat of the various subdivisions of this sphere. The New Yorker's conscientious guide will list each week all current amusement offerings worthwhile—theaters, motion pictures, musical events, art exhibitions, sport and miscellaneous entertainment—providing an ever-ready answer to the prevalent query, "What shall we do this evening?" Through The New Yorker's Mr. Van Bibber III, readers will be kept apprised of what is going on in the public and semi-public smart gathering places—the clubs, hotels, cafes, supper clubs, cabarets and other resorts.

Judgment will be passed upon new books of consequence and The New Yorker will carry a list of the season's books which it considers worth reading.

There will be a page of editorial paragraphs, commenting on the week's events in a manner not too serious.

There will be a personal mention column—a jotting-down in the small-town newspaper style of the comings, goings and doings in the village of New York. This will contain some josh and some news value.

The New Yorker will carry each week several pages of prose and verse, short and long, humorous, satirical and miscellaneous.

The New Yorker expects to be distinguished for its illustrations, which will include caricatures, sketches, cartoons and humorous and satirical drawings in keeping with its purpose.

Ross's final paragraph began with a line now famous: "The New Yorker will be the magazine which is not edited for the old lady in Dubuque. It will not be concerned in what she is thinking about. This is not meant in disrespect, but The New Yorker is a magazine avowedly published for a metropolitan audience and thereby will escape an influence which hampers most national publications. It expects a considerable national circulation, but this will come from persons who have a metropolitan interest."

The New Yorker had its debut with the issue dated February 21, 1925. It ran thirty-six pages and cost fifteen cents. Few magazines find their voice in the first edition, and *The New Yorker* was no exception. It was a major disappointment editorially and a huge flop commercially. Raoul Fleischmann later described it succinctly: "The magazine *stank!*"

The premier issue did use some section headings that have survived to this day, most notably "The Talk of the Town." The *New Yorker* "Profile" was invented—the magazine was the first to put that name to the genre—and today's "Goings on About Town" made its debut as "Going On." But while the titles later proved workable, the initial text was forced and banal. The humor was a bad imitation of the broader jokiness popular in the magazines aimed at a mass audience. It was not the high humor Ross had promised. Here are some representative samples, drawn from a now defunct feature called "Of All Things." Note the massacre of English usage.

"Mr. George Jean Nathan, who when not engaged in his more serious work of telling everybody where to get off at, finds relaxation in writing for Mr. Hearst's publications, is the author of 'Women are Playthings.' Ah there, (as the editor of our 'In Our Midst' column would say) George!"

"On general principles, this magazine expects to take a firm stand against murder. But we don't want to be bigoted. If, for instance, someone should ask you to advertise in The New Yorker, and throw out the hint that your refusal might lead to some unwelcome publicity, you wouldn't shock us much if you poured him into the nearest drain."

"Two of the big collar firms have combined. Our own Beauty Contest judges announced that the handsomest man in America is now Mister Cluett Peabody Earl Wilson."

The cartoons fell flat as well. "What's the drunk's name, Reilly?" inquired the sergeant of the cop on the beat. They peer down at a prone man, who seems to clutch a cane. "Dunno, sergeant," comes the reply. "He claims he's a unidentified body."

There was precious little advertising in the issue, and less still that was paid for, though there were glimmers of what was to be. There was a promotion for A. Jaeckel & Co., "Furriers Exclusively," one for Elgin watches, and another for "parfums Caron." The copy for Cruger's, a men's store, ran like this: "'Just like London.' It's patterned after those smart little shops that hitherto one has found only in London. You'll find the tie, hose, shirtings, etc., at Cruger's the same as those worn by the well dressed Britisher. Drop in or—if that's impossible—write us."

It was on the cover of the first issue that Eustace Tilley was born, though it would be years before he was actually named. Drawn by Rea Irvin, Tilley is the fictitious fop with the top hat who trains his monocle on a butterfly. His career would be a long one since he would go on to grace the cover of the anniversary issue of *The New Yorker* every year for sixty-three years and counting. He came to represent the pictorial embodiment of the *New Yorker* spirit, though that was not the idea when he was drawn.

The inaugural issue also sported some of the graphics that have survived to this day, including the winking owl that hovers over the Talk of the Town heading.

The costs of producing *The New Yorker* were higher than expected and the revenues lower. It was immediately apparent that Ross had vastly underestimated the funds required to carry the magazine long enough to find an audience. Most of the original cash disappeared with the first issue, a circumstance that sparked Raoul Fleischmann to take independent action, which, in turn, led to the first major rift between Ross and Fleischmann. Within days of the launch, a nervous and despairing Fleischmann sought out the advice of John Hanrahan, a precursor to today's highly paid magazine consultants who billed himself as a "publisher's counsel." Hanrahan signed on as promotion manager of *The New Yorker* and general adviser to F-R Publishing in return for payment in stock. Hanrahan set about organizing the magazine. He recruited the personnel for the advertising, circulation, and promotion departments, a task which Ross was constitutionally unequipped to handle. Later on, he penned promotion copy, aimed at Madison Avenue, that succinctly set forth the philosophy of *The New Yorker* and described its potential as a worthy forum for advertisements.

Raoul Fleischmann dug deeper into his pockets to keep the magazine afloat, forcing Ross into a financial dependency that made him resent Fleischmann all the more, even as Fleischmann dutifully paid the $5,000 worth of bills that Ross dropped on his desk each week. Ross sought new ways to raise funds, even being reduced at one point to selling a bound set of *Stars & Stripes* to Theodore Roosevelt, Jr., for $1500. With unhappier consequences he took to trying to finance the venture at the poker table. He was winning one night, at a game at the home of Herbert Bayard Swope, when Jane Grant suggested it was time to leave. Ross moved to depart with her, but his companions bullied him out of it. Grant left and Ross stayed. Ross staggered home at dawn, lurched up the stairs and into bed. As Grant helped him undress, several slips of paper fell from his pockets. Ross had written close to thirty thousand dollars' worth of IOUs that night. It was a fortune for Ross and Grant, half again more than their original investment in *The New Yorker*.

Fleischmann, who was at the game, felt Ross had been taken advantage of, and advised him not to pay. But the other players were not sympathetic, forgiving, or generous, and they insisted on collecting. Fleischmann bought up some of the Ross IOUs. It was a kind gesture, but it deepened Ross's debt to Fleischmann, as well as his dependency on him, and thus served to make him more resentful.

By May, the fourth month of *The New Yorker*'s life, circulation had sunk to below 4000 from an initial 15,000. There were a mere three or four pages of advertising in each issue. Fleischmann, Ross, Hanrahan, and Hawley Truax, a friend to both Ross and Fleischmann, meeting in an eight-hour session at the Princeton Club, were forced to agree that the outlook was grim. They discussed halting publication for a few months, then resurrecting the magazine in the fall, when magazine advertising traditionally picks up for the Christmas selling season. They were well aware that the hiatus would likely prove permanent. A despondent Ross told Fleischmann he wanted a clear message to carry to his staff. Fleischmann said he had no choice but to abandon the project.

But later that afternoon, all of the men attended the wedding of F.P.A. and Esther Root, an occasion that, by definition, represented optimism and commitment. Fleischmann relented. (Fleischmann later recalled that his decision was influenced by a chance remark he overheard. John Hanrahan told an associate: "I can't blame Raoul for a moment for refusing to go on, but it's like killing something that's alive.") He agreed to see the magazine through the summer, on the condition that it be produced unambitiously. The print run would be small, and the best stories and cartoons would be hoarded for fall. He said, too, that he wanted to limit his exposure as sole investor, and he directed Ross to find other backers. It turned out that only Hawley Truax contributed any more funds.

They straggled through the warm months. One event of importance was that it was that summer that Ross hired Katherine Sergeant Angell, who was to become one of the *New Yorker*'s greatest editors. She began as a part-time manuscript reader but soon rose to editorial assistant, and eventually fiction editor. She would be largely responsible for giving the magazine its direction in that area, and for launching the careers of many talented writers. Despite a frequently uttered Rossism—"I'm surrounded by women and children!"—Angell, later Katherine White by her marriage to E. B. White, was to become one of Ross's closest friends and most trusted advisers.

By early fall, the New Yorker issues reflected a new sensibility. It was as if Ross and his writers had decided that since they were probably going to fail anyway, they might as well do it on their terms. In the early issues, the staff tried to second-guess readers' tastes, which inevitably resulted in writing that was strained and self-conscious. The fall issues were filled with what writers wanted to write and editors to publish. They were jaunty and confident. Talk of the Town, for one, began to discover its voice.

"'Is New York a Menace? The West Wants to Know,'" read an entry. "This is the title of a Methodist pamphlet. In reply will state, 'yes,' and that we have to build fifty-five story hotels to accommodate the West during the menacing season.

"New York, too, is a contradictory place. Waiting recently in the lobby of the Waldorf, we saw more nonentities trying to attract attention and failing, than we did celebrities trying to avoid attention and succeeding.

"Visitors should be repeatedly warned that they must not form their opinion of New Yorkers from the other visitors they see."

In the fall, some of the columns, writers, and artists that would become The New Yorker's most popular and enduring first appeared. Other columns that looked promising were eventually dropped, including "Heroes of the Week," which spoofed recent newsmakers in short text accompanying purposefully silly caricatures billed as "photographs." One such accompanied this copy: "Mrs. Jessie Woolworth Donahue who is here photographed wearing a few million dollars worth of the Woolworth family jewels, several quarts of which were stolen from her at the Hotel Plaza last week, will find little difficulty in replacing the missing real gems with exact replicas from her late father's shops."

Another feature was titled "The Making of a Magazine: A Tour Through the Vast Organization of The New Yorker." Part "IX" of the series, to pick just one, concerned "The Construction of Our Sentences."

"Mining the letters that make up the words and phrases of an issue is only the first phase of the all-important work of printing The New Yorker. Before these letters may be used, they must be arranged by experts in the form of words, and these words in the form of sentences, and these sentences in the form of paragraphs; and even after they have been laid one below another in the form of stories and articles they must be placed in such order that the pages follow consecutively throughout the magazine. Six hundred trained mathematicians from Yale, Columbia, Harvard and other universities are employed in the work of numbering these pages alone." It went on from there in great zany detail, like, "Sentences in The New Yorker vary in length from six inches to six months or $100 fine or both." S. J. Perelman had not yet arrived on the pages, but you'd never know it from that last line. As for the first part, it would be right at home on today's David Letterman show. The column was dropped, but its spirit lives on.

Features destined for longer life included an abundance of profiles that were much abbreviated forebears of today's incarnation. In the early days, The New Yorker "profiled" Cecil B. de Mille, Jimmie Walker (a politician but not yet New York's mayor), and Carl Sandburg, among others.

It was in the fall of 1925 that Janet Flanner commenced writing her "Paris Letter" under the pseudonym "Genêt." (Ross in the early days wanted everyone to write under an assumed name. Some writers preferred it that way because they were on staff elsewhere.) Flanner directed her reporter's eye at all manner of subjects, from French bank tellers' strikes to which socialites were sailing in or out of Paris on what boat: "Mr. and Mrs. William Dick, with her son, John Jacob Astor, are here, the Astor lad being ill from milk drunk in Venice. Venice is a suburb of Paris for the moment. All the American princesses are there. Parisians have been running down to Venice lately as the courts of the Louis used to run out all the year to Versailles." She had a lightness of touch that was combined, often, with serious thought and incisive writing. She produced some of the finest coverage of World War II.

Helen Hokinson and Peter Arno, cartoonists whose work originally came in over the transom, were regulars by fall. Hokinson poked affectionate fun at prosperous and plump matrons. An early entry depicts a behatted member of the species demanding of the small, mustachioed shoe salesman, "Young man, just what *is* the difference between alligator and lizard?" Arno contributed the Whoops sisters, a hugely popular series that had to be toned down because it was too bawdy for Ross's tastes. Arno, the son of a judge (his real name was Curtis Arnoux Peters), had dropped out of Yale to play piano for Gilda Gray, "the shimmy girl." He deposited his portfolio of drawings at *The New Yorker* one day, not really expecting a response. What he got in return was a check. He remained, for decades, one of the *New Yorker*'s most popular artists.

It was in the fall, too, that Lois Long (who later, temporarily, became Mrs. Peter Arno) began to write "Fifth Avenue," which evolved into "On and Off the Avenue," in which she covered the retail and fashion beat. The column was controversial because there was a perceived conflict of interest when a writer discussed what was in store even as sales representatives tried to procure retail advertising. Most such columns were barely disguised ad promotions for the stores. Ross decreed that his magazine could do both and retain its integrity. The column found both audiences and advertisers with its tongue-in-cheek frothiness:

"Shopping for shoes this year is just about the most fascinating thing that you can possibly do. The fashion magazines are full of bulletins from Paris saying that subtle greens and greys and *bois de roses* and russets are to creep into footwear; that black shoes, to be really chic, should be relieved with touches of grey, beige, or a color to complement the costume; that evening slippers should be of pale apricot satin, colored brocades, or metallic kid with futuristic designs or pipings of a silver or gold kid. Which gives you a lot of leeway, and makes every show window an unending source of emotion."

Using the pseudonym "Lipstick," Long also contributed "Tables for Two," a chronicle of her life as an active member of the blooming young café society. The column was unwittingly subsidized by her string of escorts. Early "Tables for Two" entries serve today as a literary form of archeological artifacts. The frenzied gayness of the twenties gave way, of course, to the stock market crash of '29 and later to the Depression. In 1926, unaware of such gruesome eventualities, Lois Long wrote:

"All the great minds who used to be absorbed solely in worrying about whether or not to order chicken salad, whether or not to Ask Him In, and the correct method of eating asparagus, now seem to have concentrated on but one vexing problem—'Are they dancing the Charleston at the smart night clubs?' At present (not that I want to set myself up as an authority on etiquette) the answer is No. And the reason, undoubtedly, is not that nice people disapprove of this pastime, but that nice people do not yet know how to do it."

The success of café society reporting came as a revelation to Ross. Early issues of the magazine presented gossip of the warmed-over Broadway variety. Ross had missed the seismic shift in the attitudes and evening activities of a younger generation. When a woman named Ellin Mackay submitted a piece called "Why We Go to Cabarets: A Post Debutante Explains," Ross didn't like it. His ambivalence was such, though, that instead of rejecting it outright, he kept passing it around the office, asking others if they thought it should be published, hoping they would agree that it shouldn't. Happily, they didn't. The article ran; it represented a crucial turning point for *The New Yorker*.

Ellin Mackay was a young woman from an upper-crust family who was rebelling at the traditional values her parents held dear, and who was fleeing from the life they had neatly laid out for her, as symbolized by white-gloved boys in stag lines. There is certainly nothing new in generational conflict, but the youth rebellion of the twenties was more dramatic than most, the break with the past so distinct and wrenching that it would change the world. Ellin Mackay's piece was not heavy-handed, but clearly it harbored anger. Much of its success owed to the fact that she said what others her age were thinking, and that she spoke for them to "our elders" in ways they wished they could. Mackay dissected the differences between deb balls and cabarets, but the deepest chord struck had more to do with the longings to burst out of a repressive society.

"Our Elders," wrote Mackay, "criticize many things about us, but usually they attribute to us sins too gaudy to be true. The trouble is that our Elders are a trifle gullible; they have swallowed too much of Mr. Scott Fitzgerald and Miss Gertrude Atherton. They believe all the backstairs gossip that is written about us. We do not mind when they load the Seven Deadly Sins on our backs, but we object when they claim that we invented them...."

The elders, wrote Mackay, did not understand why young people would forgo small dinners and grand balls in order to "go to cabarets and rub elbows with all sorts and kinds of people." But such were not the motives of the cabaret crowd: "We do not particularly like dancing shoulder to shoulder with gaudy and fat drummers. We do not like unattractive people. But, at least, in the cabaret, though we see them and are near them, we do not have to dance with them. If our Elders want to know why we go to cabarets let them go to the best of these, our present day exclusive parties, and look at the stag lines. There they will see extremely unalluring specimens." The problem with stag lines, wrote Mackay, was that you *had* to dance with the "colorless young men" who formed them.

Mackay starts the piece on the defensive, with youth having to account for itself and its ways, but halfway through there is a switch. By then it is the elders' parties that are harrowing and nonexclusive: "We go to a party and take pot luck, and the luck is four to one against us. At last, tired of fruitless struggles to remember half familiar faces, tired of vainly trying to avoid unwelcome dances, tired of crowds, we go to a cabaret. We go to cabarets because of the very fastidiousness that our Elders find so admirable a quality. We have privacy in a cabaret. We go with people whom we find attractive. What does it matter if an unsavory Irish politician is carrying on a dull and noisy flirtation with the little blonde at the table behind us? We don't have to listen; we are with people whose conversation we find amusing. What does it matter if the flapper and her fattish boy friend are wriggling beside us as we dance: We like our partner and the flapper likes hers, and we don't bother each other.

"Yes, we go to cabarets, but we resent the criticism of our good taste in so doing. We go because, like our Elders, we are fastidious. We go because we prefer rubbing elbows in a cabaret to dancing at an exclusive party with all sorts and kinds of people."

Ellin Mackay proved loyal to her philosophy. When it came time to marry, she forsook the white-gloved boys in favor of Irving Berlin. (When Berlin celebrated his 100th birthday in May 1988, Mackay was still by his side. She died two months later, at the age of eighty-five.) Her piece gave *The New Yorker* its first sellout issue, and helped the magazine and its readers find each other. The weekly and its audience soon could be described with the same adjectives: independent, worldly-wise, fashionable, irreverent, intelligent, and looking for fun. Those qualities attracted new talent to *The New Yorker* as well.

2

Harold Ross had a welcoming attitude toward undiscovered writers that is rare among editors of both new and old publications. It is considered safer to rely on "names." Ross was willing to take chances on unknowns for two reasons: In a practical sense, he could not afford to pay famous writers. More important, he wanted to discover fresh voices. To produce something that was different, he had to try untested talent. It happened that Ross did not have to strain to find the talent because it found him, drawn to this brave new idea of a magazine. James Thurber, for one, refused to give Ross credit for assembling what turned out to be a stunning collection of writers and artists. "The moths deserve the credit for discovering the flame," he wrote in his book *My Years with Ross*.

Elwyn Brooks White arrived in late 1926 from a detested job as an advertising copywriter. E. B. White, who signed his pieces E.B.W. and was known as Andy to his friends, was a small, gentle, high-strung man who was hired to edit the humorous fillers known as "newsbreaks," to rewrite "Talk of the Town," and to oversee cartoon captions. *The New Yorker* then, as now, would often buy art but delete the artist's caption and replace it with a newer—it was hoped, funnier—one. A classic shows a small boy at a dinner table with his mother. "It's broccoli, dear," she explains as he glares downward at his plate. To which he replies, "I say it's spinach and I say the hell with it." It was pure White.

For all of his skills as an editor, White's most cherished and lasting contributions came in his writing. In addition to editing "Talk," he came to write the "Notes and Comments" prelude to it. He contributed quirky little stories that resist categorization into slots like essay or vignette. When he lent his elegance of phrase and whimsy to a subject as mundane as, for example, the waitress at Schrafft's spilling buttermilk on his suit, buttermilk suddenly became a proxy for all that was right or wrong or even just ironic about the world. White was better than anyone at making something profound out of something that was simple without sounding like that was what he was setting out to do. He wrote the book *Charlotte's Web* for children, but it has become one of the best-selling and most beloved children's books of all time because its barnyard tale of the selflessness of Charlotte A. Cavatica, a large gray spider, in saving Wilbur the pig from slaughter is a fable of friendship that tugs at adult emotions as well.

White's marriage to Katherine Angell was just one in an eternal stream of intramural hitchings at the magazine. There is a long incestuous tradition at *The New Yorker* for writers to marry writers, for writers to divorce writers and marry other writers, and for sons and daughters, brothers, cousins, and classmates to be gathered into the fold, in the business office as well as in the editorial department. All of that literary inbreeding contributed to the "us against the world" aura that *The New Yorker* would come to project.

Another of E. B. White's contributions to *The New Yorker* was to recruit James Thurber. When Thurber arrived, Ross quickly demonstrated a tendency he had to try to put round pegs in square holes. He branded Thurber an editor, over Thurber's protests that he was a writer.

"Writers are a dime a dozen, Thurber," Ross told him. "What I want is an editor. I can't find editors. Nobody grows up. Do you know English?"

Ross was a born worrier, a fidgeter, a man who was always upset by the way things were going—in life and at *The New Yorker.* He searched in vain for solutions to what may not have truly been problems, and for people to fix what wasn't necessarily broken. For his magazine, he searched for perfect editors.

"He'd get in a new 'Jesus,' as they came to be called," says a writer, "a miracle worker who would appear and be supportive and take everything over, clean it up, get it right." A veritable parade of managing and executive editors marched through the *New Yorker* offices, at an in-one-door-and-out-the-other pace. Some of them might have worked out, had Ross been less obstreperous. Others wouldn't have, like the "Jesus" who took to meandering across the street to the Harvard Club and lying on a leather couch to read galleys. Ross didn't give up, but kept constantly rummaging for new and perfect Jesuses, hiring men he met at lunch or at a party, dispatching telegrams to far regions because somebody knew somebody who knew somebody.... Ross plowed through dozens of editors in the early years, rarely disposing of them himself, but instead cowering at a distance while some subordinate lopped off heads. James Thurber was spared that fate.

It took months, but Ross eventually allowed Thurber to retire his blue pencil and prove himself one of America's foremost humorists and cartoonists. Ross grew to appreciate Thurber's written wit, but he and his art department remained befuddled by Thurber's whimsical cartoon characters, his skewed creatures—lopsided dogs, amused seals, bewildered people. Thurber could sketch thousands of the characters in one sitting, and Ross dismissed them as doodles. A now famous early Thurber cartoon shows a couple in bed. Above them, a seal is draped casually over the headboard.

"All right," says the wife to the husband, "have it your way. You heard a seal bark!"

Upon receiving an early Thurber seal, the art department resketched it and shipped it back to editorial with a brisk note: "This is the way a seal's whiskers go." E. B. White put the bristles back in their original state and shipped the cartoon back again with the missive: "This is the way a *Thurber* seal's whiskers go." That was the way they stayed.

The New Yorker came increasingly into its own in the first couple of years, but in 1927 it seemed to reach maturity. It was now consistently more humorous, and the humor was accompanied by more serious reporting. "Remember that The New Yorker is a magazine of reporting and criticism," Ross told his staff. Serious reporting did not mean advocacy journalism, however. Ross was determined that opinion would not find a home in *The New Yorker*. The Talk of the Town and other essay-type material had the informal, offhand tone that Ross sought for what he called the magazine's "casuals." In those days brevity was cherished. Ross rewarded it by paying more for the first few thousand words of a story.

Thanks to Ross, but especially to Katherine White, the magazine began to establish itself as a storehouse of great fiction. In 1928, a twenty-three-year-old writer, John O'Hara, made his *New Yorker* debut with the short story "Alumnae Bulletin." His was a type of fiction, less structured than its literary predecessors, that came to be known as "the *New Yorker* short story." The list of fiction writers given early career boosts by Ross and White eventually grew to include—in nonchronological order—Ogden Nash,

Clarence Day, Marianne Moore, Jean Stafford, John Updike, Mary McCarthy (for whom Ross lifted his ban on long, formal short stories), Irwin Shaw, J. D. Salinger, and John Cheever. Ross did not pay well—Thurber complained that he was cheap— but writers were nevertheless attracted by the nurturing creative environment at *The New Yorker*. Ring Lardner once commented, "I would rather write for *The New Yorker* at five cents a word than for *Cosmopolitan* at a dollar a word."

Alexander Woollcott became a regular columnist in 1929 under the heading "Shouts and Murmurs." Woollcott was already well known. He had been a theater critic for three newspapers— the *New York Times*, the *New York Sun*, and the *New York World*—but like other writers, he found that his greatest recognition came in writing for *The New Yorker*. *The New Yorker* made him a celebrity. His articles were reprinted more often than were those of any other contributor.

Another veteran reporter, Alva Johnston, formerly a star at the *Herald Tribune*, became known as "the man who wrote the *New Yorker* profiles." Johnston all but invented the concept, then unknown, of penning portraits that were not fawning and shallow, but well-rounded and insightful. The *New Yorker* profiles would remain one of the magazine's most popular features, though later entries would run many tens of thousands of words longer than Johnston's 3600 or so. Johnston wrote only about a quarter of the profiles that ran while he was with *The New Yorker*, but nevertheless he was the person most closely identified with them, and he was featured in stories in the *Saturday Evening Post* and women's magazines, and recognized wherever he went.

Another of the *New Yorker*'s notable early contributors was Wolcott Gibbs, an associate editor and top aide to Katherine White who wielded a surgically sharp blue pencil. He was no less a writer, best known for his parodies. *The New Yorker* in the 1930s had a famous battle of words with Time Inc. and specifically with *Fortune* magazine. The August 1934 issue of *Fortune* carried a long dissection of *The New Yorker* written by former "Jesus" Ralph Ingersoll. *The New Yorker* decided to turn the tables.

Wolcott Gibbs approached Henry Luce and requested an interview. Ralph Ingersoll tried to warn Luce off. "They hate you over there," he said. "They'll take long knives and cut you into little pieces and put you over a fire." Luce replied that it was his moral duty as a journalist to cooperate, and he did. Gibbs took great delight in skewering Luce and his company, using as his greatest weapon a perfect parody of the *Time* style of writing with lines like this: "Backward ran sentences until reeled the mind." *Time* was too easy a target. A representative sentence in the *Fortune* article read: "Certain it is that Ross's original idea was more editorial than commercial."

One of the most beloved of *New Yorker* writers, both in print and in person, was the humorist Robert Benchley, who wrote "The Wayward Press" as well as short funny pieces that were limited in subject only by his imagination, which is to say that they were not limited at all. In a piece entitled "Sex is Out," he responded to a Dr. Max Hartmann ("I used to have a dentist named Dr. Hartmann, but he was a dentist"), who had declared that there was no such thing as absolute sex: "If 60 percent of your cells are masculine, you rate as a male. If 60 percent are feminine, you sit with the girls. All combinations are possible up to 99 and 1, but the 100 percenter in either sex is a myth. Dr. Hartmann says so."

Benchley went on to detail the ramifications of such a terrible reality, arriving at this decision: "You can see for yourself, there is going to be no fun in figuring out sex on the back of an envelope. We might as well give the whole thing up and go in for hockey."

Benchley's appearances in *The New Yorker* became less frequent when, inevitably, Broadway and Hollywood, responding to his charm and humor, beckoned. He became a part-time actor. Ross considered it a great loss even though Ross's editorial comments in the margins of Benchley proofs were often greeted by Benchley's penciled remark: "You keep out of this, Ross!"

Other popular early contributors included a man named Howard Brubaker, the first-hired regular columnist, who wrote "Of All Things"; Morris Markey, author of "A Reporter at Large"; Robert Simon, who wrote about music above the initials R.A.S.; G. F. T. Ryall, who, as "Audax Minor," covered "The Race Track"; Clifton Fadiman, who wrote on books; and Lewis Mumford, who, among other endeavors, wrote the art column.

With writers came readers and with readers, advertisers, followed by large revenues and commercial success. The advertising salesmen lured in the exact category that Ross had targeted in the first place—the department and specialty stores which would become not only the financial lifeblood of *The New Yorker* but also a major contributor to its editorial success. The ads became popular among readers. The sense of chic prosperity they imparted was just right wrapped around the magazine's high-hat prose. Because the merchants were local—their hometown just happened to be Manhattan—their promos lent an aura of intimacy that national advertisers like cigarette companies could not provide. Also, store ads constantly changed as retailers featured different fashions. One week Henri Bendel might promote an organdy and velvet creation for $29.95, as it did in 1925 in *The New Yorker*; the next week it might dazzle women with the perfect little black dress. Readers began to await the surprises they might find in store fashion ads as eagerly as they did the prose, and that, in turn, sold magazines. Bonwit Teller signed on, and liked the results so much that by early 1926 it was taking a full page in nearly every issue. Then came Saks Fifth Avenue, B. Altman,

Best & Co., Bergdorf Goodman, and Macy's, all clambering into the pages.

Raoul Fleischmann occasionally solicited ads personally, as did Ross in the earliest days. Eventually, Ross left that task to the advertising department, but he retained the right to veto ads he deemed inappropriate. If he disapproved of a promotion, it didn't run. Ross did not believe that businessmen were equipped with enough intelligence or savvy to determine which ads properly belonged in *The New Yorker*. Ross largely succeeded in establishing a harmony between the ads and the editorial product which was unequaled in the magazine field, and which would prevail for sixty years. Once the magazine was launched, Raoul Fleischmann absented himself from editorial affairs, but Ross regularly took hold of functions generally regarded to belong to the advertising department. There is a popular notion that there existed at *The New Yorker* a complete separation of church and state. Obviously, it was not true. But unlike at other publications, it was editorial that was allowed to influence advertising, not the reverse.

Ironically, even as editorial was establishing one sort of dominance, Raoul Fleischmann and other executives were establishing another kind of foothold: They were amassing a controlling portion of the stock of the still privately held company.

The intention of Ross and Fleischmann when they formed F-R Publishing, as noted, was to divide the 80 percent of the stock they themselves didn't hold among the other investors and contributors. As it turned out, there was only one new investor, Hawley Truax, who put up $10,000 and received less than 5 percent of the stock. Fleischmann gave John Hanrahan 10 percent for signing on as a consultant. Top editors like Katherine and E. B. White received small percentages, as did Rea Irvin, and smaller amounts still went to contributors. The vast majority of the stock was held for future distribution to employees.

Fleischmann and Ross were not to remain equal partners for long. Ross never anted up more than his initial $20,000. Fleischmann, however, in the first year alone put up another $195,000. Over the following two years, he poured in an additional $360,000. Each time he made a contribution, he gained more stock. By 1935, he controlled 35 percent of the total, according to *Fortune* magazine. Ross still held only 10 percent.

From the start, Ross was ambivalent about concerning himself with the financial affairs of *The New Yorker*. Like many creative people, he did not feel comfortable in the realm of numbers. He was notorious for the disorganized state of his personal finances. His inattention reached such extremes that his secretary, Harold Winney, was able to defraud him systematically of tens of thousands of dollars over a number of years by forging Ross's name on checks. Ross never did notice; it was the business office that discovered the scam. Ross brought the same lack of sensibility to his financial dealings with *The New Yorker*. Initially he served on the board of directors but soon resigned, explaining that editors should not be directors. He was given to selling his stock in dribs and drabs, often to cover gambling debts. Nor did he push the case that since Fleischmann was compensated in stock for his financial contributions, so should he, Ross, be compensated for his editorial ones, not the least of which was the very invention of the magazine. He simply drew a salary. In 1927, another publisher offered $3 million for *The New Yorker*, even though the magazine was not yet profitable. Someone more attuned to business might have taken that as a clear indication not only of current worth but of future value. What's more, the following year, *The New Yorker* broke into the black with a net profit of $287,000 on gross income of $1.8 million.

It weathered the Depression better than most magazines, earning $263,000 in 1933 and twice that the following year when, for the first time, it topped the *Saturday Evening Post* in ad pages.

In 1935, revenues soared to $2 million and profits reached $600,000, according to *Fortune*. Circulation was 125,000, a figure that was double Ross's original estimate of the highest it could *ever* reach. Ross and Fleischmann were alarmed by the steady *increases* in circulation. They figured that if too many people liked you, you must be doing something wrong. They were almost superstitious in their belief that excess readers spelled certain ruin. Fleischmann went so far as to order the *New Yorker*'s telephone number unlisted in order to discourage new subscribers.

Ross, with his inattention to finance, however idealistically conceived, mortgaged the future for his editors and writers. They would never catch up with the business side. Fleischmann deemed it inadvisable to entrust writers and artists with stock. He said they were too emotional and would likely become upset if the stock price fell. In the beginning, necessity dictated that Ross pay writers with stock. Once there was available cash, they were not again offered shares. Ross did nothing to defend his staff against Fleischmann's writers-as-babies mind-set. On the contrary, recalls a former writer, "The approach was to keep people separate, especially where money was concerned." He recalls, for instance, that pains were taken to ensure that nobody knew what anyone else was earning.

The editorial department was rarely informed directly of business events that might affect them. Instead, news tended to filter slowly through to editorial and to surface in the form of rumors. A story that circulated early in 1935 was a source of particularly high anxiety. The staff learned that someone had sold a large block of *New Yorker* shares to Time Inc. It was rumored that Henry Luce wanted to buy the magazine for his bride, Clare Boothe Luce, managing editor of *Vanity Fair*. The seller's identity was at first a mystery, but editorial assumed the villain to be Fleischmann. In fact, it was Ross who sold, because, he said, with consistent Rossian logic, editors should not own stock in their own magazines.

Time executives claimed the shares had been bought purely

for investment reasons. And indeed, it would have been impossible for anyone to have bought *The New Yorker* without the co-operation of Raoul Fleischmann. When, later in 1935, Ross offered Luce the balance of his shares, Luce declined. In 1936, Luce sold his *New Yorker* stock, having by then decided that it was not good policy for *Time* to own shares in another publisher. The buyer was Raoul Fleischmann. The series of events served to make an already acrimonious relationship between Ross and Fleischmann even more so. Fleischmann was furious that Ross had not consulted him before selling to Luce, and Ross was upset that Fleischmann had wound up owning *his* shares.

The editorial department lost more ground when, in 1937, the company instituted a stock bonus plan. Under the terms of the plan, selected employees were awarded 1500 shares of the stock to be paid out at the rate of 150 shares a year for ten years. Writers were not eligible. At around the same time, there was a secondary offering of some of Raoul Fleischmann's shares that served to put the stock into more hands. Some of the buyers were not related to *The New Yorker*, so the sale made the stock quasi-public and established a market for the shares.

The *New Yorker*'s fortunes began to shift as the magazine approached and entered the 1940s. There was a sharp decline in circulation that coincided with a shift in editorial direction toward more serious reporting. The world was at war, and *The New Yorker* could hardly overlook that fact. Its writers produced superb coverage of the conflict. But Ross fretted about what he perceived as the demise of humor at what he called his "funny little magazine." Many of the weekly's early cartoonists and humorists had died. New writers who in bygone eras might have devoted their talents to humor now found it difficult to extract amusement from the world around them, and perhaps even frivolous to try. The world wasn't carefree any more.

In June 1940, after the Germans occupied France, *The New*

Yorker departed from Ross's long-standing edict against advocacy when E. B. White penned an editorial call to arms in which he urged the United States to stop waffling and enter the war.

The deterioration in circulation was accompanied by a drop in advertising. Wartime was no time to be hawking luxury items, even if they were available, which of course many were not. *The New Yorker* grew more emaciated with each passing week. It was dealt an almost fatal blow when its allotment of paper was frozen just as it reached a near-record low in the number of pages printed. At Jane Grant's urging, Ross decided to publish a smaller-scale, thinner, and lighter "pony" edition of the magazine for the troops abroad. It would carry no advertisements. The military agreed to allocate more paper toward that purpose. It turned out to be an inspired idea because, with plenty of waiting time in the military, there was time to read. And just as he had once pleased the troops with *Stars & Stripes*, Ross now did the same with *The New Yorker*. Before the war's end, the pony edition was outselling the parent.

In the midst of its wartime financial difficulties, *The New Yorker* was dealt another setback. Starting in 1935, Raoul Fleischmann had begun to invest *New Yorker* funds in two ventures. An investment in Condé Nast, publisher of *Vogue* and *Vanity Fair*, had logic in its favor. Condé Nast was a solid, established entity. Further, there was an existing tie between the two companies. *The New Yorker* was printed on Condé Nast presses. Thus, as an investor in Condé Nast, *The New Yorker* could be said to be profiting from money it was *paying* the other publisher.

The second venture was a good deal more speculative. John Hanrahan launched a magazine called *Stage*. Without consulting Ross or the board of *The New Yorker*, Fleischmann advanced *New Yorker* funds to *Stage*, eventually to the tune of $750,000. The loans were secured by Hanrahan's 10 percent share of *New Yorker* stock. *Stage* was never a success. It limped along for several years before finally folding in 1942, taking with it three-quarters of a million dollars of *New Yorker* cash. When the inevitable furor erupted, it was scant consolation to Ross and the board of *The New Yorker* that *The New Yorker* would regain 10 percent of its stock. Stock was an abstract representation of value, especially in those days when prospects seemed to be fading; $750,000 in cash was *real* money. Ross accused Fleischmann of improper handling of company funds, and the board and other shareholders, one of whom was Fleischmann's ex-wife, supported Ross. The directors threatened to oust the chairman. At first he planned to fight them. He was, after all, by far the single largest shareholder. But as prospects of a long, visible, and vituperative court battle loomed, Fleischmann capitulated. Both Ross and Fleischmann disdained publicity for themselves and their magazine. In this case, Fleischmann personally was bound to suffer the slings and arrows of public opinion if accused of financial malfeasance. In a settlement negotiated by Hawley Truax, Fleischmann agreed to place his *New Yorker* shares in escrow for ten years. He lost control of the board. Ross for a time became more involved in the business. He even rejoined the board, but then he rethought his stance and soon resigned again.

Fleischmann continued to come to the office each day, but his powers were greatly diminished, and he felt a loss. He had other businesses, but *The New Yorker* was his love. Many years later, he again became chairman and resumed an active role in the running of *The New Yorker*, but he never again made an investment. Excess cash was placed securely into interest-bearing government instruments. His and his family's philosophy would later be summed up by a cartoon that appeared in an ad for *The New Yorker*. Its caption read: "No deals is a good deal."

Naturally, Ross's disdain for Raoul Fleischmann and for businessmen in general meant that certainly members of the editorial department did not consort with businessmen. The primary contact between the two camps came at the annual anniversary parties at various hotels, and even then one has to define the word "contact" quite liberally. The parties resembled high school mixers, except that it wasn't adolescent boys and girls who were so awkwardly apart, but editorial and business employees, shuffling around at separate ends of the room. On setting foot in editorial one day, Raoul Fleischmann felt compelled to explain to an onlooker, "It's all right. I have permission to be here."

"Editorial! Don't shoot!" a writer, John McNulty, would shout on occasional forays onto a business floor. Shouting was something so frowned upon in editorial that one had to go to the business floor to do it. The business department was a place where you *could* shout. While no more modern or less shabby than editorial, it was lighter in spirit and richer in conviviality. It was a place where, if an adman landed a big new account, someone would run and clang a genuine ship's bell, then they all would hie off across the street to the Harvard Club to lift their martini glasses in liquid celebration.

It was almost sad, the disdain with which editorial personnel held business ones, because the admen tended to be great admirers of the writers. Writers, thanks in large part to the tone set by Ross but no doubt also to their own proclivities, just would not try to understand what went on in business. Admits a writer: "Editorial thought that the business guys just pasted labels on the magazine and sent it out."

There was intraeditorial disdain at *The New Yorker* as well, and a not altogether friendly notionalism to the everyday life of the place. "Everyone had a strong sense of himself or herself," a writer recalls, "and while in an odd way it worked well, it made for a feeling that it was not a team effort."

A writer recalls being surprised that not only did writers not know what other writers were working on, but they never read anyone else's stories. He remembers asking Edmund Wilson what he thought of a piece that had run. Wilson replied that he hadn't read it. "I used to read *The New Yorker* in my bath," he told the young man, "but I haven't read it in a long time." Recalls the employee: "There was no allegiance to other writers."

There was also something of a class system. At no other magazine was the function of "checkers," editorial employees who make sure that every word printed in the magazine is true, considered as important as at *The New Yorker*, yet former checkers complain of having been dismissed as strange and then ignored. They say they felt like outcasts, isolated in a small office filled floor to ceiling with thousands of reference works, ranging from the *Encyclopaedia Britannica* to volumes of the *New York Times* bound full-size to the directory of the New York Yacht Club. Rogers E. M. Whittaker, for many years the chief of the copy-editing department, was one who "treated us like dirt," says a former checker.

Whittaker's attitude may have had a lot to do with the fact that he and Fred Packard, the head checker, detested each other. Their mutual loathing was in the best tradition of the magazine. Feuds at *The New Yorker* went on for decades. Eccentricity was condoned. It was not encouraged—nothing was; the best one could hope for was tacit approval—but it was condoned, and sometimes it took mean shapes. In the early 1940s, in a startling departure from the status quo, a succession of stunning young women occupied the reception booth in editorial. It was all the more jolting because, says a writer, "No one else in the place was even remotely attractive." One young receptionist, fresh from the Midwest, proudly gave her visiting parents a tour of *The New Yorker* one Sunday afternoon, assuming the offices would be empty. She made the mistake of poking her head into the room of Wolcott Gibbs, who sat composing a review of a play he had seen the night before. Embarrassed and naive, the young woman brightly offered: "Mr. Gibbs is our theater critic." She was fired on Monday.

In contradictory fashion, there was a decency about Ross's *New Yorker*, a strong sense of loyalty toward employees. People who left and didn't make it in the outside world were gathered once more into the fold. Even if they drank or had no particular talent, a place was made for them.

"It was not sentimentality," says a writer, "it wasn't generous or even kind. It was a family sense of loyalty, like 'Let's find a place for Uncle Jim because it's our duty.'"

And for all of Ross's fabled cantankerousness, he really was the old cliché: the rough and tough editor with the heart of gold. He was also brilliant and hardworking. He took manuscripts home each night or returned to the office after dinner. He loved words and spent evenings working his way through the dictionary. When he and Jane Grant eventually divorced, he told her she could have anything but the Funk & Wagnall's. He once gave a friend a page of commas for Christmas. He delighted in bragging that he never read anything. Famous names in writers' copies would often elicit the penciled notation "Who he?" The writer William Gaddis, who was a checker at *The New Yorker* early in his career, recalls sitting at his desk, in an otherwise empty office, and being suddenly aware of a presence behind him—a tall man with a brush haircut.

"Is Moby Dick the whale or the captain?" Ross demanded.

"The whale, sir," Gaddis replied.

Ross thanked him politely, turned, and left, scratching his head and muttering to himself.

Ross once told a bar chum, "I don't want you to think I'm not incoherent."

Examining a cartoon showing two elephants in conversation, Ross exclaimed, "I can't tell which one's talking!" Speakers' mouths were a major preoccupation. They had to be open. "We're not promoting ventriloquism around here!" Ross would trumpet. He scrutinized every cartoon, examined every word; the public delighted in the result.

Ross himself mellowed considerably when, toward the end of his *New Yorker* days, an artist, Ralph Barton, committed suicide. Barton had told Ross on several occasions that he was going to do it, but Ross didn't believe him. He thought that people who *said* so didn't *do* so. He felt responsible afterward for not trying to stop him. From then on, the editor was gentler to his staff, allowing to show on the outside what most of them knew had always been on the inside.

3

The momentum of the wartime "pony" edition of *The New Yorker* carried into the postwar years as soldiers returned home, became civilians, and subscribed to the "real" *New Yorker*. The result was a massive burst in circulation. The mid- to late 1940s would prove to be the greatest of boom times for *The New Yorker*. The magazine became a journal of national importance and stature. Befitting that status, F-R Publishing became The New Yorker Magazine, Inc. It is noteworthy that despite Ross's early exclusion of the old lady from Dubuque, and contrary to popular perception, 80 percent of the *New Yorker*'s eventual readers lived *outside* the New York metropolitan area—outside of Connecticut, New Jersey, or New York.

In 1946, an editor named William Shawn persuaded Ross to devote an entire issue of *The New Yorker* to John Hersey's *Hiroshima*, the monumental opus that imprinted on the world consciousness the human consequences of atomic warfare. With that issue, *The New Yorker* served notice on its readers that it would not return to its prewar funny tone but rather would remain dedicated to publishing long, thoughtful pieces on serious issues. There is some evidence that not all readers readily adjusted to the new approach. "I've read that entire Hiroshima article from front to back," a disgruntled reader informed artist Helen Hokinson, "and I didn't see one funny thing in it!"

Until the day he died, Harold Ross would lament what he saw as a dearth of humor in *The New Yorker*. Nevertheless, he understood that the world's sensibilities had evolved, and that the editorial philosophy of William Shawn reflected that evolution.

Shawn had been hired at *The New Yorker* in 1933 as a freelance Talk of the Town reporter. As he had done on so many other occasions, Ross tried to find an editor in Shawn, and with this Jesus he succeeded. Shawn became an associate editor in 1935 and in 1939 was named managing editor in charge of nonfiction. Another newly appointed managing editor, Gus Lobrano, was placed in charge of fiction. When Shawn took control of what he called the "journalistic side" of the magazine, it was, he has said, in "disarray." The staff was tiny and there was barely three weeks of material in inventory. Shawn built both staff and stock—to excess, arguably. Shawn was a small, dignified man with a balding head, large ears, and rosy cheeks who spoke in a high-pitched, wavering voice. He took great care to select the correct words when he spoke, and his speech was filled with painful pauses, especially when he was in front of a group. He was unfailingly polite, courtly, gracious, and formal in manner. He dressed in dark suits and ties, which he neither shed nor loosened during working hours.

Everything about him was unobtrusive. His shoulders slouched some and his chin seemed to tuck toward his chest. He gave the appearance of a man who would prefer to be invisible. He disliked nothing more intensely than he did a confrontation. It was impossible to clash with Shawn, and thus he was a perfect foil for Ross. Shawn was beloved by his writers, whom he put on a much higher pedestal than did Ross. He became involved in writers' lives on the most personal of levels. He was known to travel across Manhattan at 4:00 A.M. to minister to a hysterical writer. He once wrote in a letter to a *New Yorker* executive that he had gotten involved in the staff's "affairs, illnesses, family deaths, nervous breakdowns, and everything else that affected them and therefore their work." He said that he "listened for hours or whatever it took." He explained that it was "not in Ross's nature to do that, so he delegated."

"Writers need some degree of psychological security," Shawn believed, "since all writers feel insecure."

Harold Ross died on December 6, 1951, at the age of fifty-nine, of an embolism suffered during cancer surgery. He was in the midst of his third divorce. His old friend Hawley Truax was at his bedside in the final days.

While Ross was alive, he did not publicly reveal his choice of successor, but it had long been assumed that the next editor would be one of his two managing editors: Shawn or Lobrano. It was Raoul Fleischmann who made the announcement. On January 21, 1952, a memo on Fleischmann's letterhead and bearing his signature was tacked to the bulletin board in a corridor of the editorial offices that functioned as a sort of town cryer at *The New Yorker*. It read: "William Shawn has accepted the position of editor of The New Yorker, effective today."

For all of his involvement in his writers' lives, his writers knew little about Shawn. He was an obsessively private person. When he arrived at *The New Yorker* in 1933, he did so with an identity that was somewhat changed from that with which he began life. He was born not Shawn but Chon, and he was not Irish, as the former name would seem to indicate, but rather of Russian Jewish extraction.

He was born in Chicago on August 31, 1907, to Benjamin and Anna Bransky Chon. Contrary to some lurid legends that have Shawn's father sharpening blood-soaked butcher knives in the Chicago stockyards, Benjamin Chon owned a nicely prosperous store called the Jack Knife Shop, which purveyed one of the Midwest's larger assortments of knives. He and his parents and a brother named Myron lived in a stately house in the affluent Hyde Park section of South Chicago, and William attended the private Harvard School for Boys. Described by newspapers at the time as "prestigious and fashionable," Harvard was one of a number of schools, including the Princeton and Yale schools, that were founded in the late nineteenth century to prepare young gentlemen to go east to college. The Princeton and Yale schools have long since been shuttered, but Harvard still operates out of the red brick building at 4731 Ellis Avenue on Chicago's south side. The school is more racially mixed now, and inevitably it has gone coed. The neighborhood, one of the most elite at the time that Shawn lived there, later decayed, but it seems now to be enjoying something of a regentrification. Many of the rambling old mansions have been torn down or subdivided into apartments, but others are being restored by families.

William Shawn is a lost alumnus of the Harvard School. No one currently there was aware that he had attended. Douglas Ginsburg, another graduate, is the most recently discussed alumnus of Harvard—he was President Reagan's second unsuccessful candidate for appointment to the Supreme Court in the fall of 1987. (He withdrew from consideration when it was reported that he had tried marijuana.)

An update on the class of 1925, written in 1940, leads off: "Who would have thought that quiet Billy Chon would be on the staff of the New Yorker Magazine? But that is what they tell us, and they say he is a 'big shot' on the editorial staff." But Shawn, while at Harvard, gave every indication of the editor and leader that was to be. He was president of both his freshman and senior classes, secretary of the junior class, manager of the football team, president of the debating society, editor in chief of the senior yearbook (his father placed an ad—"Congratulations to the Seniors from 'Dad' Chon"), and by far the most prolific writer, at least if the volume of his prose and poems published in the yearbook is representative.

In an essay called "First Night," he described the thrill of a theatrical opening: "For some vague reason, it has become a signal for slight heart tremors in certain ones of us who not only love the theatre for what it has to offer in the way of diversion but also relish the thrill that its premier porformance [sic] affords."

In "Reflections," Chon mused on three writers who "have helped considerably in making my first few months of school enjoyable." They were Upton Sinclair, Stephen Leacock, and Joseph Conrad. "Each is an artist in his own particular field and is likely to know more about it than any other contemporary. All that I knew of the Sea and its men, before reading Conrad, was what I had learned from Eugene O'Neill, whose vision was seen to be slightly obstructed after my reading Conrad's sea stories."

Chon's classmates wrote poems describing death in the Yukon and helmsmen pulling on oars. Chon's efforts clearly were more influenced by the likes of Byron and Shelley and others of that ilk. In the poem "Iris" he wrote:

In your mother's breast, my sweet,
While each little throb and beat
Of your heart drew fresher blood
From another, you, a bud,
Oh! A thousand flowers died
And passed on beyond this side,
And the angels made a prayer

49

THE LAST DAYS OF THE NEW YORKER

> That this host of flowers fair
> Bear a kiss from God above
> For your soul, my purest love.

Chon was twitted by his schoolmates for his idealistic approach to love. His write-up in his junior year annual reads: "Bill's ideals of the fair sex are somewhat a mystery to us, and we often wonder whether he actually lives up to them." His sophomore description read: Chon "finds no amusement in the gentler, fairer, et cetera. He is a great theatre fan." Shawn wrote the junior class poem and said of himself:

> Then Bill Chon, who frequently said
> That surely he never would wed.
> He understood, too,
> That he'd never be blue,
> Because he was very well-'red.'

When Shawn was at Harvard, the school was at the center of one of the most notorious, grisly, and puzzling episodes in American crime—the Leopold and Loeb case, frequently referred to as "The Crime of the Century." Nathan Leopold and Richard Loeb were nineteen-year-old sons of millionaires who in 1924 kidnapped and murdered Bobby Franks, fourteen, a Harvard freshman. Leopold himself had graduated from Harvard.

A story that has become attached to Shawn is that he was the intended victim of Leopold and Loeb. Shawn has denied there is truth to the legend. According to Brendan Gill in his book *Here at The New Yorker*, Shawn said that he was too old for Leopold and Loeb's purposes. It is difficult to see why two years would have made a difference to the kidnappers, especially since Shawn was small for his age. Still, the Chicago newspapers of 1924 and 1925, following the case in minute detail, made no

THE LAST DAYS OF THE NEW YORKER

mention of a William Chon. Leopold and Loeb, when the evidence mounted up against them, confessed to the crime in several days' worth of testimony, and both claimed that they had chosen Bobby Franks at random.

According to Joseph Anzek, the current headmaster at the school, there has always been a rumor that Leopold and Loeb *did* have another boy in mind, someone they didn't like, but that he was absent that day. But at the school, the name Chon has never been put forth as that of a potential victim. A wealthy industrialist, Armand Deutsch, who was the grandson of the founder of Sears Roebuck, where Loeb's father was an executive, believes himself to have been the intended victim. In any case, those who choose to believe it was Shawn attribute his famed shyness and bouts of paranoia to the incident. The murder in itself was sufficiently horrifying to have a lasting psychological effect on all of the adolescent boys who were close to it.

Bobby Franks had been engaged in the most wholesome of American pastimes before he left school that day—he umpired a baseball game. On his way home, a car pulled up next to him. He spoke briefly to its occupants, got in, and was never again seen alive.

He was murdered that night and was later discovered face down in a Hyde Park swamp. To prevent Bobby from screaming, the murderers stuffed acid-soaked rags in his mouth, which burned out the inside of his mouth and a portion of his face, and later poured acid on his body. It was speculated that the perpetrators were "male annoyers of boys" and might have hoped, with the acid, to destroy evidence that they had molested Bobby. They then bludgeoned him to death with what the police described as a small tool.

In the manhunt that followed, the police scoured the city in search of "cocaine fiends" on the premise that only a drug-crazed fanatic could have committed such a heinous crime. But a pair of glasses found by the swamp led them to young Nathan Leopold. His seemingly solid alibi—on the night of the murder he was with his friend Richard Loeb—soon collapsed. Under intense questioning, Leopold began to crack and then finally confessed.

Through it all, the Harvard students were hounded by the press and faced daily with every sordid detail of the case. It was never determined beyond a shadow of a doubt if Franks was molested, but the discussion was enough to terrorize young boys, as, certainly, were accounts of acid-soaked rags and bludgeonings. The school's approach was to pursue business as usual. A former student recalls a sixth-grade teacher's telling her class that the murder was a subject that would not be discussed. It's hard to believe that as sensitive and poetic a young man as William Chon emerged unscathed.

Shawn attended the University of Michigan from 1925 to 1927, dropped out, and for all of his protestations about marriage, wed Cecille Lyon, a woman as ebullient and outgoing as he was reserved, on September 1, 1928, the day after his twenty-first birthday. The couple have three children: Wallace, the actor and playwright who is perhaps best known for a movie he wrote and acted in: *My Dinner with André*; Allen, a composer, who is married to a *New Yorker* writer, Jamaica Kincaid; and Mary, Allen's twin, who is retarded and lives in an institution.

Shawn reportedly changed his name from Chon to Shawn, a near homophone for his birth name, because he thought he might want to be a writer, and he figured acceptance would come harder if people believed he was Chinese. At the time he switched, the writers most highly regarded by romantic young aspirants were Irish. It may not be pertinent, but it is certainly worth noting that while Shawn was at the Harvard School, its predominantly Jewish student body was subjected to heavy doses of anti-Semitic verbal abuse and on occasion physical attacks by boys from neighboring schools.

In 1928, Shawn found work as a reporter for the Las Vegas, New Mexico, newspaper *Optic*. The following year, he joined the *International Illustrated News*, in Chicago, as Midwest editor. Early in his career, Shawn was torn between pursuing writing or music as a career, and for a while, he played jazz piano in a bar in Montmartre. Pete Spelman, a former *New Yorker* executive who has heard Shawn play, says, "It's a little like watching Billy Talbert play tennis." The game is rusty and the age shows, but what remains is ample proof of the talent that was.

In his career at *The New Yorker*, Shawn produced only one piece that ran above his byline, and not even a full byline at that, but rather the initials W. S. It was a work of fiction entitled "The Catastrophe." Published on November 14, 1936, "The Catastrophe" told the tale of the destruction of New York by a meteor. It is interesting that it was a humor piece, though hardly a competitive challenge to a Benchley or a Thurber. As the tale begins, a meteor grazes the Manhattan skyline and falls "into either the sea or the outskirts of Carlstadt, New Jersey." No harm was done, and, in fact, the event went all but unnoticed. "All astronomers having been asleep at the time, the world had to rely for data on such unscientific observers as two giddy airmail pilots, a scattering of cops, several nonunion millworkers on the night shift, and a man going home from El Morocco."

The next day, however, another meteor fell. This one failed to disintegrate: "It landed, nice and tidy, on all five boroughs of Greater New York."

As an editor William Shawn was meticulous about proper usage. He and his band of copy editors terrorized writers into employing proper word use and grammar no matter how contorted the resulting sentence. Thus it is noteworthy that as an author Shawn got away with this: "Mayor Kelly of Chicago long-distanced Mayor La Guardia to offer sympathies."

But La Guardia received no long-distance call because La

Guardia, of course, was a casualty. "Approximately seven and a half million New Yorkers, and over a half-million visitors from out of town (who cared very little for the city anyway), had been annihilated. The only New Yorkers who had escaped were those who chanced to be at Miami Beach, and there they remained, shaking their heads and trying to find someone who would cash their checks.

"It was not until the newspapers, in simultaneous spurts of fancy, decided to reprint the New York telephone directories as an obituary notice that the country began to grasp the scope and connotations of what had happened. New York City, like Pompeii, was through."

There followed a period of "readjustment. Boston took over as the Eastern shipping center. The gap in the American League was filled by the Baltimore Orioles; in the National, by the Toledo Mud Hens. . . . Then there was a wave of Catastrophe jokes (Catastrophe who?)."

After five years, New York was gone from the last map. After twenty, "there was a full generation without a single first-hand New York memory. Eventually, the few old timers who still claimed to have seen New York were regarded as cranks. They had to be humored when they talked about the electric signs on Broadway, the shops along Fifth Avenue, the subways, the Metropolitan Museum and Central Park and Harlem, the lobby of the Waldorf, the view from the Empire State Building. Nobody had the heart to tell them that New York had been invented by H. G. Wells."

Shawn has told associates that he did not particularly like "The Catastrophe," that it was not the kind of writing he wanted to do. Though he did not sign future articles, he did sometimes write segments of Talk of the Town, and he wrote many obituaries of *New Yorker* staff members. But most of his energies were channeled into editing. It was his editorial skill and his ability to work with people that earned him Harold Ross's chair.

Shawn did not heighten his profile to correspond with the exalted new title of editor of *The New Yorker*. Indeed, the polarity between the visibility of his position and the invisibility he seemed to wish upon himself led him to be described by columnist Brendan Gill as the best-known unknown man in America. He did not attend celebrity-thronged events or the kinds of Literary Lions dinners that other New York editors aspired to. He rarely went anywhere in public where he was likely to be reported on. He eschewed the usual publishing watering holes and instead lunched on corn flakes or coffee cake and Sanka at a corner table in the Rose Room of the Algonquin Hotel. The table had often been occupied by Ross as well as by Fleischmann—though not together—and the Algonquin had always served as a kind of corporate cafeteria for *The New Yorker*. It was geographically desirable, just steps away from the magazine's offices.

Shawn also retained his air of formality. Only a very few people called him "Bill." To the vast majority of the staff he was "Mr. Shawn."

Shawn, like his mentor Ross, had a number of personal idiosyncracies. He was opposed to talking in elevators and whistling in hallways. He avoided confined spaces. He did not like elevators, especially self-service ones. When the elevator operators in the *New Yorker's* building went on strike, Shawn stayed home. When the lobby of 25 West Forty-third was renovated, so too were the elevators. They were converted to self-service, and the glass doors were replaced by metal ones. One elevator, however, was left as it was, with glass and operator intact, in deference to Shawn. *The New Yorker* assumed the cost of paying the operator. On occasion a group of *New Yorker* staff members would travel by train to Connecticut to visit a printing plant. Shawn would take a cab to 125th Street and board the train there, instead of getting on with the others at Grand Central on Forty-second Street, just a couple of blocks from *The New Yorker*. The train travels underground out of Grand Central and up the East Side, and Shawn does *not* travel underground.

Shawn had an unusual approach to problems. For instance, when discussing with a member of the business department whether or not a certain ad should run, he would go back to a root question. "Should we have any advertising at all?" he would wonder aloud. Then he would proceed to the next step. "Assuming we have advertising, what *kind* should we have?" And finally, "Now, what of this particular ad?"

He was extremely persuasive, even while broaching topics in such a way that it did not appear as if he was trying to persuade. He could couch a suggestion that a writer change a word in such a way that the writer ended up thinking it was his or her own idea. "He could talk you out of your socks," a former associate recalls. Some people who have worked with him believe the impression of timidity is a calculated one, that he is even manipulative. "Beneath that benign exterior," says a colleague, "there is an egomaniac lurking." Shawn is not so shy, they say, as he works at appearing in order to ward off unwelcome intrusions from the world. What no one doubted was that the sweetness and shyness masked a strong will. Somehow, Shawn got his way. Writers called him "the iron mouse." Mostly they admired him and even idolized and idealized him. Dozens dedicated books to him.

In 1953, Raoul Fleischmann paved the way for another generation of Fleischmann involvement in *The New Yorker* when he appointed his thirty-one-year-old son, Peter, a stockbroker at Smith Barney, to the board of directors. In 1956, Fleischmann further strengthened the family's hand by bestowing the title of president of *The New Yorker* upon Stephen Botsford, his stepson and the son, by a previous marriage, of Raoul's wife, Ruth, who was also the mother of Peter Fleischmann. Stephen's brother Gardner worked at *The New Yorker* as an editor, and married a writer, Janet Malcolm.

Stephen Botsford was popular with the staff. He was, says a man who worked for him, "incredibly brilliant, flip, world-weary, wry, amusing and sarcastic." The employee pauses, then adds a line that is inevitably uttered in any discussion of Stephen Botsford: "He was also a hopeless drunk." In Botsford's tenure as president, the magazine became saddled with a reputation that it would not shake for decades: It was a place where top management was often drunk.

In those days, neither the perception nor the reality hurt the magazine, which flourished as its postwar boom continued throughout the 1950s. By the middle of that decade, *The New Yorker* was running more than 4000 pages of advertising a year, ranking it third among all magazines even though it was only seventy-second in circulation.

The meager circulation bothered no one. The business department clung as ferociously as ever to the notion that where subscriptions were concerned, less was more. The original premise of the magazine was working beautifully. If you produced a quality product, you attracted a quality reader, and the reader, in turn, would lure advertisers who were willing to pay more to reach an affluent audience. *The New Yorker* was still virtually alone in catering to people with intelligence and wealth. It was, and would be for decades to come, the only literary publication that consistently made money.

The magazine business had turned a corner into a future full of unknowns. The new miracle of television meant that advertisers could now find their way into millions of homes electronically. Just as it was predicted that radio would become extinct, so, too, was it prophesied that magazines would suffer. To some extent, they did, but it was not *The New Yorker* that felt the impact, but instead mass magazines like *Life* and the *Saturday Evening Post*, which were trying to appeal to everyone. In their struggle to prosper, and in some cases just to survive, magazines were still going after numbers. Stephen Botsford, in a 1958 speech to magazine editors, deplored the state of the industry. He said, "How healthy it would be if magazines tried to get better instead of bigger. They seem to have lost interest in quality in the race for size."

It was lucky for him and for his magazine, though, that the others had not yet tried to emulate the *New Yorker* formula. Nor should he have wished such an occurrence upon *The New Yorker*. Competition would come soon enough.

*   *   *

In 1961, Raoul Fleischmann, in a reaction to Stephen Botsford's refusal to separate himself from the bottle, fired his stepson. (The official account was that he resigned.) Stephen, then forty-two, left, saying, "I'm old and tired, and I don't want to be president of *The New Yorker* anymore." He pursued his first love, writing, but with no great success, and he continued to drink heavily. He died six years later of pneumonia.

At around the same time he forced Botsford out, Raoul persuaded his son Peter to join the staff. Peter began to work his way through the ranks, stopping at least briefly in every business department so that he could learn how the company as a whole operated. He was smart and he worked hard. He was intent on learning. He developed a particular fascination with production and manufacturing, and could discourse at length and with great enthusiasm about types of paper and machines and processes in a way that was oddly touching. His fellow workers liked him. He was perfectly capable of behaving like one of the guys—as opposed to the boss's son. Potential resentment that might have been aimed in his direction was softened by his willingness to work and learn as well as by tradition—the concept of nepotism had always been embraced at *The New Yorker*.

Stephen Botsford's successor as president was A. J. "Joe" Russell, whom Fleischmann elevated from ad director. Russell, with his actions, did nothing to alleviate the hard-drinking reputation of *New Yorker* executives. In fact, he exacerbated it. It became a given among employees as well as in the advertising community that you didn't try to do business with *New Yorker* executives in the afternoon. They were approachable and even reasonable in the morning, but following a long liquid lunch, anything could happen. "It was like the shoot-out at the OK Corral on the seventeenth floor in the afternoon," says a former executive. "They might just as soon fire you as look at you. On the other hand, they might give you a raise. You never knew what was going to happen." But again, the perception didn't hurt business. As the sixties progressed, *The New Yorker* grew increasingly fat and prosperous. The business department was reveling in it. By 1965, in the business departments, but especially in advertising, a group of new "Young Turks" had assembled. Their aggressiveness and ambition exceeded the bounds of those qualities seen in previous generations at *The New Yorker*. In contrast to the editorial department—which still retained a kind of quietness and even, as one writer expresses it, "creepiness" under Shawn—there was a team spirit and a camaraderie in business.

They formed a softball team, calling themselves "Tilley's Tigers." At least once a week in the spring and summer, weather permitting, they rented a hotel room where everyone would go to change into shorts and Tilley's Tigers T-shirts. Then they would charge up to Central Park to take on other teams from ad agencies or magazines. The players were all male and included the upwardly mobile group of George Green, who had been an ad salesman, was now assistant treasurer, and would later become president; Bob Young, an ad salesman on his way to becoming ad director; and Fred Jackson, an adman who would eventually become publisher of *Mademoiselle* and later *Town & Country*. Ken Bosee, formerly research director, then treasurer, older than the others and entrenched at *The New Yorker* since 1948, played too. A group of women headed by Elaine Matteo, a former secretary who was by then assistant to Bosee, cheered from the sidelines. Peter Fleischmann never played, but he often showed up to watch and cheer. After the game, the players returned to the hotel to shower and change, then they'd all go off to dinner together. George Green wrote a newsletter, *Speaking of Softball*, which was distributed to all employees the morning after the game, bearing headlines like "Tilley's Tigers Trounce Ted Bates."

Nor did they need softball as an excuse to convene. They also played football, once with Lindsay's Lancers, the City Hall team, and if they didn't play football, they got together anyway, a band of them socializing so frequently that they become one large roving group date. Unlike the eerie quiet of editorial, advertising was still filled with yelling in the halls and the traditional ringing of the ship's bell. The flood of advertisers was so strong that it had to be dammed. Ads were turned away. Some were rejected on altruistic grounds. In 1965, following the release of the surgeon general's report on the hazards of smoking, *The New Yorker* adopted a new policy banning cigarette ads from its pages. The cigarette manufacturers had been substantial advertisers, yet in that year, *The New Yorker* carried 6092 pages of ads, making it number one in ads among all magazines. Its nearest rival for the position, *Business Week*, wasn't even close with only 4808 pages. In 1965, *The New Yorker* shrugged off a total of $750,000 worth of business. Cigarettes were not all that were found unsuitable. They also rejected some advertisers other magazines would have been thrilled to showcase. Sears Roebuck, for one, was deemed not in keeping with the kind of advertisers *The New Yorker* wanted to publish. The magazine didn't *need* Sears. It had Bergdorf's, Bonwit's, Bloomingdale's, Saks, Peck & Peck, and Trimingham's of Bermuda, as well as Jaguar cars, Rolex watches, Tiffany jewels, Revillon furs, Portraits by Bachrach, and nearly every conceivable expensive brand of liquor.

The rejections engendered ill will in the advertising community as the magazine's staff began to be perceived as arrogant. Some salesmen *were* arrogant and abrasive in their dealings with would-be advertisers. The media buyer for a cruise line was told by a salesman, "I don't need to talk to you, I can talk to the president of the company. And I don't need to talk to anyone, because no matter what I do, you'll continue advertising in *The New Yorker*. You need us more than we need you." Other sales-

THE LAST DAYS OF THE NEW YORKER

people were not arrogant but were perceived that way because they were turning business down. They were saying, "We can't make room for you." No matter how prettily it was put, nobody liked rejection.

Because even after the magazine rejected advertisers for specific reasons, there was still not enough room for ones that would otherwise have been quite desirable. In the glory days a salesman might, as early as May, tell a client, "We can't take your ad in October, November, or December, but we'd be happy to run it in January." Clients found it insulting. The fall was the important selling season; January was a consumer wasteland, reserved for the less-than-elite ads for sales and clearances. Furthermore, it was embarrassing for ad agency account managers to have to turn around and explain to their clients, the advertisers, that they couldn't get space in *The New Yorker* for the clients' products. The rejection grated most on agencies with longtime associations with the magazine. Nevertheless, in 1966, the sales force sold— or, more appropriately, accepted—6143 pages of advertising, an all-time record high that would never again be achieved.

Against great odds, the *New Yorker's* prosperity did not go unnoticed. The New Yorker Magazine, Inc., was technically public, but the shares rarely traded. The line on Wall Street used by the few investment people acquainted with the stock was that "it trades by appointment only." Security analysts, who concern themselves only with stocks that are of interest to large institutions, didn't follow it because it was too small. There was not enough stock available. Also, many investors didn't even realize that *The New Yorker* was a public company. The belief was that the Fleischmann family owned it. The Fleischmann family and their trusts controlled around 25 to 30 percent of the stock. Related friendly insiders, like E. B. White and Jane Grant, among others, owned another 15 percent or so. Hardly anyone ever sold. The rest of the stock was held by people who were equally committed. It wasn't the sort of stock you traded in and out of. It was the kind you married.

Nevertheless, a discerning few were interested in buying. One such was William S. Paley, the founder and chairman of CBS. There was a joke around the *New Yorker* offices that if it was spring, it must be Paley, because each year CBS came around with an offer to purchase the magazine. In 1963, Paley had actually believed that he had a deal, but it fell apart because the Fleischmanns kept insisting on inserting a clause in the contract that would, in effect, allow *The New Yorker* to divorce CBS if it didn't like the corporate marriage. Heir apparent Peter Fleischmann explained to a reporter, "It was just too damned complicated."

Also in the mid-1960s, an Omaha, Nebraska, investor named Warren Buffett began, through two companies that he controlled, to accumulate *New Yorker* stock. Buffett had formed a private investment partnership in 1956 with $100,000 borrowed from family members. By 1969, when the partnership was broken up, it would be worth $100 million. In the interim, in 1965, Buffett bought a New England textile company, Berkshire Hathaway, which he would use as his investment vehicle. Subsidiaries of Berkshire Hathaway would buy *New Yorker* stock, as would subsidiaries of another company of which Buffett was CEO, Diversified Retailing Company.

It comes as no surprise, with financial results like Buffett's, that he developed a reputation as a shrewd investor and even became a legend in the investment business. Buffett had been a student of Benjamin Graham, an investment pioneer who, with David Dodd, wrote what remains the definitive text on security analysis, aptly titled *Security Analysis*. Buffett's approach was to accumulate a lot of stock in a very few companies that lent themselves to analysis. If there were variables that made the future harder to predict, such as government regulation, he was not interested. Buffett liked to invest for the long term. He wasn't given to overnight trades. Like everyone else in the investment business. Buffett wished to buy stocks at prices that would turn out to be bargains. Unlike most people, Buffett was nearly always successful in that last aim. But *The New Yorker* turned out to be one of his losing ventures.

The Fleischmann family was not unduly alarmed by Buffett's advances, nor were they threatened by CBS or any other would-be buyer. The business and investment environment of the mid-sixties was very different from that which exists today. The corporate raiders who launch hostile takeover bids, then plunder companies and pick through the carcasses once they have succeeded, were not yet a phenomenon twenty years ago. Warren Buffett seemed content to sit with his investment.

5

William Shawn was sixty years old in 1967, an age that signifies approaching retirement for most mortals. Raoul Fleischmann instructed Shawn to find a replacement for himself. Fleischmann was in his mid-seventies and in poor health, a circumstance that prodded him to put his house in order. Former *New Yorker* treasurer Ken Bosee recalls that in several luncheon conversations, Fleischmann told him that "the main assignment" that he had given Shawn was to find a successor. But Shawn was decades—and maybe longer—away from willingly relinquishing his job. He was at the height of his power.

There is a popular belief that *The New Yorker* didn't change much under Shawn. Tom Wolfe, writing in 1965 in the *New York Magazine* Sunday supplement of the *Herald Tribune*, called Shawn "the museum curator, the mummifier, the preserver-in-amber, the smiling embalmer—for Harold Ross's New Yorker." It was a common misperception that Shawn existed as some sort of editorial manservant, dedicated to preserving his late master's literary belongings intact. Shawn himself often conveniently harkened back to Rossian theory when he needed to buttress his own arguments, and on occasion he referred to himself as "custodian" of the magazine. But that was the "iron mouse" talking. Shawn's *New Yorker* was as different from Ross's as Shawn was from Ross. Some of the differences were cosmetic, others went to the very definition of the magazine.

Many years later, in November 1983, Shawn would make an unusual pilgrimage, via elevator, to the sixteenth-floor conference room of the business department, to talk to *New Yorker* sales staff. The answers he gave to their questions that day serve to illustrate his philosophy throughout his reign.

When Ross was editor, *The New Yorker* ran humorous and whimsical covers. Shawn's covers tended to be more serious and often bland. An advertising man said to Shawn that all the covers seemed to have a sameness to them; they were, he said, "dull." Shawn replied that they may have seemed that way to "the reader or to some outside observer," but that "to us who have to do with developing the covers... what we see is a succession of beautiful covers." He admitted that "we have fewer covers today that have humor than we did years ago. We can't explain that. They just don't seem as appropriate." Instead, "They tend to be more aesthetic and the subject matter for the most part is New York City or the country around New York City. The suburbs, the countryside. Sometimes they're just a still life of flowers or a plant.... It's not supposed to be spectacular. When it appears on a newsstand, it's not supposed to stand out. It's a restful change from all the other covers, I'd say."

Shawn carried on the Ross tradition of reviewing questionable advertisements before they ran, but he was stricter than his predecessor in defining what was appropriate. Ross allowed lingerie advertisements. Bras and girdles were not just displayed in abstract drawings, but photographed on live models. "Does Your Girdle Have a Crush on You?" Warner's wanted to know in 1950.

An ad for Vanity Fair lingerie showed a model in a lacy "night dress," and another racier one featured the bare back of a woman wearing only a half-slip. Shawn put a stop to such ads. He didn't think they were appropriate.

Likewise, Ross had rejected or toned down cartoons that were too suggestive, but he was more liberal than his successor. A Peter Arno cartoon that appeared in 1950, for example, showed a big-eyed, bountiful-breasted young blonde admiring the mink coat that has just been bestowed upon her by a portly, balding gentleman whom kind interpreters might take to be her "uncle." "Gee, Mr. Payson!" the blonde exclaims. "Mere words can't express my appreciation—I guess." Ross ran it. Often, it seems, the cartoons slipped through because a naive Ross didn't quite grasp the meaning. A famous Arno cartoon showed a couple in a police station carrying the backseat of an automobile. The caption read, "Officer, someone has stolen our car." Ross confessed after it ran that he hadn't gotten the joke.

Though the official policy was to shun profanity, under Shawn the language of the magazine got a bit spicier. Ross himself was a profane man, but, as Shawn explained to the *New Yorker* sales force, "He didn't like obscenity in the magazine. He didn't like even profanity in the magazine. There were very few damns and hells. He just didn't like it. He felt that the magazine was going into the home. It was a family magazine." Under Shawn, the "hells" and "damns" crept in, but by the time they did, other magazines had gone on to far saltier words that made *The New Yorker* seem chaste in comparison.

Shawn disapproved of the fashion industry, and unlike Ross, he didn't see any virtue in reporting on skirt lengths or what designer was making which fashion statement. In the 1983 conference with the sales force (to jump forward in time to illustrate Shawn's philosophy), Shawn was asked why Kennedy Frazer, a writer whom Shawn called "the best fashion writer I guess there has ever been," didn't write more. Shawn replied that fashion was "now a combination of commerce and, to use a terrible word, hype." He said that Frazer's past writing had proved that "there was very little real and consistent true fashion as an art. There are some very fine designers but even they are caught up in a world of publicity and business." Not only was Shawn revealing his hand where fashion was concerned, but he also seemed to be making a value judgment about any product that promotes itself. What that translated to in his philosophy about *The New Yorker* was that he would probably rather have only five people reading it than to knuckle under to crass commercial considerations.

With light fashion reporting gone, whimsical covers a thing of the past, and the waning of humorous writing, *The New Yorker* had become increasingly serious. The most substantive change came in the length and breadth of the stories. Shawn did not embrace the Ross dictum that *The New Yorker* was no place for editorial advocacy, and *certainly* he did not share Ross's love of brevity. As noted earlier, it was Shawn who persuaded Ross to dedicate an entire issue to the Hiroshima article, which was both serious and long. Shawn allowed the subjectivity to show through in nonfiction pieces that numbered among them some of the most important ever written. He published Rachel Carson's "Silent Spring," which sounded the alarm on the potentially devastating effects of pesticides at a time when the assumption of most Americans was that they represented welcome progress. The book is often credited with having launched the environmental movement. In 1962, Shawn ran James Baldwin's passionate essay on racial discrimination, "The Fire Next Time." Truman Capote's "In Cold Blood" first appeared in *The New Yorker*, and while it was not strictly journalism, the riveting account of the murder of a Kansas family was the first, and probably still the best, example of the journalistic novel.

Along the way the magazine published articles on the dangers of asbestos, the effect of aerosol propellants on the ozone layer, and nuclear testing. Shawn seemed to have a prescience for discovering topics that would become imprinted upon the American consciousness, in some cases many years before they became national issues.

Shawn erected a literary empire of around two dozen editors on the payroll and 140 writers under contract, divided approximately evenly between fiction and nonfiction. The only writers receiving what could technically be defined as a weekly salary were a handful of columnists, like Brendan Gill and Edith Oliver, who in those days covered Broadway and Off Broadway, respectively. Around half of the writers under contract had offices at *The New Yorker*.

Shawn professed great admiration for his writers. *New Yorker* writers "are doing creative work," he told the *New Yorker* sales staff in his visit with them. "They are literary as much as they are journalistic. They are not like writers for *Newsweek* or *Esquire*. They are *writers*."

He cossetted them and wrapped them in a blanket of financial security unknown at other publications. Their contracts, drawn up on an individual basis, were among the more distinctive features of *The New Yorker*. Writers received a nominal annual stipend—say, $100 or so—in return for which they granted *The New Yorker* right of first refusal of their work. If Shawn chose not to buy a piece, the writer was free to peddle it elsewhere. At least, that was how it worked in theory. In practice, that system applied really only to fiction writers. Nonfiction ideas were approved before the writer went to work. According to Shawn, "Every piece is developed in collaboration between the writer and the editors. Whether the idea is his own or comes from the editor, it has to be something that the writer has a real and deep enthusiasm for. But that enthusiasm has to be shared by the editors or editor. So it isn't just a lot of writers running around loose, writing exactly what they want to write and then we publish it."

Under Shawn, while writers were researching and reporting a piece, they had the benefit of a drawing account which allowed them to obtain generous advances of cash to live and work on. Around half of the nonfiction writers took advances in the form of a weekly paycheck.

It was an exemplary system when it worked, because it granted writers the peace of mind that comes with some sort of financial security, and it afforded them the luxury of time to tackle subjects which might not necessarily be commercial but which deserved to be explored. It worked less well when writers became too comfortable, even lazy, and exploited the system by taking five or ten or fifteen years to finish an article.

Remuneration was solely at the discretion of Shawn, though he did entrust the details to one person, Milton Greenstein, a lawyer who acted as an intermediary between editorial and business. Greenstein was a rarity at *The New Yorker* in that he stepped with ease and agility back and forth over the line between the two departments. He served on the board of directors, yet writers trusted him to negotiate their book deals and prepare their tax returns. (He took over those tasks from Hawley Truax.) But Shawn did not share with the business department details of his methods of compensation. Shawn told the advertising department, in the question-and-answer session with them, that the writers "are all treated equally and they're all paid the same amount for the same work."

Even many writers at the magazine believed that there was a set per-word rate. A word payment system might seem alien to as highbrow a journal as *The New Yorker*. While it leads to the inevitable jokes—"no wonder the stories are so long"—it's a practice that seems more appropriate to a magazine like, say, *Ellery Queen*. And in fact, Shawn could call the system what he would, but all of his writers were not equally compensated, and who got what was a common topic of discussion. Elizabeth Drew, the political reporter, was rumored to be compensated in the hundreds of thousands by Shawn. A former *New Yorker* top executive says that Shawn paid upwards of $25,000 for profiles, he *thinks*. It is indicative that a major executive wasn't even sure what the going rates were. Shawn's way around the stated system was to tack bonuses on for articles he especially liked.

Susan Cheever wrote in a biography of her late father, the writer John Cheever, that he received only forty-seven cents a word from *The New Yorker*, and couldn't get by on what he earned there. That statement directly contradicts a stated Shawn principle that writers should not *have* to write for other publications.

Once compensated, however handsomely, writers still had to get published, and under Shawn, there was an important distinction between getting bought and getting published that irked writers. Shawn was obsessed with building an inventory of works, countless of which never appeared in the pages of the magazine. Others could molder for as long as ten or fifteen or twenty years before publication. The record is believed to belong to a short casual by John Updike that was published twenty-one years after it was accepted.

Writer E. J. Kahn, Jr., who has spent half a century at *The New Yorker*, complained at an Authors Guild seminar in 1985 that he found it quite distressing that so many of his pieces never saw print. The money he was paid provided little solace. Many writers write more for the satisfaction of being published than they do for the money. If it were otherwise, they would pursue a more lucrative career.

Kahn said, "One of the reasons that quite a few of us who are not regular columnists... spend a great deal of our time writing books now is that it's almost impossible to get your pieces into the magazine no matter how good you may think they are, no matter how good the editors may think they are... and no matter how well they pay you for it.

"No matter how handsomely one may get paid for a piece that isn't published," Kahn continued, "the subject of the piece, particularly if it's a profile and one has spent days, hours, weeks, months bothering the hell out of a subject, the subject will never quite believe that you wrote the piece, that it got bought, that it got praised, and that it isn't going to run because there are fifty other writers competing for the space."

Kahn imagined that Shawn lived in fear of press time—and nothing to publish. So, went Kahn's thinking, Shawn stocked up inventories and refused to admit that a piece was never going to run. By the time the editor got around to printing it, the war was over or the profile subject was dead. Shawn once closed the poetry department for two years because the pile of accepted but unpublished poems had grown beyond what even *he* considered acceptable. The inventory of cover art was always around a hundred pieces—or two years' worth.

Still, the *New Yorker* writers found little sympathy for their plight among other writers or the publishing world at large. They were blessed with many of the freedoms of free-lance writers but had to face few of the anxieties about where the next check would come from, or when. Whether or not the story ran, they were paid. "If you started it, it was bought," says a former executive. At other magazines, free-lance writers receive only a "kill fee" of 10 to 20 percent of the agreed-upon price for a story that doesn't run.

New Yorker writers drew checks that were meant to represent advances against future earnings. That is rare in the field at large. *New Yorker* authors and artists under contract were included in the company's health and life insurance plans. In 1944, when the magazine instituted its first retirement plan, the contract authors and artists were in it. The benefits were based on career average salary to reflect the fact that artists and writers had rather bumpy pay charts. The contract creative people were also participants in a profit-sharing plan set up in 1963. Further, they retained all rights to the sale of their articles in the "aftermarkets," meaning that if the article became a book, or was optioned to the movies, or was included in an anthology, the proceeds were theirs alone. They did not have to split them with the publication or forfeit them altogether, as is the case at many magazines. Furthermore, *The New Yorker* paid two full-time employees to assist in the secondary sales.

Perhaps the greatest luxury was that they were allowed to write about what interested them. As Shawn put it in his talk with ad people, "Nobody is sent out on an assignment as you would be at many magazines or at all newspapers." They were allowed to explore their subject at length—even up to fifty or sixty thousand words. *The New Yorker* was the only magazine left in America that would publish such lengthy opuses. Furthermore, there were no real deadlines, nor even a lack of funds to make writers hungry and pressure them to produce quickly. And last, on top of time and money and security, they toiled at a magazine that was considered the most prestigious literary vehicle among American writers and readers. They wrote for a magazine that received a quarter of a million unsolicited manuscripts a year, one that every young aspiring writer saw in his dreams. There evolved an ivory tower smugness, and a feeling of security. *The New Yorker* was a safe harbor. It is little wonder that the artists, and especially the editors and writers, were lulled into the mistaken notion that they owned the place.

But even as they believed that, Raoul Fleischmann clung more tenaciously than ever to the notion that stock should not be entrusted to members of the editorial staff. At an annual meeting, in response to a question, he said that he thought "highly of our editors, but don't think they understand business. If things go sour, a drop in our stock price could have a bad psychological effect on them."

Shawn, nevertheless, got on well with Fleischmann. Shawn, like Ross, believed in separating editorial employees from those in the business department. He would not, for example, allow any editorial conferences to be held in the sixteenth-floor business conference room. But he didn't detest businesspeople the way Ross did. Shawn, in fact, broke radically with Ross precedent by joining the board of directors in 1951 and staying on it until 1962. The reason most frequently proffered by editorial staff for his quitting the board was that he decided that boards were no place for editors. No explanation is offered for why it took him more than a decade to reach that conclusion. His abdication from the board, however, happened to coincide with a new SEC ruling that required corporations to publish in their annual reports the salaries of the five highest-paid directors. Perhaps that circumstance influenced Shawn's thinking.

Shawn also engaged in a detente of sorts with the advertising department. Fred Jackson and Pete Spelman, two members of the enemy camp, posed the idea of organizing a series of lunches in which advertisers and members of the advertising community would talk with Shawn's writers and artists. Shawn said, "I would like to think about that, Mr. Jackson and Mr. Spelman." He thought about it for three years, then sanctioned the symposiums in the late 1960s. In one such lunch, John Brooks, a New Yorker financial writer, spoke to the heads of banks and brokerage houses. In another, the cartoonist Charles Saxon communed with art editors. In a particularly popular session, Pauline Kael, one of the magazine's movie critics, had lunch with two hundred leading advertising copywriters in the upstairs room at Sardi's. The attendees became so enthralled that at 4:15 P.M., most of them were still there, analyzing Citizen Kane, frame by frame. Vincent Sardi finally had to tell them, "Unless you want to be joined by the one hundred members of the New Rochelle B'Nai Brith who are arriving in an hour, you'd better get out!"

It turned out that the banner year of 1966 had been the zenith for advertising pages at *The New Yorker*. In 1967, Tilley's Tigers disbanded, because that was the year that business went bad. Instead of frolicking at night, some advertising sales staff worked late trying to dredge up business. The magazine lost 500 ad pages in 1967, another 400 in 1968. The initial bloodletting could be blamed on a sliding economy. *The New Yorker* could not help but be affected as advertisers slashed budgets. But it would get worse before it got better.

In 1968, Joe Russell retired as president of *The New Yorker*. Raoul Fleischmann replaced him with the company treasurer, his son, the only issue of three marriages, forty-seven-year-old Peter. Raoul Fleischmann endured a long illness related to a series of debilitating strokes. Many *New Yorker* employees donated blood to their boss. In May of 1969, the elder Fleischmann died. His death caused great sadness throughout the magazine, even in editorial, where those writers who had known him had liked him, even those who thought he was stingy and who noted his refusal to give them economic participation in the magazine. Fleischmann and Shawn had shared cordial enough relations that Fleischmann remembered Shawn generously in his will. After Raoul Fleischmann's death, Peter Fleischmann and family trusts set up by Raoul Fleischmann would control around 25 percent of *New Yorker* stock, according to company proxy statements. The company would later report that another 7 percent belonged to family members whose holdings did not have to be spelled out in proxies.

A few months after Fleischmann's death, the board bestowed the additional title of chairman of *The New Yorker* upon the company's president, Peter Fleischmann. It was a step that caused barely a ripple and certainly no alarm among editors and writers. Changes in administration had never affected the lives of the creative staff, and even more soothing, the business side continued to rest comfortably and securely in Fleischmann hands.

6

Peter Fleischmann wore his new title with the ease of one who had been born to it, which, of course, he had. *The New Yorker* had always been part of the family. A former school chum remembers a Fleischmann household constantly populated by *New Yorker* luminaries. In the living room of the town house in the East Sixties in Manhattan or on the croquet lawn of the mansion in Sands Point, Long Island, one was apt to bump into Alexander Woollcott or Robert Benchley or Hawley Truax.

The friend recalls that the relationship between Raoul and Peter was one of "formal respect." Raoul and Ruth divorced when Peter was young, and Raoul proved an elusive parent. "He didn't have much time for sophomores," says the friend.

Peter attended Hotchkiss, an exclusive boys' prep school in Connecticut, and later Yale, where among his fellow graduates of the class of 1944 was future New York City Mayor John Lindsay, as well as two men who would be senators, two destined to be governors, and several ambassadors-to-be, including Walter

J. P. Curley, a close friend of Fleischmann's who later became United States ambassador to Ireland.

Peter Fleischmann was good-looking and game, a heavy smoker and drinker who enjoyed partying and being boisterous but never loud. Like his father, he was a gentleman of the old school. Though slight in build, he was an excellent college athlete—a swimmer and a hockey player. After graduation, during the war, he enlisted in the army and was sent to Europe, where he served with an artillery unit. He was a forward observer, his job to scramble ahead of the troops, hiking up mountains and climbing to the top of steeples to see if shells were finding their marks. He fought in and survived the Battle of the Bulge, the decisive Belgian battle that turned back the Germans but left legions of American soldiers dead. It was the second most costly battle, in terms of American lives, of any in United States history. Fleischmann never truly recovered psychologically from that experience. He would often suddenly begin to speak of it, in the midst of unrelated conversations, and to relive it in his own personal kind of shell shock. He was later wounded in the war, but that would prove to be the least of the injuries and illnesses that would plague him throughout his life. Back in the States after the war, he broke his neck in an automobile crash and spent years convalescing.

A man with a naturally sardonic approach to life, he became even more so after the war and as the injuries began to mount up. He became more introverted than he had been in his college days. He was often described as shy, but close friends said that it was not so much shyness as it was a tendency to step back and observe what was going on around him, rather than enter the fray.

As president and chairman of *The New Yorker*, he was more approachable than either his father or Joe Russell had been. He socialized with the staff and kept his door literally and figuratively open to them. But Peter Fleischmann took over at a time of crisis.

Ad pages, already down substantially in 1967 and 1968, fell another 500 in 1969. It is impossible to separate the reasons for the free-fall. Magazine advertising in general was hard-hit through the late sixties and early seventies. But numerous people affiliated with the business side of the magazine at the time say the *New Yorker's* problems in overcoming a weak economy were further aggravated when the publication ran smack up against Nixon and the Vietnam war, and faltered even more. *The New Yorker* turned political. The more political it became, the more both ads and circulation plummeted. Advertising dove another 700 pages in 1970, while circulation drifted downward to 460,000 from 478,000 two years earlier.

The magazine first grappled with the topic of Vietnam in 1967 when it published a series of three reports from the Vietnamese villages of Ben Suc, Quang Ngai, and Quang Tin. The stories were written by Jonathan Schell, Shawn's pet among a clique of young men who had been Harvard College friends of Shawn's son Wallace and who had all ended up at *The New Yorker.* Some readers and politicians hailed the series as a landmark piece of reporting that changed the course of American intellectual thought on Vietnam. But "The Village of Ben Suc," the powerful and indicting portrait of the destruction of that village by American soldiers, was discredited by other foreign correspondents, who claimed that Ben Suc was not a quiet place inhabited by noninvolved and peace-loving villagers, but instead was a Viet Cong stronghold. The debate could never have a clear winner, since the very nature of the war made it impossible, often, for soldiers to determine who was the enemy. On the home front, Americans could not agree on who the aggressors were and, indeed, if there really was an enemy, or if the enemy was ourselves.

Nevertheless, *The New Yorker* became more emboldened, running more savaging on-the-scene reports from Saigon as well as a searing castigation, by Richard Harris, of the pre-Watergate

Nixon justice department. In 1970, following the American bombing of Cambodia, it moved from subjective reporting into a full-fledged editorial attack on the Nixon administration. As the war escalated, so too did the tone of moral outrage and the accusations. Editorials in Notes and Comments, penned primarily by Jonathan Schell, compared America under Nixon to a totalitarian regime, attributed to the administration "a form of official deception that may be altogether new in American political life," and charged that America was engaging "in a brutal and oppressive campaign in another country."

Today the editorials seem almost tame, and certainly *The New Yorker* was not alone in its thinking. But in 1970 the writing was considered incendiary, and opinion of the rightness or wrongness of the *New Yorker* stand was as divided as opinion on the war. William F. Buckley, the conservative editor and columnist, later summed up his camp's opinion when he accused *The New Yorker* of "high colonic conscience-flushing." He wrote that its writers "tend to make the rather common mistake of identifying their own conscience with that of the republic. During the Vietnam years the screech of pain became all but unbearable, and some of us came close to suggesting to the publishers that they bring out two editions of The New Yorker, one with, one without opening pages"—he was referring to Talk of the Town—"charging double for the shorter, unencumbered version."

The New Yorker received hundreds of angry letters from readers who demanded that the magazine cancel their subscriptions, citing as their reason the pro-Communist, anti-American bent it had followed of late. *The New Yorker* had been serious for a long time, and that was accepted. Articles on pesticides might be hotly debated, but in a more controlled, less emotional, and more intellectual manner. Whether or not readers agreed with the conclusions, they somehow understood that *The New Yorker* was venting a subject that needed to be considered. But with Vietnam, the magazine went from serious to outright political, and if you didn't happen to agree with their stand, you weren't happy.

On the other side, the magazine actually found new readers in those days among college students and young, politically liberal, and aware people in their twenties and early thirties.

Between the two camps of the conservatives and the college students were what probably constituted the majority of the readers: people who weren't so much infuriated as they were bored or let down. *The New Yorker* had once been a gentle respite from worldly cares. Now it was bringing the world into the living room. When readers opened its pages, they found less humor and pleasant diversion and more of the same ugly news that confronted them when they read the paper or switched on the television.

The New Yorker had always run what it pleased. A former staff member sums up the philosophy like this: "We don't care what our readers want to read. It is not one of the things that has made us successful. The reader has to want what the editors have to say. This is not normal publishing philosophy, but it is successful." Or was.

J. Kennard "Ken" Bosee, at the time treasurer of *The New Yorker*, believes that the Vietnam coverage caused an irreversible trend to a lower common denominator of reader at *The New Yorker*. "There was a change in the character of the readers," he says. "The numbers didn't change, but where before there were top executives of Fortune 500 companies, now they were replaced with a bunch of kids. The thrust was to a lower audience. The demographics never went up again." That theory, in hindsight, should have proven faulty over time. Yesterday's hippie is today's aging baby-boomer. However, for that moment he was correct. The new audience was less appealing to the *New Yorker*'s traditional advertisers.

Furthermore, while advertisers offered all sorts of excuses for failing to buy space in *The New Yorker*, many of them, without admitting it, feared alienating their more conservative customers. And in any case, a serious and opinionated political journal didn't seem like the proper stage on which to display the wares of a Fifth Avenue department store. Not least, some media buyers, still smarting from the sting of the cavalier treatment previously accorded them by the *New Yorker* sales force, were more than happy finally to get their revenge by *not* advertising. The revenge was made all the more sweet by the fact that they didn't *have* to. There were plenty of alternatives emerging. Counter to the balance of power that had prevailed only a handful of years earlier, now it was the advertisers who could afford to be arrogant.

The success of the *New Yorker*'s approach, targeting itself at a narrow, affluent audience, could not be kept a secret forever, and gradually other magazines began to experiment with the same formula. An early threat was *New York* magazine, which became a glossy after springing, in 1968, from between the pages of the Sunday edition of the *New York Herald Tribune*, which had folded. *New York* seemed a natural advertising vehicle for local advertisers, and especially retail stores, just as *The New Yorker* had been forty years earlier.

The pressures on Peter Fleischmann were enormous. He himself was a political liberal, but while he did not disagree with the views expressed by the writers, he felt that *The New Yorker* had become too much of a "political journal," as he put it to Shawn and others. It was difficult not to blame the dismal state of affairs at the magazine on the unrelenting political bent it had embraced. It seemed as if every time Fleischmann went out in public, someone castigated him about the editorial caterwauling at his magazine.

Raoul Fleischmann had instilled in his son the belief that the editorial department was not to be tampered with. Peter himself had long been a champion of editorial freedom. He used to tell his executives that his primary role at the magazine was "to protect the editorial side." But in 1970, unable to restrain himself, he not only expressed an opinion to William Shawn, but he asked the editor to pull a cartoon. Artist (and writer) James Stevenson had drawn a political cartoon that was a series of panels depicting and skewering Spiro Agnew. Fleischmann thought it was overly incendiary and told Shawn so. He asked him not to run it. Shawn was upset at the request. He told Fleischmann he would like to have lunch to discuss it, which they did.

In a booth at the Algonquin, Shawn told Fleischmann that he was uncomfortable with his "meddling."

Fleischmann replied, "Are you asking me not to interfere?"

Shawn was. But Fleischmann was not swayed. Testament to that is the fact that the cartoon never ran. Business—the owners—won the round. It is significant that Fleischmann had his way and breached the sacred separation, but it is equally significant that as far as anyone can remember, it was the first and last time that a Fleischmann or anyone else then in the business department intruded in editorial affairs. There were many occasions on which executives would roll their eyes and shake their fists in the general direction of the editor's office, but they never again "meddled."

Lost ads were always cause for worry at *The New Yorker*, but the seventies marked the first time that anyone worried when circulation fell, which it did, steadily, through the late sixties and early seventies. Peter Fleischmann was not quite the intellectual snob that his father and Harold Ross had been. On one hand, he believed in what executives at the magazine called "a natural level" of circulation. The *New Yorker*'s audience would somehow find the magazine. There were no concessions made to lure subscribers. There were no reduced-rate subscription offers, except in the case of college students and Christmas gifts, and there was no credit offered. Subscription forms did not bear the notation "Bill Me Later." No discounts and no credit made *The New*

Yorker an oddity in the field. But for Peter Fleischmann, none of that contradicted experiencing a sinking feeling when you actually began to *lose* readers.

In the magazine business, circulation departments had traditionally been treated as poor relations of advertising when it came to garnering revenues. At *The New Yorker* specifically, it was easy to overlook circulation, because there was so much money being made in advertising. Then came the late sixties. Not only did advertisers slash budgets and give more pieces of the pie to television, but at the same time, there were more magazines going after what was left. Publishers began to look to circulation revenues as a way to make up the shortfall. The number of magazines sold—both at the newsstand and through subscriptions—and the efficiency of their sale and distribution took on greater importance. Circulation couldn't drift anymore but instead had to become a sophisticated, modern part of the business. Peter Fleischmann was cognizant enough of that fact to fire four circulation managers in a row.

In April 1971, after the fourth dismissal, Fleischmann tapped George Green to take over the circulation department. Green, like Fleischmann a Yale graduate, had also grown up in a publishing family. His father was Monroe Green, who, as the top advertising executive at the *New York Times*, had become a legend in the industry for his innovative approaches to the business. Green had been hired at *The New Yorker* in 1962 as an advertising salesman covering retail accounts. The morning he arrived he was told that the man who hired him had committed suicide the day before. It was a sad beginning, and an inauspicious one, but it was not, as it turned out, an omen.

Green moved quickly through the ranks, becoming, in succession, a salesman in the Atlanta regional office, assistant to the treasurer, and assistant treasurer. But swift as his rise had been, Green was apprehensive about taking on the circulation job. First, he knew nothing about circulation. And he was aware of the demise of the four previous contenders. The prospect seemed risky at best. Nevertheless, it was too good an opportunity for an ambitious thirty-three-year-old to reject. Besides, Peter Fleischmann had great confidence in him. Unknown to Green, Fleischmann had begun telling others at The New Yorker that Green would someday be president. A former salesman recalls Fleischmann's saying, "Everyone thinks I'm crazy. They don't believe me. But George is the one."

The circulation department was in chaos. Simple yet vital tasks were not being executed. Renewal notices, for instance, were not being mailed out on a timely basis, resulting in interruptions in service (The New Yorker, remember, sent magazines out only on receipt of money) and distortions in the circulation numbers.

When he first joined The New Yorker, Green had guessed that circulation must consist of only three people, because that was the number that toiled away behind the door marked "Circulation" down the hall from his office. Early in his sales career, though, he learned that there were another seventy-five people closeted in an office two blocks away on Forty-fifth Street, pounding out mailing labels from Speed-o-Mat stencils. They were performing "fulfillment" work—the paperwork that has to do with filling subscriptions. To have seventy-five clerks doing that job by hand was almost the equivalent, then, of bypassing the Xerox machine in favor of monks. Today it would be the equivalent, because the task is farmed out to large fulfillment companies that rely heavily on computers. (That is why, if you call Vogue, for instance, with a change of address request, you are provided with an "800" number which connects you to a voice in Colorado.) The fulfillment workers at The New Yorker were held in such low esteem that they weren't even invited to the anniversary party.

In the late 1960s, a New Yorker executive, Marvin Rosenthal, contracted the fulfillment effort out to Neodata, a subsidiary of

A. C. Nielsen based in Boulder, Colorado. With that move, *The New Yorker* made a giant step toward modernizing its processing of subscriptions, but there were still major problems with circulation promotion. Green, when he became circulation chief, made some moves that could be placed under the heading of commonsensical rather than brilliant. By his own admission, "It was pretty basic stuff." The magazine was spending over a million dollars a year on circulation promotion. Most of that was being poured into a direct mail campaign in which letters of solicitation were sent to thousands of names on mailing lists bought by *The New Yorker*. The campaign was not well conceived because the lists for the most part were not compatible with *The New Yorker*, and the returns were so low that each subscriber who signed up cost the magazine $100. Green halted the campaign.

He also set about renovating the renewal process. Renewal notices were mailed on time, accompanied by letters festooned with cute little *New Yorker* cartoons. The first letter would begin, "We hope that The New Yorker has given you pleasure...." The second would read, "Have you forgotten to renew?" The third would assume desperate tones: "This is your last chance! To avoid interruption of your subscription...."

In 1971, the first year that Green took over the department, circulation rose by 15,000. The following year copies were up 3000, then another 6000 in 1973 and 3500 in 1974. Given that the political atmosphere was less charged through those years, circulation might have risen even without Green's tinkering. But Green must at least be given credit for having pulled the department into the decade in which it belonged, as well as for making it more profitable.

Green called the circulation years "the happiest period of my professional life. I would tinker here and tinker there and the costs would go down and the circulation up." Fleischmann left him alone to tinker. In the midst of it, though, came the worst half year of

Green's life. *The New Yorker* had, incongruously enough, branched out by founding a company called Boulder Enterprise, a printer of computer forms and letters that had proved a major money loser. Fleischmann sent Green and another executive, Sam Spoto, to Colorado for six months to turn the company around. Working day and night—"I never even saw the goddamned mountains!" Green recalls—they put it on track. They hired Jim Noel, a smart young executive at Neodata, to run it, and eventually it became one of the *New Yorker*'s most profitable businesses.

Even through the lean and troubled years at *The New Yorker*, the magazine continued to attract potential buyers. Peter Fleischmann fielded a steady influx of proposals, often inviting the hopeful buyer to visit him in his office or to meet for lunch. He would listen politely to the pitch, then promptly forget it. Fleischmann was often described as a man who would tell people what they wanted to hear just to get them out of his office.

A group that came calling in 1972 was led by a magazine consultant named Monroe Pofcher and included editors from *Newsweek* and the *New York Daily News*. The men knew they were rapping on a door worn thin by the knuckles of others in pursuit of the same prize, but they regarded themselves as more suitable candidates than most. They had capital, having secured lines of credit from the Morgan Guaranty bank, the old-line institution with which *The New Yorker* had close ties, and a major insurance company. Yet they were not a large, monolithic organization like CBS or Time Inc. that would engulf *The New Yorker*. They could ensure that the character of the magazine would not be diminished.

Like CBS a decade earlier, the Pofcher group thought it was closing in on a deal. Fleischmann seemed to encourage them. They had *several* lunches with the chairman. Pofcher recalls one comical episode. He and Fleischmann met for lunch at the Sky Club, one of those ubiquitous New York eating clubs, near the

THE LAST DAYS OF THE NEW YORKER

top of the Pan Am building. Fleischmann was a member there. He had by then established his reputation as a heavy drinker in the *New Yorker* tradition. He had a particular fondness for J&B scotch but would occasionally drink wine with a meal. Also in keeping with tradition, with Fleischmann as chairman, it was accepted in the office and in the advertising community that you didn't do business with *New Yorker* executives after lunch.

In any case, on that particular day, Pofcher, feeling strong and hearty, decided to match Fleischmann drink for drink. He chose as his poison martinis, three of which he downed in rapid succession. Then nature called. Pofcher excused himself and made his way to the men's room. It was on the way back out that the liquor hit him and his internal homing device broke down. He couldn't find his way back to the table. He wandered frantically through a series of rooms before finally stumbling onto his seat. He clutched for safety, sat down, and somehow made it through the rest of the meal, peaceful in the knowledge that Peter Fleischmann had poured down so much scotch himself that he couldn't possibly have noticed what happened. Fleischmann made no remark.

Ten years later, Pofcher and Fleischmann met again for a friendly social lunch at the Sky Club. They exchanged a warm greeting. As they sat down Fleischmann said, "Remember that lunch we had ten years ago when you got so drunk you couldn't find the table?"

The deal with the Pofcher group did not go through, unrelated to the Sky Club episode. Fleischmann decided he didn't want to sell. He didn't need the money, and he wasn't eager to let control pass out of Fleischmann family hands. The Pofcher group had nothing to offer that could motivate him.

Looking through the narrow crack in the door that Fleischmann opened to them during "negotiations," the Pofcher group had come to an ominous conclusion about *The New Yorker*:

There was a serious dearth of both management talent and potential management talent. Pofcher told Fleischmann that he saw only one bright spot on the horizon: the young circulation director, George Green. He wasn't telling Fleischmann anything he didn't know. At the magazine and in the industry, Green began to be referred to as the heir apparent.

In editorial, William Shawn gave an indication that he might be cognizant of his own mortality. While he had no immediate plans to step down, at the age of sixty-six, he did begin to search for a successor. In 1972, he appointed as "executive editor" Robert Bingham, a forty-six-year-old nonfiction editor. Thus anointed, Bingham became what writers and editors took to calling "the current focus of the experiment."

7

By early 1973, Omaha investor Warren Buffett's companies' position in *The New Yorker* amounted to 23,053 shares, or about 9 percent of the total then outstanding. Buffett was in an awkward and unaccustomed situation. He owned a large portion of the company, yet he had no control over its fate or, consequently, the fate of his investment. He hadn't even been offered a seat on the board of directors. Furthermore, the stock price had drifted downward during those troubled years, with the inevitable result that the Buffett shares were worth less than what was paid for them. Buffett was not used to experiencing feelings of helplessness when dealing with companies in which he was heavily invested. In a practical sense, he had two options: He could become more involved—own more of the stock, a controlling portion, even, and obtain a seat on the board—or he could sell his stake and make a graceful exit.

At the time that Buffett was mulling his alternatives, another

THE LAST DAYS OF THE NEW YORKER

investor was eagerly and confidently buying *New Yorker* shares. Philip Messinger, a forty-three-year-old stockbroker with the firm of Herzfeld & Stern, had, in 1968 and 1969, liquidated a large position in an electronics firm and was casting about for a place to invest the proceeds. He did not have much confidence in the direction of the market as a whole, and, like Warren Buffett, he did not believe in taking a "market basket" approach to investing. He wasn't even interested in accumulating positions in five or ten companies, as Buffett was. He searched for one special situation. He came upon *The New Yorker.*

"When I found The New Yorker," Messinger says, "it was not like being in the stock market." The fundamentals, it seemed to him, were so solidly intact that there was little risk involved.

"Here was a company," recalls Messinger, "that had a trade-mark publication, an important name, reputation, prestige, and it was selling at only sixty-five percent of its book value. There just wasn't any comparable situation around. And there were growth prospects." The *New Yorker*'s balance sheet at the end of 1972 showed $12 million in cash or cash equivalents, and those figures don't give the total picture. The company kept a segregated account of millions of dollars in cash-equivalent short-term investments to apply against the unearned portion of subscription payments it had received. It was a *very* conservative approach. For all intents and purposes, the cash was readily available.

Messinger noticed all of the cash, and noticed, too, that "it was not money that was needed for working capital. It was pure excess cash. To me it was like shooting fish in a barrel."

In 1972, Messinger embarked upon the slow process of accumulating the stock in the open market. By early 1973, he had amassed several thousand shares at that price. The offer to purchase at $75 was a generous one, since the stock at the time was selling at around $50 a share. But Messinger immediately refused the sale. He wanted to be invested in *The New Yorker*. He began to forage for other investors in hopes of forming a group that might seek to buy out Buffett at $60 a share.

At around the same time, Buffett contacted Peter Fleischmann and expressed interest in buying The New Yorker Magazine, Inc., outright. Fleischmann politely turned him down. And lest his own rebuff prove unpersuasive, Fleischmann set up a meeting between Buffett and editor Shawn. The editor told the investor that *The New Yorker* was a fragile thing, that few owners could understand it as the Fleischmann family did. He added that he himself would not want to work for anyone but the Fleischmanns. Buffett needed no more convincing. He told Fleischmann, in what observers describe as an exceedingly civilized and gentlemanly fashion, that he would not attempt to buy the magazine but instead would sell his shares. *The New Yorker* accommodated him by scheduling a tender offer in March 1973, though accommodating Buffett was not the stated purpose of the offering.

A stipulation in the will of Raoul Fleischmann required that any *New Yorker* stock to be sold by the trustees of his estate must first be offered to the employee profit-sharing plan or to the company. In early 1973, following that dictum, the trustees informed management that they wished to sell 27,000 shares. Peter Fleischmann and the board expressed interest in buying the stock, but they worried that to buy it outright would be to incur lawsuits by shareholders who wished to dispose of their stock as well. And, of course, not only were they aware that Buffett wished to sell 40,000 shares, but they were more than happy to say good-bye to such a large outside owner. To allow Buffett and other shareholders to exit, management extended to all shareholders an offer to buy their stock at $56.25 a share, to a limit of 89,000 shares. According to Buffett, "It was a close decision with me as to whether or not to tender our shares." But in the end he did. Another shareholder, Philip Messinger, had no intention of selling. He bought into the tender offer.

On the morning of March 27, 1973, Messinger called a Herzfeld & Stern trader and instructed him to buy a few thousand shares of *The New Yorker*. He then left his East Side apartment to run errands. He went to Tiffany's, on Fifth Avenue, to buy some presents. When he left the store, he found a phone booth and called his trader. He had bought a thousand shares. "Keep buying," he said. He headed south on Fifth Avenue, browsed through a few more stores, then found another pay phone and called the trader. He had bought another thousand. "Buy more," said Messinger. Then down to Saks, another booth, another thousand. Before day's end he had added several thousand shares to his holdings, and in the days and months to follow he would add still more. Eventually he would own 13 percent of the company, making him the second largest shareholder after the Fleischmann family.

Warren Buffett, a man with near perfect pitch when it came to investing, sold his shares at a loss, by his reckoning, "in the neighborhood of 12 percent." Had he held on, he would have eventually wound up with an enormous profit. But then again, he invested that same year in another media property, the Washington Post Company, with equally excellent results. According to Buffett, his appreciation in Washington Post stock between 1973 and 1985 was 18-for-one, identical to The New Yorker's gain over the same period. What's more, the *Post* proved far more hospitable to Buffett. He became a financial mentor to its chairman, Katherine Graham, who invited him on her board, appointed him to the executive committee, and even entertained him at her house in Martha's Vineyard.

As for *The New Yorker*, it was rid of Buffett, but it had acquired in his place Philip Messinger. He would prove far more vocal, more active, and more difficult to shake.

Later in 1973, Peter Fleischmann appointed George Green to the board of The New Yorker Magazine, Inc. In March of 1974, in an unusual sequence of events, he made Green a vice president. Green had become a director before he was an officer.

Green and Fleischmann had grown close. They had lunch together at least once a week, and often dinner as well. They belonged to a small, tight-knit group of executives who formed an informal club they called "Sam's Club," named for production manager Sam Spoto. Two of the group's members, Fleischmann and newsstand sales manager Frank Ogden, met every afternoon at the Berkley bar, out the *New Yorker*'s back door on Forty-fourth Street, for an hour or two of social drinking. The other members, including treasurer Ken Bosee, Spoto, and Green, would drop in and join them a couple of times a week. Peter Fleischmann delighted in Sam's Club. His face glowed when he talked about the official club tie, which had become a prized possession. But casual as the clan was, it caused some resentment among other executives, who felt excluded.

Green and Fleischmann also saw a good deal of each other on weekends. Fleischmann lived with his wife, Jeanne, on Madison Avenue in the East Sixties in a large and grand apartment in a landmark building. He also had a gracious shingled home in Quogue, Long Island, a dignified seaside town where some of his relatives lived, as did a number of *New Yorker* employees. Fleischmann and Green shared an unabashed enthusiasm for the

New York Giants. On Sunday afternoons in football season, Green would travel the ten blocks from his East Side apartment to Fleischmann's, where the two men would sit in the cozy paneled library, drinking, chatting, and watching their team. Green always noticed that Fleischmann's library had many lamps. It struck him that this was the room of a true reader. On infrequent occasions, Stephen Fleischmann, Peter's son by his ex-wife, Nancy, was present. Young Fleischmann seemed to Green to be an amiable and charming fellow, like his father.

In early 1975, conversations between Green and Fleischmann took a serious turn. There was one particular lunch at the Sky Club at which the chairman seemed depressed, as if the world were weighing heavy on his shoulders. Fleischmann told Green that he had not been feeling well, that his health was not what it should be, and that his doctor had been lecturing him about his smoking and drinking habits. He was only fifty-three. His father had lived to be eighty-four, but his health had gone steadily downhill for the last decade of his life, to the point that he was incapacitated for years. Peter Fleischmann did not mention that fact, but Green had a feeling it was lurking in the background. Fleischmann was at the age where many men start to worry about repeating their fathers' health patterns.

Fleischmann, who still carried the dual title of chairman and president of *The New Yorker*, told Green, "I need someone to handle the day-to-day running of the company." He said that he was no longer up to the task and wanted Green to get more involved. He made no specific offer, provided no more details, just opened the topic to future discussion.

The New Yorker celebrated its first half century on February 21, 1975. New York City Mayor Abraham Beame proclaimed the occasion "The New Yorker Day." Ceremonies marking the occasion were to be held at City Hall. Columnist Brendan Gill, taking advantage of the timing of the anniversary to promote his new book, *Here at The New Yorker*, suggested to the business department that Peter Fleischmann attend the event and present a $50,000 check as a gift to the New York Public Library. He said it was obvious that the *New Yorker* company could afford such munificence since it had just raised the shareholder dividend while at the same time continuing to pay menial wages to writers. He added that if the donation were not made, Fleischmann needn't bother showing up at the ceremony. It wasn't and he didn't.

As for William Shawn, he disapproved of making a big fuss over anniversaries, and he did not attend the City Hall festivities, instead sending as envoys the four most junior members of his editorial staff.

That night, the business department feted 350 employees at a dinner dance in the Grand Ballroom of the Plaza Hotel. There were no spouses allowed except those who also worked at *The New Yorker*, which many did. Shawn commented that the occasion was being celebrated more austerely than the twenty-fifth had been because it was "against a background of rising unemployment." Topic A at the party was Gill's book. Shawn disapproved of the book, as did many other editors who were irked that Gill had omitted their contributions and other worthy ones as well.

Roger Angell took the opportunity to point out that humor pieces were flooding into the office again: "It all started the day Nixon left office," he explained. "I think people suddenly started to cheer up."

The Sunday *New York Times* marked the occasion with a business article entitled "The New Yorker: Mannerly Maverick at 50." The subtitle was: "Neither a Borrower Nor Seeker of Diversity." The piece, an examination of the magazine's long-standing conservative fiscal policies, was written by Marilyn Bender, who came to this conclusion: "When the party is over, the magazine will go right on doing what it has been doing week in and week out for half a century, proving unintentionally that 'to thine own self be true' is a sound formula for business success."

The *Times* hadn't counted on George Green.

In three months' worth of lunches that Green and Fleischmann shared through that winter and spring, Fleischmann repeatedly returned to the same subject, saying again and again that his health was bad and he needed to slow down. He began to get more specific about the kinds of duties he had in mind for Green, and when he did, both men realized that they were the sort that came with the title of president.

In June, one month after Green's thirty-seventh birthday, Fleischmann officially offered him the job. He told Green that he had had him in mind for the spot for a long time, saying, "I recognized your potential almost the first day you walked in the door." Others on the staff were less pleased with the appointment, and not a little surprised. It was unusual in publishing to move directly from the circulation department to what was in effect the publisher's role. Publishers more frequently advanced from a position as advertising chief. But Green had for many years been an advertising salesman, and he was the only candidate who had worked in nearly every business department.

Ken Bosee, the treasurer, was particularly disappointed. He had been at *The New Yorker* for twenty-three years and was considered the number two executive, after Fleischmann, and thus the leading candidate for the job. Bosee didn't begrudge Green the position—he thought the young man was smart—but he didn't think Green's time had come. Bosee figured that he himself had been ruled out because, at fifty-five, he was older than Fleischmann, and that Fleischmann wanted someone in the job who could ensure continuity for more than ten years, perhaps long enough that the next transition could be a smooth one to his son Stephen. But Bosee was a gracious man, and he became a supporter of Green. The same could not be said for a number of other executives, who refused to acknowledge Green as their leader and who often countermanded his instructions. Fred Jackson, by then publisher of *Mademoiselle*, recalls asking Green, "Why don't you *fire* these guys?" A former associate of Green's recalls that some of the objections to him took on anti-Semitic overtones. It is interesting that despite the fact that both Raoul Fleischmann and William Shawn were Jewish, *The New Yorker* was perceived as a WASP enclave, even by many who worked there. This perception perhaps developed because Peter Fleischmann was raised in, and practiced, his mother's Presbyterian religion, and Shawn's name sounded Irish. But Green was "thick-skinned," the colleague remembers, and he decided to ignore the naysayers. He figured that if he did a good job, they would come around, and most did, though clear resentment would linger in others.

The New Yorker had never seen a president like Green. He was ambitious and aggressive and fast out of the gate. He later told author Jane Adams, "I was straining at the leash...I wanted to move fast, move this company fast, not to change it radically but to evolve it."

Walter Curley, Fleischmann's close friend, said, "George Green hit the ground running with the attitude 'Let's take a good thing and make it better.' He saw a platform, a launching pad. His attitude was 'When I see something, I want to make it grow.'" It was not the attitude that had traditionally been found at the magazine.

Green moved from the circulation office on the eleventh floor into a typically shabby windowed office on the seventeenth floor that was just across from Fleischmann's, with a shared secretary, Terry Duenzl, in between. One of his first unofficial acts was to "resign" from Sam's Club. Green had been aware since before he arrived at *The New Yorker*, thirteen years earlier, that its top executives had a reputation for getting sloppy drunk by afternoon. He resolved to project a more professional image. Further, he felt it set a bad example for the staff if the company president retired to a bar in the afternoon.

Green and Fleischmann continued to fraternize, though, and shared a working lunch every Monday at either "21" or the Sky Club. In the beginning, Green drank as heavily as Fleischmann did; he preferred "21" to the Sky Club because Mario, the Sky Club bartender, had a heavy hand. Later the president switched to Tab and maybe a beer. Fleischmann preferred the Sky Club, and that's where they usually went, strolling over together past the camera shops and the restaurants, occasionally stopping into J. Press, a men's store, to check out the sales or buy a new suit, then into the Pan Am Building. They arrived at the club at around twelve-thirty and had drinks at the bar until the last call for lunch at one-forty-five. Peter Fleischmann rarely ate his food in restaurants, but rather just stared at it and pushed it around on his plate. He took his main meal each night at 3:00 A.M., when he would rise from his bed and foray to the kitchen to eat a ham and cheese sandwich, à la Dagwood Bumstead. When he traveled, his secretary arranged in advance for a sandwich to be waiting in his hotel room so he could have his middle-of-the-night meal.

Fleischmann was true to a pledge he had made when he gave Green the higher post—that he would allow him to run the business. At the Monday lunches, Green filled Fleischmann in on everything that had happened the week before, be it trouble with the printer or disappointing ad sales or a personnel change. Once the briefing took place, Fleischmann left Green to his own devices.

Green's association with William Shawn, whom he called "by far the most intelligent man I have ever known," was formal and respectful. They addressed each other as "Mr. Shawn" and "Mr. Green," never Bill and George. Nothing that transpired between them did anything to either narrow or widen the schism between business and editorial. Early in Green's tenure, there was a flap about a new switchboard. Some modern-minded technician had discovered that the *New Yorker*'s phone setup was antiquated, and the business office decided to invest in a new one. Editorial and business had each had their own switchboard, which was not cost-effective, so it was decided that they would be incorporated into one. But editorial refused to share a switchboard with business, offering a variety of reasons. Some editors feared that the operator from the business side would not be nice to callers to editorial. Others were obsessed with the notion that the business staff would listen in on their calls. The editors at *The New Yorker* took the separation of church and state seriously, to the point of separate switchboards. The tangle was resolved when the two boards were incorporated into one, to be located on the *editorial* floor.

Green and Shawn met at least once every week or two, when Green would travel the two floors to the editor's office to discuss issues of mutual importance. Shawn was an expansionist for editorial copy and was always trying to get more column space. No formal budget was imposed on Shawn. Once a year, Milton Greenstein would tell George Green how much money editorial needed for the coming year. It was generally a few percentage points above the year before. "I would just gulp and say 'Fine,'" says Green. Then Shawn would spend the money as he saw fit.

Shawn also made his feelings about particular advertisements clear. The advertising department by then had become such a strict policer of its own standards that Shawn rarely had to object to anything they accepted. They actually had a printed book of advertising policy. They shunned Jockey shorts and toilet paper. They took it upon themselves to airbrush out of a travel ad from

Australia a part of the anatomy of a kangaroo they found distasteful. They pulled an ad for Chase Manhattan, after it had run once, because they learned that all of the signs on a Japanese street that Chase had chosen as a backdrop for its message translated into English as "Specialist in Sexual Diseases." From that day forward, the ad department had every foreign word translated before running the copy.

They also knew better than to accept promotions that were too enthusiastic (superlatives were discouraged), or ones for "active ingredient" products like aspirin, or for South African tourism, feminine hygiene products, or downscale stores. Those were all stated policy, as was a ban on advocacy ads. Shawn did not want to air oil companies' arguments against a windfall profits tax, for example. Occasionally a new concept would slip in because no precedent had been set in the policy book, but *The New Yorker* usually learned in those instances that if the staff didn't censor themselves, their readers would do it for them. When the magazine first carried a "scent strip," one of those ubiquitous and smelly inserts that advertise perfumes, it was greeted with a flurry of angry letters, and Green and the advertising department decided they wouldn't run one again.

Years later, animal-loving readers reacted with fury at promotions for a book, *101 Uses for a Dead Cat*, that showed dead cartoon cats being used as tennis rackets and lamps. *The New Yorker* stopped running it.

One ad that slipped by Shawn and made its way into the *New Yorker* pages was for a "pooper-scooper," a device for picking up dog debris. Shawn, upon seeing it, summoned Green to his office.

"Mr. Green," Shawn asked, "how could you accept this ad?"

Green explained that New York City had just passed a law requiring dog owners to clean up after their pets. This was a product that helped them do that. The ad, he said, was tastefully presented, putting across the message about what it was without becoming too specific. Shawn listened patiently to the discourse, then said, "But what does it do, Mr. Green?"

Green said, "Well, you take it with you when you walk your dog and use it to clean up after your dog."

Shawn seemed dissatisfied with the answer.

"But, Mr. Green," he pressed, "*exactly* what does it *do?*"

"It collects *shit*, Mr. Shawn, that's what it does," said Green.

Shawn seemed to relax slightly, having finally elicited the response he sought.

"Mr. Green," Shawn asked, "does a product like that belong in *The New Yorker?*"

"No, sir," said Green.

"Good," said Shawn. The ad was dropped.

Shawn was aware that he was being allowed to hold sway in an area most editors have little or no influence upon. In his 1983 question-and-answer session with advertising personnel, he said, "We seem to have achieved at *The New Yorker* what almost no other publication has been able to achieve. People who work at other publications are just struck by our actual separation, by the fact that the advertising department goes its own way, the publishing office does not intervene with how the editorial department is run, or what is published. There's been a consistent and notable adherence to that policy by the publishing office and it has permitted *The New Yorker* to develop as it has." Shawn went on to admit that "there's been perhaps more effort by the editorial department to interfere with the advertising department" because editorial was more sensitive to "what will bother...and disturb readers."

Shawn did not always get his way with Green. For instance, he objected to "advertorials," units of several pages of ads wrapped around text on a subject related to those ads. The text is also ad copy, but it is written and laid out to resemble the feature articles in a magazine. An advertorial on, say, "Tennis in America" would feature a "story" on the history of tennis, accompanied by ads for Wilson rackets and Fila shirts. Shawn disliked the idea of ads masquerading as New Yorker stories, and asked Green not to run them. Green partially overruled him. He accepted an advertorial from the state of Hawaii, for example, because the subject was clearly not a New Yorker story.

Also over Shawn's objections, Green broke the taboo against lingerie by accepting ads for Victoria's Secret, the mail-order catalogue that showed nubile models in scanty underthings. The New Yorker turned down another catalogue that was identical except for the fact that the models were "oversized." The advertising department deemed fat unaesthetic.

At the same time that Shawn's control over advertising was waning, he was also finding his influence over his editors and writers slipping somewhat. In 1975, three years after he bestowed upon Bob Bingham the title "executive editor," Shawn decided that Bingham was not going to work out as a replacement for him, and began to consider other possibilities. Shawn had been working very closely with Jonathan Schell, then thirty-three, who had authored the controversial "The Village of Ben Suc" and was a regular reporter on Notes and Comments. Shawn had known Schell since he was five years old; Schell was roommate to Shawn's son Wally at the Putney School and was a classmate at Harvard. The Shawn–Schell writer–editor relationship developed to the point that Shawn was spending roughly half his time with Schell, and the more he knew of him, the more sanguine he became about his potential to be editor.

Shawn discussed Schell with Gardner Botsford, one of his top editors and Raoul Fleischmann's stepson. He said that he wanted to give Schell a promotion to audition him for the top slot. Botsford was skeptical. He told Shawn that he did not think it would be a popular choice. He said, though, that he would not voice any public objections if Shawn was adamant. Shawn said that Schell was "the only person in the world" who could do the job.

Shawn summoned to his office other editors, including senior fiction editor Roger Angell, executive editor Bob Bingham, art editor Lee Lorenz, and fact editor Patrick Crow, and informed them of his intentions. He knew that none of them would be thrilled, because Schell's getting the nod by definition meant that they had been passed over, but he was unprepared for the vortex of fury that he encountered. The objections were swift and strong. Within hours, word had spread throughout editorial that Shawn had chosen Schell to be the next editor, and that Shawn would impose Schell on the rest of the staff whatever their objections. The editorial floors were in turmoil.

The editorial staff felt almost as one that Schell was not a logical choice because he had no editing experience and he was too political. He was best known for what some of his colleagues called "stiff political tracts." They worried that *The New Yorker* would become the ideological organ that some critics claimed it already was. They worried, too, that Schell would not concern himself with aspects of the magazine that made it great, like humor, aesthetics, culture, and the arts. A weak-hearted joke made the rounds: One writer moans to another, "Schell would make *The New Yorker* like *Partisan Review* with cartoons." To which the other replies, "What makes you think there would be cartoons?"

Shawn tried to quell the fears. He admitted to his staff that he knew some of their doubts were real, but, he said, he believed that any potential problems could be overcome. The staff doubted it. A delegation of editors called on Gardner Botsford and pleaded their case. They could not work with Schell. Botsford, in turn, passed the word on to Peter Fleischmann, and Fleischmann told Shawn that it didn't seem to be a workable proposition. He had better find a new candidate. An amazed and bitter Shawn in late 1976 dropped the notion of grooming Schell. Three months later, in early 1977, he resurrected it, only to be greeted by the same barrage of objections. He again scrapped the notion in May 1977, though that did not still the speculation. In late 1978, Shawn was forced to circulate to the staff a two-line memo in which he said he was staying on. The editor, in a letter written years later, mused that it was just as well that Schell didn't get the job, because if he had, he would never again lead a normal life. Shawn was commenting on his own existence with that statement. While editor of *The New Yorker*, Shawn rarely took vacations or "played" on weekends. Even away from the office, he worked. To relax, he edited.

The Schell incident shook Shawn, who was further rattled when Gardner Botsford, then in his early sixties, approached him and offered to be managing editor, which Shawn took to mean that Botsford was setting himself up to be *the* editor. At around the same time, Milton Greenstein, the lawyer who sometimes played Mercury, messenger of the gods, between business and editorial, told Shawn that Peter Fleischmann's confidence in him had eroded. Fleischmann was worried that editorial was so badly demoralized by the Schell episode that peace would not return unless Shawn resigned.

In addition, Fleischmann was fed up with the unrelenting, all-consuming *presence* of the succession question. It was being built up out of all proportion. A lot of Fleischmann's executives believed that the chairman considered Shawn all but irreplaceable, but in truth, Fleischmann was much more practical than that. Shawn, after all, was seventy-one years old, and *probably* not immortal. Nor was Fleischmann overly in awe of the writing staff. He used to tell fellow executives that the writers "don't make a bad wage for a half day's work."

Shawn also got the message that Fleischmann believed Shawn thought himself to be the only person capable of editing *The New*

Yorker; that Shawn remained intent on the idea of Schell, despite the fact that the choice was clearly unpalatable to the rest of the staff; and that the magazine was deteriorating badly, adrift editorially.

A distraught Shawn took a drastic step: In December 1978, he submitted his formal resignation to Peter Fleischmann. At the same time, he made a proposal to Gardner Botsford that he be allowed to stay on for two more years, until the end of 1980, to aid in the search for a successor. Botsford replied that the proposal was unacceptable; it would be better if Shawn left immediately. Fleischmann, in turn, was inclined to accept the resignation which he had precipitated.

But Shawn, for all his vaunted timidity, was not one to be quietly ushered out. He wrote Fleischmann a long, anguished letter in which he refuted each of the charges against him. It was not true, he wrote, that his staff was demoralized: "No writer has left." As for editorial criticisms, those went back twenty-five years, to the time when people started complaining that *The New Yorker* wasn't funny anymore. He noted that ten or fifteen years earlier, there were many unfavorable reviews of *New Yorker* books that had gone on to criticize *The New Yorker* itself. But in defense of his magazine, he quoted sources he clearly considered worthy and astute. J. D. Salinger, "who is a genius and who admires almost nothing about our contemporary culture," had spoken of his pleasure at reading *The New Yorker*, and his hopes that it would not change. (Shawn spoke by phone to the reclusive Salinger on a weekly basis. Shawn was pleased that Salinger continued to write, for to Shawn, to write was more worthy than to publish.) Saul Bellow had recently sold a story to *The New Yorker*, even though he would receive far less money than another magazine had offered him.

Every time he had lunch with S. J. Perelman—and they had only recently had lunch—the writer complimented him on "the brilliant humor pieces of our young writers." Even A. W. Clausen, chairman of the Bank of America, had extolled the merits of *The New Yorker* in a speech before the Magazine Publishers Association. McGeorge Bundy, the president of the Ford Foundation, had written Shawn a letter expressing concern over rumors that *The New Yorker* was going to be taken over. Bundy told Shawn that foundation policy prevented it from owning companies, but that perhaps a grant could be offered to *The New Yorker* to ensure "the maximum of protection for continuity of editorial policy." The Ford Foundation, Bundy had written, could provide "a basis for... long run protection of an independent journalistic voice which is of great value for what passes for civilization around here."

Shawn outlined for Fleischmann the qualities that made a great editor. He must have art sense, editorial instincts, the feeling for a good story, but most important, the ability to establish a good relationship with writers on the staff, and the skills to help writers cope with their inevitable insecurities. Botsford didn't have a rapport, Shawn declared.

Shawn recited his résumé. With Ross's encouragement, he had broadened the magazine's journalistic scope, given it new dimensions, both intellectual and spiritual. He had served as editor for twenty-seven years; he had built a staff. "Gardner doesn't have that," Shawn protested. "But when it's time to make the most important decision [in the magazine's history], you turn to him, not me."

Were Botsford to become editor, declared Shawn, it would be "a disaster." Botsford would bring in more writers, try to make the magazine more popular. Botsford would delegate to the editors. The editors, Shawn wrote, were "incompetent."

"I am seventy-one," Shawn told his chairman, "but I am neither old nor tired." He listed the great contributions throughout history of men of advanced years. Verdi, he pointed out, wrote *Falstaff*, one of his greatest operas, when he was seventy-nine. Picasso and Titian painted masterpieces in their eighties. Casals and Stokowski conducted when they were ninety. Balanchine directed the New York City Ballet at seventy-four.

Yet he, Shawn, was being dismissed. "I am not being gently eased out," he stated. "I am being brutally thrown out."

Later events would prove that much as they disliked the choice of Schell, Shawn's writers and editors still loved Shawn (the editors did not know that he termed them "incompetent"), and while there was a rising tide of sentiment that the editor had overstayed and should find a suitable replacement, writers would have been upset by an unceremonious dumping. But even so, creative dissatisfaction was growing. Some staffers believed that Shawn was purposefully choosing as "focus of the experiment" candidates who really weren't up to the job. "Shawn wanted to die the editor of *The New Yorker*," says a staff member, "and then he wanted to take *The New Yorker* with him."

One could quibble with some of the arguments presented by Shawn in his letter. If Gardner Botsford had no rapport with the staff, why was it that the staff turned to him to protest the choice of Schell? It is true that he was thought to have influence with his half brother Fleischmann, and this was one case where the editors didn't mind business interference, but, too, he was considered approachable and sympathetic. In any case, history attests to the fact that Shawn won that round with Fleischmann. He seemed so ensconced and in control that neither the world nor his writers ever knew how close he had come to toppling. But in the total scheme of things, his power was diminished. The battle of 1978 represented Shawn's last major victory.

Before the year was out, another major misunderstanding developed between business and editorial. That year, the Internal

Revenue Service refused, for the first time, to accept the *New Yorker's* retirement and profit-sharing plans because they included artists and writers who were under contract and thus were not defined by the IRS as employees. The news filled the creative people with white-heat anger. Many became convinced that it was some kind of trick on the part of the business side to dump them from the plans. At the very least, they didn't understand why *The New Yorker* couldn't have protected them from the evil influence of the IRS.

George Green, in an attempt at conciliation, visited with the authors and artists in a meeting on the eighteenth floor. He explained that *The New Yorker* had no control over the actions of the IRS, and that they were now stuck with a ruling that none of them liked. He proposed a solution—a simple way around the problem. *The New Yorker* would provide each of them with financial compensation equal to what they were losing. The writers and artists were not interested in equivalents. They demanded what they had before, what was rightfully theirs.

The New Yorker engaged the law firm of Proskauer, Rose, Goetz & Mendelsohn to prepare a private bill for an exception to the IRS rule. The lawyers advised the company management that the chances of getting some kind of relief were virtually nil. *The New Yorker* asked for, and received, help from Senators Bill Bradley of New Jersey and Daniel Patrick Moynihan of New York. George Green testified before a House committee that the *New Yorker's* system was an unusual one. It had been in place since 1944, and contract employees had come to rely on it. At *The New Yorker*, said Green, writers and artists not only were real employees, with permanent offices in many cases, but also were *New Yorker* family, both literally and figuratively. He pointed out that Congress was in the process of trying to expand the universe of individuals receiving benefits, yet the IRS ruling would serve to narrow the number at *The New Yorker*.

It took three years and $100,000 worth of legal fees, but in the end President Carter signed a piece of special legislation allowing for New Yorker contributors under contract to be treated as employees and allowed to participate in the pension and profit-sharing plans, despite the IRS rulings. However, *The New Yorker* was barred from including in the plans any *new* contract artists and writers. The old employees were, in effect, grandfathered in. The outcome did not dispel the rancor that had built up over the three years. Some writers were still livid at what they perceived as a betrayal. It floated back to George Green that one writer in particular, Richard Harris, was telling anyone who would listen that Green had sold the writers out. Green, in turn, was surprised and unhappy that some creative people did not appreciate the lengths to which he had gone to rectify a law that he had not imposed. The result was a widening of the gulf of misunderstanding and enmity between business and editorial.

8

George Green became a historic exception among *New Yorker* executives when he began to play a gregarious "Mr. Outside" role. He gave speeches. He became active in the Magazine Publishers Association, the "trade group" for the consumer magazine industry. Green was invited on the MPA board, and five years later he was elected chairman, a nonpaying but prestigious job in the industry. Green, then a bachelor, also fraternized constantly with media people. He spoke annually at the Radcliffe publishing course and gave frequent speeches as well as interviews to the press. Raoul Fleischmann never gave a speech in his entire career, and his chats with the press were short, infrequent, and gruff. Peter Fleischmann adopted his father's policies as his own. Green called attention to himself and to the magazine. He was fully aware that he was breaking two long-standing rules. One was that *New Yorker* executives should keep a low profile, consistent with the dignity of the magazine. The other was that no person should be individually identified with the magazine. No one should stand out. The rules applied in editorial as well, and explained, for example, the fact that *The New Yorker* never had a masthead. A writer recalls that there was always a lot of gnashing of teeth when it came to bestowing titles, such as managing editor or executive editor, because a new title implied that someone had been elevated above others: "There was a kind of Red Army approach to organization."

George Green was aware, when he became president of *The New Yorker*, that the magazine and the company had an image problem. The reclusive nature of management, their storied drunkenness, the past arrogances of members of the advertising department all combined to create an unpretty picture of life at the weekly. When Green told people he was the president of *The New Yorker*, their first response was, "How can a magazine have a president?"—a reflection of the fact that hardly anyone realized that *The New Yorker* was a public company. The second comment was, "I hear things are really bad over there." They were referring as well to the stories floating out of editorial about the anti-Schell insurrection and a rising tide of ill will toward Shawn.

Green could do nothing to improve the image of editorial, but he could present a different picture of business, one that indicated there was a professional management intent on running The New Yorker Magazine, Inc., like a real company, not a men's drinking club.

The Fleischmanns could not have found fault with the message that Green carried. He was a great cheerleader for the magazine, fond of telling his audience that being president of *The New Yorker* was the greatest job in publishing because you never had to worry about the quality of the next week's issue. But the Fleischmanns had always been great believers in tradition. If Raoul hadn't given speeches and Peter hadn't given speeches, then Green shouldn't give them either.

Reaction in the business department to Green's visibility was split. Some people thought that the president was on a long ego trip. A lot of the old-timers embraced the Fleischmann philosophy that it was somehow undignified to tout the magazine, let alone yourself. Green met a couple at a party in Long Island who asked him what he did. He told them that he was president of *The New Yorker*. A pleasant conversation ensued. The couple mentioned the meeting to Hoyt R. "Pete" Spelman, the *New Yorker*'s business public relations chief, and he wrote his boss a long angry letter in which he gave him a lesson on how he should present himself. He was not to tell anyone he was the president of *The New Yorker*. If asked, he could say, "I'm with *The New Yorker*," but only if pressed should he reveal his status. Green should not single himself out as someone in an operating position. He should not stand out.

William Shawn several times complained to Milton Greenstein that Green was too visible, and Greenstein, in turn, took the grievance to Fleischmann. "You've got to control him, Peter," Greenstein pleaded with the chairman. Fleischmann would remonstrate with Green, "You've got to control yourself, George." Green would reply, "The magazine business is not a passive business anymore, and I don't intend to sit back and behave passively." Fleischmann, having delivered the editor's message, would leave it at that. Fleischmann may have come from the old traditions, but the necessity of occasionally employing modern methods was not lost on him.

There was a large contingent of *New Yorker* employees who felt that Green represented the proverbial breath of fresh air, and who were stimulated by the thought of shaking the rotting foundations.

To put it in perspective, it was not as if Green were a Hugh Hefner or a Helen Gurley Brown, stumping the country making speeches and exchanging late-night pleasantries with Johnny Carson. He remained a relatively unknown publisher. To find his name in the magazine, one had to search through the United States Post Office–mandated fine print at the bottom of the contents page. By the standards of the industry, Green's behavior was as understated as his dark suits and wire-rimmed glasses. By the standards of *The New Yorker*, it was positively egregious.

Green's personality was equally controversial. He could be sharp-tongued and blunt. Elaine Matteo, the company secretary and assistant treasurer, says that he was often unnecessarily cruel in his criticisms. She adds, "He was the most frustrating person I've ever had to work with, but working with him was the most rewarding experience of my life." He had a problem delegating, according to some employees. Pete Spelman believes that "George wanted all the marbles." But Stuart Jason, the comptroller, says, "As long as you were doing a good job, he left you alone." "If he didn't like your performance," says another employee, "he could be very heavy-handed."

In the advertising community, Green was well received and respected. Advertisers and publishers seemed to grasp that he was trying to undo damage done in the past, and his methods were not alien to them as they were to some *New Yorker* employees, because they were mainstream in the rest of the industry.

Green also got support from shareholders, among them Philip Messinger and Charles P. Schwartz, Jr., a Chicago businessman. Both men had bought stock while Fleischmann was chairman, and both knew what they were getting into, but they nevertheless had become annoyed at management. Messinger would ask two or three questions at the annual meetings, and Charles Schwartz was something of a gadfly, taking the floor for what seemed to management interminable hours of queries. At the 1975 annual meeting, while Green was still circulation manager, Schwartz had pressed so persistently for the answer to a question that an exasperated Peter Fleischmann exclaimed, "Oh, Mr. Schwartz, for goodness sake, is there going to be a war in the Middle East?"

Neither Schwartz nor Messinger approved of the *New Yorker's* conservative approach to cash management. They thought that the excess cash in the treasury should be used to make acquisitions. Fleischmann disagreed. He told the *New York Times,* "It's difficult enough to get out a magazine once a week without fussing around with other things. It confuses you, or anyway it confuses me." But Green was sympathetic to the Messinger/Schwartz stance. Since the days that he was an assistant in the treasurer's office, he had wondered why the company let so much idle cash build up. Every year the figure rose. At the end of 1974 there had been $6.2 million in cash or cash equivalents. In 1975 there was $7.3 million, in 1976 $8 million, then $9 million in 1977. It was not much money by the standards of other companies, but it was a hefty chunk for *The New Yorker,* on the order of a quarter of total revenues and more than five times net income. And, as noted earlier, cash figures were higher when the funds segregated for subscription liabilities were added in. In any case, Green wanted to put the cash to work.

In 1978, he hired a young lawyer named Janet Muir, who had worked for him as an intern on an MPA program the summer before. Her job was to oversee special projects. Muir's principal activity was to search out potential acquisitions, but her first task was unrelated to that. She was to study measures that *The New Yorker* could use to ward off unfriendly takeover attempts. Media properties had begun to change hands with dizzying frequency, and while most of the acquisitions were friendly, others were not. Attention in the industry had been riveted on *New York* magazine only one year earlier, in January 1977, when Australian press lord Rupert Murdoch waged a winning proxy battle against editor Clay Felker for control of the weekly. It had once been a gentlemen's game, publishing, but Murdoch's preemptive strike raised the suggestion that it might not remain so. The acquisition proved to be a catalyst that sparked a frenzy among publishers and nonpublishers alike to scoop up magazines at ever-escalating prices. A reporter asked George Green if the Murdoch acquisition had affected *The New Yorker*. "Yes," Green replied. "The effect of Mr. Murdoch is that a week doesn't go by that someone doesn't call me and ask about buying *The New Yorker*. Mr. Murdoch has stimulated interest in magazines. He paid $8.25 a share for a stock that was selling at $2 when he decided to take it over, and the company wasn't making any money." Murdoch turned *New York* into a virtual money machine, which further served to inspire other potential buyers.

Despite the acquisitive environment, Muir's task was considered an academic exercise since nobody, including Fleischmann and Green, believed *The New Yorker* could *really* be bought. Too much stock was in friendly hands.

Nevertheless, Muir wrote a report outlining various options. One was to split the stock. The bid price at the time was around $70 a share. A split would put it in a trading range considered more popular, somewhere between $15 and $45, which would make it more accessible to small shareholders. Smaller shareholders meant more shareholders, and that meant it would be harder for any investors on the prowl to buy up enough stock to give them leverage in going after the whole. But stock splits were considered racy gambits at *The New Yorker*. As Raoul Fleischmann once sputtered to some unfortunate soul who had dared, at an annual meeting, to inquire about the possibility of a split: "This is not a Wall Street racket! We're an old-fashioned business!" It was not lost on longtime holders sitting in the audience that *New Yorker* stock had split many years earlier. "Now that it's popular it doesn't," grumbled a back-row shareholder, according to the *New York Times*.

Muir also recommended that *The New Yorker* split the stock if it wanted to set up a stock option or purchase plan for employees. Green had become fixed on the notion of getting stock into the hands of editors and businesspeople alike, because employees care more and work harder when they own the company. But a split was rejected for now.

Muir also explored the possibility of taking *The New Yorker* private. In theory it was the most sensible course of action. The Fleischmanns never acted as if their company was public, so why should it be so? It was relatively expensive for a small company to remain public: The costs related to being public—paying lawyers to file forms, registering with the SEC, and such—ran into the hundreds of thousands a year, no matter how big or small you were. On the other side of the equation, there were advantages to being able to determine a current market valuation for the stock, particularly when it came to estate taxes. But that was a minor problem. There were enough publications—some private—being bought and sold that an investment banking firm could certainly have evaluated the worth of *The New Yorker* by studying other activity. Nevertheless, management passed on the idea of going private. Peter Fleischmann worried that to do so would be to invite lawsuits.

Green, in the meantime, continued to press Fleischmann about diversifying. Since Raoul Fleischmann's ill-fated investment in *Stage*, *The New Yorker* had not made an investment in an outside property. It owned Boulder Enterprise, but that was launched internally, not bought, and it had been a major drain until only recently. It had also once started, internally, a company to market magazines to college students, but that was now defunct. William Shawn was adamantly opposed to getting involved in anything that was not *The New Yorker*. He would come up with many reasons, over the years, for ruling out investments in other properties, but in the end they all came down to one: *The New Yorker* should be management's only concern. Green had several discussions with Shawn in which he explained that it could work to the benefit of *The New Yorker* magazine if the company owned other properties, because it would provide a financial cushion. When the *New Yorker*'s business was weak, another subsidiary's, it was hoped, would be strong. *The New Yorker* would not have to bow to financial pressure. Diversification would help the weekly remain independent. He assured Shawn that *The New Yorker* would always be the center, the most cherished and cared-for part of the whole. Shawn was unmoved.

Fleischmann, though, saw the sense in the argument, and Green was wearing him down. So, in 1978, he allowed the president to take the plunge in a deal that actually came to their attention through an acquaintance of Fleischmann's. For $300,000, a pittance even for *The New Yorker*, which had revenues that year of $44 million, they bought 35 percent of Teleram Communications Corp., a manufacturer of text-editing display devices that were used by reporters. The product was endorsed by the American Newspaper Publishers Association and used by, among others, the *New York Times*. Green thought there was a natural fit with Teleram since it produced machines that *New Yorker* staff members could write and edit on, were they not so resistant to technology. Nevertheless, a Smith Barney investment banker, Robert Garrett, thought the deal was too small, and told Green so. Green said, "You have to walk before you can run."

Shawn objected on the grounds that the machines that Teleram produced emitted a dangerous radiation that had been the subject of *New Yorker* fact pieces.

Teleram did not prove an inspired investment. Instead of sticking to its niche business, the company dove aggressively into head-to-head competition with IBM, Apple, and other such muscular contenders by entering the portable computer field. It would later go bankrupt. Teleram was not a financial repeat of the *Stage* disaster, though. When the company went public, *The New Yorker* recovered loans it had made, though it did not recover its initial investment.

The year 1978 was groundbreaking on another front. Since becoming president, Green had agitated for the appointment of outsiders to the board. The *New Yorker*'s directors were all officers of the company, which Green thought was incestuous and unhealthy. After countless discussions, Green obtained Fleischmann's permission to invite on the board William C. Eiseman, fifty-four, a senior vice president at Morgan Guaranty. Morgan had long-standing business ties to *The New Yorker*, as did Eiseman himself. Early in his career, he had been manager of the Morgan branch at Fifth Avenue and Forty-fourth Street where *New Yorker* paychecks were drawn, and he had become acquainted with many of the employees. Green and Bosee traveled to Eiseman's Wall Street office to extend the invitation. The banker said that he would be delighted to join the board, but he found himself wondering if Fleischmann endorsed him. He didn't understand why the chairman of the board hadn't come as well, or at least phoned.

Green also asked Philip Messinger to join the board. Messinger had left the brokerage business and was now what is known in Wall Street parlance as "a private investor," handling only his own and his family's investments. Both Messinger and Eiseman endorsed the idea of putting *New Yorker* funds in other businesses, and both set store in Green. Messinger wanted to invest more aggressively, and Eiseman wanted to hire an investment banking firm to advise on appropriate avenues of diversification. Eiseman thought Green was smart and had the right instincts, but he also recognized that he lacked experience in buying other companies, and needed guidance. Eiseman wanted to see a more organized approach and a clearer plan about what kinds of companies to invest in. Green's stated objectives—he wanted only minority interests in other companies and, of course, prospects for long-term capital appreciation—seemed a bit broad. Also, neither Eiseman nor Messinger thought highly of the Teleram investment. They didn't see much synergy between Teleram and *The New Yorker*.

They did not complain about the company's financial results, though. In 1975, the year Green took over, ad pages had sunk to a recent low of 3353. By 1979 they had climbed to 4159. Circulation was creeping back, moving from around 490,000 in 1975 to 499,000 in 1979. Ad revenues rose nearly 70 percent, circulation revenues grew 65 percent, earnings per share more than doubled. The dividend was hiked by a dollar a year per share, from $4.75 to $8.75 between 1975 and 1979. The stock price mirrored the results, nearly doubling from a high of $45 bid in 1975 to $86 in 1979. It was difficult to find stock, but those who managed to "get an appointment" to buy it were rewarded for their patience.

There was still no security analyst who tracked the company's progress, but there was an investment manager who had become intrigued. He would eventually become enamored of both the magazine and the investment to the point of emotional attachment.

William J. Reik, Jr., handled investments for more than one hundred wealthy clients from a desk at Paine Webber Mitchell Hutchins. Reik, forty-one in 1979, a man of towering height, with long gray hair and a gregarious personality, was a lawyer and former law professor who had decided, well into his career, to switch to the investment management business. He grew up in Cincinnati, "in the shadow of Procter & Gamble," as he describes it, and "was always conscious of marketing and consumer products." While in the sixth grade, he began to send away for annual reports and prospectuses, and he read them as avidly as other kids perused the Hardy Boys. He could tick off the names of directors of major corporations as easily as he could list baseball players, and the money his investment skills earned him would enable him later to merge his interests and fulfill a dream by buying a piece of the Cincinnati Reds.

Reik liked to invest in what he called "upscale consumer franchises," companies selling a quality product, preferably to people of means. He had taken major positions for himself and his clients in Tiffany & Co., the jeweler, and Sotheby's, the auction house, before each of those companies was bought out, garnering a large profit for Reik and his clients. Certainly *The New Yorker* could be defined as an "upscale consumer franchise." It also satisfied Reik's other requirements. He preferred that a company be free of debt, which *The New Yorker* was. He was happy if the stock was at least 25 percent owned by the family who founded the company. He reasoned that there was more attention to results when the fortunes of executives and their heirs were tied to the bottom line. He liked, for example, Smucker's, the jelly and jam company.

"The Smucker's name is on every building!" he'd exclaim to his clients. "On every jar. Kim, Tim and Paul on every label!"

Finally, he searched for companies that did not have a large institutional ownership. He didn't want a lot of the stock in the hands of insurance companies or banks. "Institutional investors make me nervous," he'd say. "They don't do their homework." They were too obsessed with short-term results. Unwilling to wait with an investment, they would cut and run at the first sign of trouble, causing the stock price to reel.

The New Yorker passed all of Reik's tests, and it was, thought Reik, "the ultimate in publishing, a commanding presence in the field."

He left an open order with his trading desk, and bought *New Yorker* stock every chance he got. In 1979, he went to the annual meeting and introduced himself to George Green. After that, from time to time he would drop by Green's office to talk about the magazine. They joked about the fact that there was always a thunderstorm when they got together.

Over a period of years, Reik had amassed more than 18,000

shares of *The New Yorker*, which resided in his and his clients' accounts. Reik loved his investment. He used to say to Green, "Wouldn't it be great if we could buy the whole thing and own it ourselves?" Reik still missed Tiffany's; he wished it didn't belong to Avon. He wished that he had thrown himself across the desk of Tiffany chairman Walter Hoving and convinced him to remain independent.

In March 1980, *The New Yorker* made its second investment plunge, buying a one-third interest in Raven Press, a publisher of medical books and journals, for one million dollars. The deal was brought in by Monroe Pofcher, the magazine consultant who eight years earlier had tried to buy *The New Yorker*. Raven was a growing company that required an infusion of working capital, but management didn't want to borrow at the 20 percent rate the banks were demanding of small customers at the time. Shawn objected to the deal. He claimed that medical publishers were crooks. Also, he had a horror of anatomical discussions or graphic descriptions of body parts. Shawn didn't like the kinds of photographs medical books carried.

Peter Fleischmann carried Shawn's message to Green, saying, "The editor would prefer that we not do this deal."

"But it's a *great* deal," Green insisted. Fleischmann delved more deeply into the details and decided that Green was right, and gave him the go-ahead. Fleischmann was partly influenced by the fact that Raven's offices were just down the street from *The New Yorker*, next to the Algonquin. That had to be a good sign. Raven turned out to be an excellent investment.

But Fleischmann may have acquiesced in part, too, because of his health. He wasn't up to a fight. The years of heavy smoking had taken their toll, and Fleischmann had developed cancer of the larynx, the structure at the top of the trachea in which the vocal cords are located. The chairman underwent a laryngectomy, surgery to remove the larynx, which left him voiceless. He had to learn how to speak by holding against his throat a small box-like microphone that transmits the vibrations, producing a robot-like sound. What was fascinating to a lot of people who knew Fleischmann was that he did not become shyer and more withdrawn when he had to use the instrument, as they expected he would, but was instead a good deal more outgoing. The thing looked and sounded conspicuous; Peter's words were difficult to understand. Nevertheless, he wasn't self-conscious. It was as if he now had an excuse to be eccentric. A friend recalls watching him grab for a ringing telephone, pushing his wife's hand out of the way so that he could be the one to answer. He took a tour of an R. R. Donnelley printing plant and chatted enthusiastically and charmingly with the workers.

His Monday lunches had a change of venue. Green met with Fleischmann in the hospital, and then later at his apartment, and as always, Green would brief the chairman. Fleischmann never again resumed a full office schedule, but when he had recovered enough to go out, he and Green had lunch almost every Monday at the Sky Club, where the tables were far apart and it was easier than at "21" for Fleischmann to talk using his microphone.

It was at one of those lunches in early 1980 that Fleischmann told Green it was time for his son Stephen to join *The New Yorker*. Stephen, now twenty-eight, had lived mostly with his mother after she and Peter had divorced. After high school, he worked at a variety of jobs. In 1977, he worked for six months at the South Bend, Indiana, *Tribune*, then left to go to his father's alma mater, Yale. He dropped out after two years and was living in New York. Peter Fleischmann asked Green to find a place on the staff for Stephen.

It would have been difficult for Green to refuse or fight Fleisch-

125

mann's request. *The New Yorker* was a Fleischmann tradition, the Fleischmanns were a *New Yorker* tradition, and besides, the family controlled 25 percent of the stock. In his brief encounters with Stephen at the Fleischmann apartment, Green had been favorably impressed. Stephen seemed "very nice, very personable, attractive. He exhibited all the positive characteristics you'd hope to find in a young man." Nevertheless, Green had some independent views on the subject of nepotism. He was, as noted, the son of a *New York Times* executive. Green had worked for the *Times* during summers as a student, but he had purposefully steered clear of it after graduation because he wanted it said, down the road, that he got where he was on his own merits. That was the prejudice he brought to the discussion of Stephen.

A couple of years earlier, Fleischmann's daughter Ruth had considered working for *The New Yorker*. When she came to see Green at his office, he found her "intelligent and attractive—she could have made a very good executive." But Green impressed upon Ruth the fact that she would not be given any special treatment. She would be expected to show up every day, work regular hours, and take only the allotted vacation time. Ruth decided against joining the magazine. Stephen, when presented with the same ground rules, accepted them.

Stephen Fleischmann would not be interviewed in person for this book, but instead agreed to answer questions in writing. One question concerned whether or not, when growing up, he had been aware of the *New Yorker's* exalted place in American letters, and whether he was conscious of the important literary heritage his family enjoyed. He replied: "The Fleischmann family was proud of our association with The New Yorker Magazine. On the other hand, we did not regard ourselves as enjoying an 'important literary heritage'...since most of us had no literary accomplishments, or ambitions."

The answer is disappointing not only in its lack of imagination but also because the writer seems so rote and uninspired. His father had a profound feel for the history of the place, and both father and grandfather had assumed the self-appointed task of protecting their literary heritage. Stephen Fleischmann somehow missed the point. He did write, though, that "I definitely looked forward to working at The New Yorker Corporation when I was growing up."

Stephen went to work in June 1980 in what he terms a "junior position" in circulation, reporting to department head Douglas Florenzie. In his letter Stephen Fleischmann explained, "I helped with the adjustment of subscription rates and mailing patterns, answered correspondence and complaints from the readers, and dealt with payroll problems." He worked hard, and while he and Florenzie didn't particularly hit it off, there were few objections about Stephen's performance.

In 1981, another outside director was elected to the board, this time at the invitation of Peter Fleischmann. He was Walter J. P. Curley, Peter Fleischmann's Yale friend. Curley had been a partner at the investment firm of J. H. Whitney, then became ambassador to Ireland from 1975 to 1977, and was now a private venture capitalist. Fleischmann had invited him on the board years earlier, but Curley couldn't accept because he had a government job. Curley was a charming man who could more than live up to the term "diplomat," and who would often be called upon, in his tenure as a New Yorker director, to do so.

9

There is a law of physics, here casually defined, that says that if an organization doesn't change over time, then when change comes, it will do so with a great explosion. By the early 1980s, all but one of the catalysts were in place that would spark *The New Yorker* into being the Mount St. Helens of publishing. There was an impatient president, a resistant major owner, an unmovable editor, two *very* interested large investors, and a recalcitrant heir.

Even in editorial, there was growing unrest. The department had received a demoralizing drubbing at the hands of the press in 1979 when two articles turned out to harbor inaccuracies. In one instance, John McPhee, one of the *New Yorker's* most popular and prolific writers, wrote about a nameless restaurant whose proprietor charged, apparently falsely, that Lutece, the world-reknowned citadel of culinary excellence, served *frozen* turbot. It is difficult to imagine that such a small slip would elicit much attention at any other magazine. At *People*, for instance, it might provoke a flurry of letters at most. But because it was *The New*

Yorker, it was treated almost as if it were an international incident. *The New Yorker* had long prided itself—to the point of gloating—on its factual accuracy, and there were more than a few critics ready to remind it of that fact.

More serious were charges by the British novelist Graham Greene that a profile of him by movie critic Penelope Gilliatt in the March 26, 1979, issue of *The New Yorker* was inaccurate. Greene said that Gilliatt had fabricated whole portions of the piece. Separately, Gilliatt was accused of plagiarizing parts of the profile from an article in the *Nation.*

In a letter to the British publication the *New Statesman,* Greene wrote of Gilliatt: "Her imagination extends from recording the presence of vultures in Antibes to a mysterious Czech official of the Ministry of Foreign Affairs who, she writes, abused me on the BBC.... An even more mysterious Englishman apparently invited me to visit an internment camp in Argentina, but I'm afraid both the camp and the Englishman are products of Mrs. Gilliatt's rather wild imagination."

Shortly after the charges were aired, Gilliatt took a leave of absence from *The New Yorker* for "reasons of health," according to Shawn.

The Gilliatt episode provided ammunition to some staff writers and artists who felt that William Shawn lost his objectivity when dealing with certain women writers. Says one staff member, "Shawn idolized writers, but he especially idolized insane or overbearing women writers." For decades there was speculation, founded or unfounded, fair or not, that his relationship with writer Lillian Ross went beyond friendship. Such things didn't matter, until an incident like that concerning Gilliatt arose and proved embarrassing to the staff as a whole, because it brought into question the magazine's overall credibility.

Also demoralizing was the fact that Shawn entered another decade without naming a successor. He was seventy-three years old in 1980, yet he was not ready to move aside to make room for a new generation. There was a bottleneck at the top that led to at least one important defection that year. William Whitworth, a well-liked editor sometimes cited as a potential successor to Shawn, left to become editor in chief of the *Atlantic Monthly*, which had recently been purchased by real estate developer Mortimer Zuckerman.

In the business department, too, there were growing morale problems related to succession. Many employees now believed that Stephen Fleischmann was being groomed by his father to become president or chairman. (Stephen Fleischmann says he was not.) In the middle of 1981, the younger Fleischmann, having served a year in the circulation department, was moved into another "junior position," in his words, in the production department, reporting to production chief Sam Spoto. In his letter to this writer, Stephen Fleischmann wrote, in résumé fashion, that in production he divided his time between "the traffic division, arranging freight contracts for deliveries and dealing with distribution patterns and delivery problems, and the production division, working primarily in quality control of the printing of the magazines." It was in the production department that his grades began to slip. Production work was not glamorous—it could even be grubby—and while it was one of his father's particular areas of fascination, Stephen's impatience and disdain for it became obvious to his co-workers. A boss's son often has to work twice as hard to earn the respect of his peers. His co-workers thought Stephen didn't work half as hard. He developed a reputation as someone who *said* he wanted to work hard to excel and eventually earn his father's title, but who seemed to want the title, not the duties. Some people doubted he even wanted the title. He didn't seem that interested. Stephen wrote that "if anyone resented my ancestry, those feelings were successfully hidden from me."

Disgruntlement about Stephen filtered down to Green, who

wondered if Stephen was capable of the kind of determination, perseverance, and intelligence his father had displayed in a similar situation thirty years earlier. Peter Fleischmann had successfully overcome the "boss's son" stigma, partly with hard work, partly with his engaging and sweet personality. Stephen tended to be on the prickly side. Relations between Green and young Fleischmann are described by Green as "cordial," by Fleischmann as "formal." On rare occasions, the two had lunch together. But Green was not skilled at hiding his coldness toward a subordinate he deemed incompetent, and Stephen Fleischmann, in turn, was not one to keep his thoughts to himself. He began complaining about Green to other employees.

Each of the men has his own interpretation of events. In late 1981, Green offered Fleischmann a job he calls "the opportunity of a career." Fleischmann's interpretation was that Green was trying to get him out of town. In October of that year, *The New Yorker* bought 60 percent of *Horticulture*, "The Magazine of American Gardening," previously published by the nonprofit Massachusetts Horticultural Society. *Horticulture* seemed a natural fit for *The New Yorker*. It was understated and even austere, with a look of quality that seemed to complement *The New Yorker*. The editor and coinvestor in *Horticulture* was Elliott Wadsworth, who also owned White Flower Farm, a well-known nursery and marketer of garden seeds in Litchfield, Connecticut. (White Flower Farm, coincidentally, had once been owned by Jane Grant, the first wife of Harold Ross, and her second husband, William B. Harris.) *Horticulture* was unprofitable when *The New Yorker* bought it, but Green believed it could be turned around. The "price" *The New Yorker* and Wadsworth paid was the assumption of the subscription liability—the amount the publisher had collected from subscribers, and against which it owed them magazines.

Shortly after the purchase, Green called Stephen Fleischmann into his office and offered him the top business slot at *Horticul-*

ture. His prime responsibility would be to sell advertising, but he could have any title he wanted, even publisher. Fleischmann had spent time in circulation and production; now Green was proffering an opportunity to learn advertising. Green thought the offer was very generous. Stephen, after all, was only twenty-nine years old, and he lacked the depth or length of experience that would generally be required for a position like that.

Stephen rejected the job. He said he wanted to be involved with *The New Yorker*, not an ancillary division. He felt that Green was trying to brush him aside. Green agreed that he was, in essence, shipping Stephen out of town, "but to an opportunity," he said. Green himself had spent a couple of years working in the *New Yorker* sales office in Atlanta, and he looked back on it as a learning experience. Stephen didn't see it that way. Green assured Stephen that it was not a lifetime appointment. If he didn't like it, he could say so and Green would take him back. Stephen said no.

A frustrated Green asked Ken Bosee, Elaine Matteo, and Peter Fleischmann to intervene. Green, while not always the most sensitive boss, nevertheless realized that there was some friction between himself and Stephen, that Stephen didn't trust him, and he asked the others to explain to Stephen what a golden opportunity this was. They did, but to no avail. Stephen refused to go. He remained in production for a few months more, then moved to administration, where "I reviewed the company's administration of its pension and profit-sharing plans and performed other tasks," he wrote in his letter.

Green and Peter Fleischmann began to argue about Stephen. In countless exchanges, Fleischmann would tell Green that he wanted the truth about Stephen. Green would bluntly respond that he thought Peter's son was a quitter. He never finished anything—jobs, Yale, anything. He wanted all of the glory with none of the sweat.

Green would say, "He's got the right last name, Peter, but he doesn't have the smarts."

Fleischmann invariably replied, "You just don't like Stephen."

Green said, "It's not a question of liking him or not liking him. Stephen has to help himself. I can give him an opportunity but he has to earn the respect. It's discouraging to other employees to watch Stephen get ahead without earning it."

Fleischmann told Green, "You don't treat my son as well as I treat your father's son."

Beneath it all there seemed to lurk some complicated emotional underpinnings. Green felt that Peter Fleischmann thought of him almost as a son, and many friends and associates of the two men, in observing them, reached the same conclusion. Fleischmann was obviously quite fond of Green, and he encouraged him the way a father would. In addition to nurturing and furthering Green's career, Fleischmann took an interest in his personal life, meeting his girlfriends, dining frequently with Green and his father, and throwing a fortieth-birthday party for him at his apartment. Some of Green's achievements were ones Fleischmann had wished for his own son: Green graduated from Yale, and he excelled at *The New Yorker*.

Some friends and associates of the two Fleischmanns, father and son, sensed that their relationship was not close. Peter's marriage to Stephen's mother had broken up when Stephen was still a child, and some said Stephen blamed his father for the divorce. Nancy Fleischmann, Stephen's mother, had married again. Her husband was Benno Schmidt, a partner in J. H. Whitney, Walter Curley's firm, and father of the current president of Yale. Stephen's sister Ruth married a Whitney partner as well. The invitation to Ruth's wedding bore her stepfather's name, not her father's. Green wondered if perhaps Peter Fleischmann worried that he hadn't done enough for his children, or had somehow lost them along the way, and wanted to make up for it and win Stephen's affections.

In late 1982, Stephen tendered his resignation from *The New*

Yorker to production head Sam Spoto. He explained to Spoto that he wanted to leave to start his own business. But he expressed bitter feelings about George Green, and in the letter to this writer he said, "Mr. Green regretted my presence at The New Yorker and viewed it as a threat to his continued control over the corporation's business affairs. Certainly many observers would say that Mr. Green did his best to force me out of the corporation entirely."

In the midst of the Stephen debacle, *The New Yorker* split its stock. It had gotten as high as $230 bid in the third quarter of 1981, and in November of that year it was split five for one. It immediately resumed its upward course. But it was still thinly traded. There were fewer than 800 shareholders. The company was joined by another big investor in 1982, the last catalyst for the explosion. Jane Grant, in her will, had left her *New Yorker* stock to her second husband, William B. Harris. When Harris died, he had bequeathed it, in turn, to the University of Oregon to fund a chair, quite fittingly, for the study of women's rights. The university sold the stock in 1982 to Donald Pels, who bought it as an investment for the company of which he was chairman, LIN Broadcasting, a media company that owned and operated television stations.

Like Bill Reik and other investors, Pels felt a kinship with *The New Yorker*. "My family were not only subscribers, but readers," Pels says. Pels had met Peter Fleischmann in the early 1960s, and from time to time he had offered to buy the magazine. Fleischmann would not sell. When Pels learned that there was a block of stock available, he asked Fleischmann if he would mind if he bought it. Fleischmann said he would be delighted to have Pels as an investor. He added that the stock had been offered to *The New Yorker* first, but that he personally found it a bit pricey.

Later, Pels bought stock from the estate of E. B. White, and at another time, from Fleischmann himself. Fleischmann sold 5000 shares to buy property upstate for his wife's daughter and her husband, who wanted to be a gentleman farmer. Fleischmann was close to his wife's children, closer, many people thought, than he was to his own, and he seemed eager to give the land to his stepson-in-law. LIN wound up with 5.1 percent of *The New Yorker*. Despite Fleischmann's remarks about the price being inflated, Pels was not worried. He says, "We felt that both readers and advertisers had a high regard for *The New Yorker* and that it was not, in fact, overpriced. By that time I had also come to know George Green and held him in high esteem."

Green had less confidence in the future than Pels did. Green was nervous about the business environment, and still intent on acquiring other properties as a hedge against slides in advertising at *The New Yorker*. His acquisitive instincts were dampened by a late 1982 contretemps with Fleischmann.

Monroe Pofcher, the magazine consultant, had introduced George Green to Ralph Ingersoll II, the president of a developing chain of newspapers, mostly small-town weeklies. Ingersoll's father was one of Harold Ross's "Jesuses" in the 1930s before he couldn't take it anymore and hightailed it off to Time Inc. Ingersoll was searching for a partner to invest with him in the *Orange County Daily Pilot*, a paper in Costa Mesa, California. Green and Janet Muir analyzed the deal. Orange County was a growing area, and prospects for the paper seemed good. They decided to buy a minority interest.

Peter Fleischmann was ill, during the Costa Mesa negotiations, with diverticulitis, an intestinal inflammation that was quite serious in his case, even life-threatening. Green visited him regularly in the hospital and later at home, and, he says, provided the chairman with a full set of details. Fleischmann had no objections to the Orange County deal, except to say that Shawn was opposed; by now, that was a given.

The deal progressed to the signing stage, with contract papers drawn and awaiting signatures. At the last minute, Fleischmann refused to sign. He didn't want to go through with it, providing as his reason his belief that Orange County was "where all of those ultraconservatives live." He may have been remembering the misery that ilk caused him and his magazine in the Vietnam years. He was not moved when informed that the paper, in fact, was quite liberal in its editorial stance. He didn't want to do the deal.

Green said, "Why don't we bring it in front of the board? Let them have an opinion."

Fleischmann replied, "Go ahead and bring it to the board. I've got the votes."

Ken Bosee, then treasurer, attributes the collapse of the deal largely to Green's attitude. "It was probably a good buy," he says, "but George was awfully abrupt about the way he put it. I felt he was trying to railroad it through. I would have wanted to do more thinking."

Janet Muir, Green's assistant in charge of acquisitions, remembers a lot of preparation and paperwork, and a brilliant presentation by Ingersoll. In her mind, nothing was rushed through.

It came down to a clash in styles. Green accused Fleischmann of being antideal, but Fleischmann was just more considered or, depending on one's interpretation, more plodding than Green. Considering that the Fleischmann family had a "no deal" approach to investments, Fleischmann had already allowed Green an enormous amount of leeway. He had approved several investments. But Green was nevertheless impatient. He and his team wanted to move fast. It was hard to imagine that the different approaches could ever be reconciled.

It would be many months before Philip Messinger learned of the events surrounding the Orange County deal. The outside directors had never even known it was a prospect. He was unhappy, of course, at the news. Messinger liked Ingersoll's approach to publishing—bypassing big-city dailies in favor of small weeklies with monopolies in their towns. And in general, Messinger was not enthusiastic about the kinds of investments *The New Yorker* had been making. He called them "little dots." He says, "You had investments of $250,000 to a half million dollars, finally you got to a million-dollar size. They were very small. They didn't have much impact."

In addition to disappointment, Messinger felt anger at not having been consulted. He realized, though, that even if the directors had been asked, they no doubt would have nixed the deal, because they were afraid to confront Fleischmann. With the exception of Green, Eiseman, and himself, he figured, the other directors—Bosee, Curley, Greenstein, Matteo, and Spoto—would all vote the Fleischmann party line.

Messinger felt frustrated at what he saw as a dearth of information from management. He had frequent discussions with Green, as did Reik, and Green was communicative, but it was nevertheless clear that important issues were not being raised in the boardroom. When they were, they were always presented as a *fait accompli*. He was beginning to resent the fact that he was expected to function as a rubber stamp for management. Whenever he or the other outside directors pushed for something that was not on the Fleischmann agenda, they were ignored. Green had gotten Fleischmann to agree to the formation of an audit committee constituted of the outside directors, and later a compensation committee to review executive salaries. That had been standard procedure at most public corporations for decades, but Green had to fight for it. Now that the committees were a reality, the outside directors found that a lot of their recommendations were disregarded. The audit committee had been pressing the company to hire an internal auditor, for instance, but they had been ignored for over a year. There was still no internal auditor.

When Green and Fleischmann didn't like a compensation committee recommendation, they asked the committee to reconsider. Messinger blamed it on pressures Fleischmann exerted on Green. He figured, too, that Green had not mentioned the Orange County deal because he was embarrassed at his own lack of control. It was the first time that it occurred to Messinger that ties between Green and Fleischmann were strained. "In effect," says Messinger, "Fleischmann was castrating George."

William Eiseman was not as aligned with Messinger as Messinger might have thought, because Eiseman found Messinger's approach abrasive, even though he often agreed with what Messinger had to say. Eiseman, like all of the officers and directors, was conscious that Messinger's sentiments were heightened by the fact that most of his net worth was tied up in *New Yorker* stock. His finances were inextricably intertwined with those of *The New Yorker*. Messinger, naturally, has a different interpretation. He says he was motivated, too, by the knowledge that he had assumed liabilities and responsibilities when he became a director. Furthermore, he resented being made to feel "like an outcast for asking questions which a director *should* ask."

But Eiseman, too, felt excluded, and he, too, was aware that he was being hindered in carrying out his directorial duties. Eiseman, a calm, bankerly presence, is described by all of his colleagues as assiduous and conscientious. He took the job seriously. He knew that directors were being held ever more accountable for what went wrong in a public corporation. Shareholder suits more frequently named directors as well as officers, and courts were tending to side with the shareholders in finding that directors were as culpable as management. But it was impossible for a *New Yorker* outside director to figure out what, exactly, was going on. The first day that Green and Bosee had invited him on the board, Eiseman had guessed that they had done so without the whole-hearted endorsement of Peter Fleischmann; the chairman's demeanor at board meetings had done nothing to change that perception. If anything, it had become even more apparent that Fleischmann viewed outside directors as intruders.

The quarterly board meetings were exercises in nondisclosure. They were called for 10:30 A.M., with the understanding that they would end by noon, no matter how many issues remained on the agenda. If the other directors wished to continue, Fleischmann left anyway. He did not like meetings, especially ones with strangers present.

The stock market was unaware of the growing turmoil at *The New Yorker*, as evidenced by the seemingly inexorable rise in the share price. By the fourth quarter of 1981, it had risen to $50 bid, the equivalent of $250 on the presplit stock. By the end of 1982 it got to $89, or $445 a share on the old stock. In 1983 it hit $139, or $695. It made no sense to Green, and he began advising people that it was overpriced. They paid him no heed. The advance in the stock price owed in no small way to Bill Reik's purchases. At times he was the only buyer of the stock. He and Green would have long late-afternoon meetings at which Reik would listen solemnly to Green's sermons that the stock was overpriced. As soon as Green finished his cautionary tale, Reik would say, "Okay, how many shares will you sell me? How many will Fleischmann sell me?"

Reik and the market were reacting as if the operating results of the last few years would continue forever. Ad pages rose only gradually from 1979 to 1981, but thanks to rate increases, advertising revenues increased out of proportion, by 35 percent. Earnings per share went from $3.95 to $6.51, and the dividend was raised from $1.75 to $2.25. But in 1982, pages began to slip.

The problem was a barrage of competition. The rewards to be reaped from selling upscale products to an affluent audience were no longer the *New Yorker*'s rich little secret. Advertisers had many years earlier begun to turn away from journals that reached mass audiences, which contributed to the fall of *Look, Life,* and the *Saturday Evening Post,* instead targeting narrower bands of readers. *New York* magazine, as could be expected, made a dent in the *New Yorker's* business. When *New York* was first published, *The New Yorker* considered suing to prevent the use of the name, believing that it infringed on its own, but Peter Fleischmann decided against it. The similarity of the names has proved a source of confusion over the years, if not to avid readers, at least to more casual ones. More damaging, though, was that *New York* was a natural outlet for the department store ads that had once been the lifeblood of *The New Yorker. New York's* audience was composed of hip Manhattanites, careerists on the go. The readers were the kinds of people who loved to spend money

Through the late sixties and into the seventies, a host of other publications aimed at wealthy consumers sprang up, among them the airline magazines, like *American Way* and the *Eastern Review,* which reached affluent readers while they were strapped captive in their seats; *Travel & Leisure; Food & Wine;* and an improving *Gourmet. Architectural Digest* moved beyond the editorial confines of its name and was transmogrified into a glossy glimpse into the residences of the rich and famous that appealed to moneyed readers and advertisers, and those who wished they were.

But never before had *The New Yorker* been so potentially battered as it was in the early eighties. Hearst Magazines repositioned *Town & Country* from a small circulation monthly that was of interest to the wafer-thin slice of society that could be found in its pages to a more broadly appealing, glitzier catalogue of conspicuous consumption. It featured posh resorts by emerald seas, sumptuous couturier clothing, and famously beautiful people. The obvious advertisers were Rolex watches, Tiffany jewelry, Revillon furs—*New Yorker* advertisers. Hearst also started an American edition of its British monthly, *Connoisseur,* a general-interest magazine that covered art, the Paris couture, travel, and other subjects of interest to people of elevated tastes, both intellectual and acquisitive.

In 1983, Condé Nast, the magazine empire owned by the Newhouse family, repositioned *House & Garden*. It had been in competition for many years with another "shelter" magazine, Hearst's *House Beautiful*, in a middle-level category. The houses and rooms featured were ones to which readers could aspire. They could adapt the ideas to their own life-styles. At the back of the book there was a shopping guide for furniture, fabrics, and accessories. The new *House & Garden* was upgraded to compete against the more socially voyeuristic *Architectural Digest*. It featured fantasy places—glorious hundred-acre English gardens, palaces in Marrakech, and penthouses on Fifth Avenue. The new pictures were splashed on higher-grade paper, and accompanied by more sophisticated text often written by celebrities or recognized writers.

With the change in the editorial approach, *House & Garden* cut its circulation by 50 percent and hiked its cover price from $1.50 to $4.00. The median household income of the new *House & Garden* reader was $50,000, double that of the old. Because it was reaching a higher demographic audience, it could still charge the old rate of $23,500 for a four-color, one-page advertisement, while reaching only half as many people. It was Harold Ross's concept all over again—it wasn't how many, it was how much.

The most direct attempted hit on *The New Yorker* came with the 1983 revival by Condé Nast of *Vanity Fair*, a magazine that had competed with *The New Yorker* sixty years earlier. Some early *New Yorker* writers, like Dorothy Parker and Robert Benchley, had previously written for *Vanity Fair*, but it folded while *The New Yorker* continued to thrive. S. I. Newhouse, chairman of

Condé Nast, in 1981 announced the rebirth of *Vanity Fair*. There followed one of the longer gestation periods in publishing history; the magazine did not come to life until March 1983. For eighteen months, Condé Nast worked at whipping potential readers and advertisers into an expectational frenzy.

If other magazines had gone out of their way to actually target the *New Yorker*'s readers and advertisers, they did it with some subtlety. It was the concept they were after. Enough publications had embraced it that *The New Yorker* was no longer the only one to embody it. *Vanity Fair* made it blatantly clear that it wanted *New Yorker* readers and advertisers; its business department used comparisons with *The New Yorker* as a selling tool. Condé Nast even placed a series of ads for *Vanity Fair* in *The New Yorker*.

One ad, running in 1982, provided some comic relief around the *New Yorker* offices, if not necessarily in priggish Mr. Shawn's office. It was a photograph of Hollywood-handsome writer John Irving clad in a skimpy, tight, bulge-revealing wrestling outfit. The copy read: "Vanity Fair. Coming in March." An "outraged" *New Yorker* reader wrote George Green a "disgruntled" letter of complaint. Throughout the years, she wrote, *The New Yorker* had displayed continuing integrity not only in its articles, but in its advertisements as well. But it was evident that the standards about truth in advertising had been lowered. Referring to the *Vanity Fair* ad, she wrote that it was quite obvious from the photograph that "John Irving is coming a lot sooner than March!"

Vanity Fair's launch provided a case history of how *not* to start a magazine. In the beginning, it was intended to be a sophisticated and highbrow journal, filled with enlightened prose on the ballet, literature, and esoteric aspects of art. From the beginning there were clashes between the first editor, the arrogant self-perceived intellectual, Richard Locke, and writers and editors, as well as between Locke and his own publisher, Joseph E. Corr, Jr., who called Locke "petulant" in print. The magazine that resulted was shallow, strained, and pseudointellectual. Condemnation of the effort was fast and fuming. The *New Republic* said that it was "so crude, so wasted, so trumpery an effort" that the best thing about it were the Ralph Lauren ads.

Locke was fired after three issues and replaced by Leo Lerman, a charming bearded man who resembled Sheridan Whiteside, the man who came to dinner in the play of that name. Lerman, who had been with Condé Nast since 1941, was put in charge of *Vanity Fair* on an interim basis, and indeed was removed less than a year later and replaced by Tina Brown, who had edited *Tatler*, a British magazine that was a glossy scandal sheet for London's yuppie equivalent—the Sloane Rangers. Under Brown, *Vanity Fair* turned into a very different magazine from what it had set out to be. It was shorter on intellect and longer on glitz, with movie star covers and stories on society murders and the Beverly Hills Hotel.

Brown seemed to stumble for a time in her attempts to find a voice for *Vanity Fair*. The magazine was emaciated for lack of ads, and what circulation there was began dwindling. Industry rumor constantly had Newhouse closing it down, though a contrary rumor had him too proud to admit failure. But Newhouse had the luxury of huge stores of capital on which to draw, and he gave Brown the commodity she most needed—time. He did not afford the same to publishers, a succession of whom he hired and fired, employing methods that were, to say the least, blunt. When he fired Joe Corr, he summoned him into his office and launched into the old "good news, bad news" routine. The good news was that he was going to keep *Vanity Fair* alive. Corr started to say how happy that made him, how hard they had all worked. Newhouse cut him off. "The bad news is that you're fired," he said.

When Tina Brown hit her stride, *Vanity Fair* developed a surer, clearer sense of itself. Some of its critics denounced it as an upscale *People* magazine. Brown defended it against those who would call it frivolous, and in print took an apparent slap at *The New Yorker* when, in her editor's letter, she wrote, "Once in a while...I run into a flabby old cliché about what constitutes a 'serious' magazine. It's the mealymouthed idea that visual excitement is somehow at odds with intellectual content, and that reading material can be deemed worthwhile only if it is presented as a wad of impenetrable text with a staple through the side."

Vanity Fair would become a striking turnaround story. It began a steady rise in both circulation and ads starting in 1986.

At the same time that competition for ads was heating up, advertiser budgets were being whittled down, resulting in more magazines chasing fewer dollars. Particularly damaging to *The New Yorker* were cutbacks by liquor companies, which themselves were experiencing lagging sales. Since the repeal of Prohibition, liquor had been a crucial advertising category for *The New Yorker*.

Further, as time went on, the business side of *The New Yorker* was more inclined to believe that ads were also suffering because of increasingly negative perceptions of the editorial product. A Greek chorus of criticisms greeted the ad sales staff and executives as they made their business and social rounds: The articles were too long; the cartoons weren't funny; the stories weren't funny; the writing was opaque. There was nothing the business side could do about it. Green could only influence the course of *his* domain.

In 1983, Green went on an investment spree. In February, *The New Yorker* bought 51 percent of *Cook's* magazine, a monthly aimed at the serious gourmet that had a circulation of 100,000, nine full-time employees, and 160 ad pages in 1982. Shawn opposed the deal, but once it went through, he offered his editorial assistance on the project. Philip Messinger also didn't like *Cook's*, but for a radically different reason: It was too small. "I wanted *The New Yorker* to go after bigger fish," he says.

Peter Fleischmann, in what appeared to Messinger to be an

attempt to compensate for not allowing Green to invest in the Costa Mesa paper, approved a deal in which *The New Yorker* took 10 percent of a Ralph Ingersoll investment in the Terre Haute, Indiana, newspaper *Tribune-Star*. *The New Yorker* paid $900,000 and agreed to make a $300,000 loan to the paper.

In June, the magazine entered into a joint project with Edi Sept, Inc., the American subsidiary of French publishing giant Hachette, to publish an English-language version of Hachette's *Elle* magazine. Hachette (which has since, by acquisition of other properties, become the world's largest magazine publisher) was owned by Daniel Filipacchi, a flamboyant man who was the French equivalent of *Penthouse* publisher Bob Guccione, except that Filipacchi printed serious magazines in addition to "skin" publications.

Filipacchi had tried to break into the U.S. market before, with little success. He resurrected the defunct *Look* magazine, losing $10 million before letting it fold again. Later he sold *Look* to Jann Wenner, publisher of *Rolling Stone*, who also could not make it work.

Filipacchi figured that in order to gain a foothold for *Elle* in the American market, he would need a partner that was already established, and that was accustomed to marketing to the kind of affluent readers and advertisers he envisioned for *Elle*. He approached George Green, and with a little discussion, the men decided to embark on the venture. Green and Filipacchi closed the deal with a handshake at Filipacchi's modern East Side high-rise apartment. Also present were Didier Guerin, an Edi Sept executive who was to be publisher of *Elle*, and Janet Muir, who was named associate publisher. The "contract" consisted of two lines that Muir and Guerin composed standing in a hallway. It provided for one or more test issues of *Elle*. *The New Yorker* would handle advertising, Edi Sept would foot the circulation bills, certain expenses would be netted out, and a profit, if any, would be split fifty-fifty. The deal was celebrated with a cross-cultural minifeast provided by Green: champagne and David's chocolate chip cookies.

William Shawn objected to the *Elle* deal. *The New Yorker* shouldn't be involved in any publication that wasn't *The New Yorker*. Also, as noted, he didn't like fashion. Once it was done, though, he did meet with Filipacchi to discuss an idea the publisher had for a French edition of *The New Yorker*. Shawn was enthusiastic and agreed to go ahead with the project as long as he could edit it. His French, however, was not of that caliber, so the idea was dropped. (Shawn refused to allow a Braille edition of *The New Yorker* for the same reason: He couldn't edit it.)

There was another revolution at *The New Yorker* that year. In the eight years that he had been president, Green had fought without success to be allowed to institute a program to put *New Yorker* stock into the hands of the rank and file of employees— *all* employees. There had never been a stock purchase program, and what little stock was given away was granted almost exclusively to business employees. Green had been bucking tradition in his quest for some kind of purchase or option plan, especially as it applied to editors, writers, and artists—the nervous creative types. But Green found support for his cause among the new outside directors who constituted the compensation committee— Curley, Messinger, and Eiseman. Eiseman was particularly adamant that a plan should be formulated. He had been a prime mover behind such programs at Morgan Guaranty, where he was in charge of personnel, and he was at least as strong a believer as Green that employees should have an equity participation in their organization.

The company hired the independent consulting firm of Towers, Perrin, Forster & Crosby to devise employee stock plans. The firm suggested three. The first two were stock purchase programs. One of those would offer shares to payroll employees at a price that represented a 15 percent discount to the market. The eligible employees included everyone from secretaries to editors and advertising staff. The second plan extended essentially the same terms to authors and artists under contract.

Green visited Shawn to explain how the plans worked and why he thought it was important to let the editorial department participate. Shawn raised no objections but instead invited Green to visit the eighteenth floor and talk to the staff. There was no conference room on eighteen, but Shawn would not let his people travel to sixteen, because editors and writers might be corrupted if they set foot on a business floor.

A time and date were selected and the message relayed to artists and writers, however far-flung. When Green and Elaine Matteo arrived on eighteen, they were astonished to find a large crowd waiting for them. It seemed as if everyone had come to the office that day, a most unusual occurrence. Green had expected apathy. Instead, he got rapt attention. He stood at a spot where the corridor bulges out to form a landing for a flight of stairs leading to nineteen. Both Green and, later, Elaine Matteo, who played a crucial role in administering the plan, were struck by how involved the editors and writers were. Many seemed quite grateful to have the opportunity to buy stock, and they asked interested and intelligent questions.

"If I die," some wondered, "can my children inherit the stock I still have coming to me?" And "What are the tax ramifications of buying this stock?" They were the kinds of questions businesspeople might have asked.

Of the 177 authors and artists eligible for the plan, 85 signed up. Among employees, the number was 193 out of 331 eligible. Those numbers were not out of line with the experience of other companies, including large financial corporations. Some employees were not willing to dedicate part of their paycheck to buy stock. Green and Matteo were both elated at the acceptance rate.

THE LAST DAYS OF THE NEW YORKER

It was the third program devised by the compensation committee that proved controversial. It was called "The 1983 Incentive Stock Ownership Plan." Simply put, it represented grants of stock to certain "key" employees of *The New Yorker*, on both the business and editorial sides. The point of the plan, as far as Eiseman, Green, and other executives were concerned, was to make *The New Yorker* competitive, in its incentives and total compensation, with other publishing companies. Moreover, it simply seemed right and just to give additional thanks to people who had worked hard and pulled themselves up through the ranks. The creative side in particular had been left out far too long by managements that took advantage of their lack of assertiveness. It was time for management to atone for past sins.

Green made the trek to Shawn's office on the nineteenth floor. Green and Shawn usually met after 5:00 P.M., and that evening was no exception. Green was filled with foreboding. His instincts told him that Shawn was not going to embrace the plan. Green greeted the editor, then launched into his sales pitch. Key employees in both business and editorial were to receive stock awards. Each would be granted a stated amount, which would be allotted over a period of five years. If they left the company, they forfeited their right to the balance of the shares. But if the company was acquired, they would receive the entire allotment at once. It was a standard program.

Shawn listened patiently, as he always did, but when Green had completed his sales pitch, Shawn's response was swift: He said no. He seized on the word "key," telling Green that among writers and editors, no one was "key." Creative people were all equal. Once again, he espoused what others called the "Red Army" doctrine.

Green pleaded his case. He pointed out that Shawn gave titles to editors—there was a fiction editor, an art editor, there had been executive editors. Those all represented a singling out of individuals. "Shouldn't someone who has served for a long time, who has clearly taken on more responsibilities, and carried them out with more talent and energy, be allowed to be compensated for it?" he asked. What of writer and fiction editor Roger Angell, or longtime columnist Brendan Gill? Were they really meant to be lumped into the same category as the newest member of the checking department, or a writer only recently given a contract? Surely the amount of money represented by the stock could provide a cushion, and surely they had earned it.

There was nothing Green could say to move Shawn. There were no "key" editors or writers. Green suggested that Shawn solicit the opinions of his top editors. Shawn was not willing to do that. He rejected the plan out of hand.

It was six-thirty when Green returned to his office. Elaine Matteo recalls passing by on her way out and noticing that Green was slumped in his chair, an anguished look on his face. She thought he might be ill. She poked her head in the door and asked, "Are you all right?"

He said, "I couldn't convince Shawn. I just couldn't convince him that there were people who deserved to be rewarded for their service to this magazine. Who deserved to be singled out. There was nothing I could say to make him go for it."

When Green reported back to the compensation committee, they were appalled at Shawn's unilateral decision. Bill Eiseman, in particular, was upset. Someone suggested that the board consider going over Shawn's head and picking the key editors themselves. But they decided against it, because to intrude on editorial turf would be to breach the trust that had prevailed for nearly sixty years. The shares were put aside and held in abeyance in case Shawn changed his mind.

10

In 1984, *The New Yorker* was like a gifted child who is surrounded by well-meaning adults, all of whom know what is best for the child, but none of whom can agree. There is no doubt that Peter Fleischmann, George Green, and William Shawn all had the best interests of the magazine in mind and in heart. There was no right or wrong, but instead a clash of approaches and wills. There was never any question of who would win. Peter Fleischmann was chairman and apparent owner.

The truth was, Peter Fleischmann was wearying of his battles with Green, and Green, in turn, felt held back by the chairman, and frustrated and beaten down by the *New Yorker* system. What seemed to Green like getting nowhere fast struck Fleischmann as moving forward too aggressively. It is a testament to the affection they felt for one another that their breakup didn't come sooner.

In early May, Green and Fleischmann clashed over an advertorial on computers that Green was determined to run. The text of the promotion centered on the history and technology of computers. It was surrounded by ads for software programs, IBM, and retail outlets. The advertorial passed Green's tests: It was presented in a classy way, and the subject, he believed, was not likely to be covered in a *New Yorker* feature.

Shawn, seeing the ad in the dummy, objected. He didn't like advertorials. Fleischmann presented the editor's objections to Green and endorsed them. Green said that it was a mistake to turn down a six-page spread in such a competitive advertising environment. The ad looked *fine*. The companies represented were all solid and prestigious. They were all advertisers that *The New Yorker* would *welcome* on an individual basis. It would be foolish and self-defeating to turn them away. It didn't seem rational.

"We're not running it," Fleischmann said.

Fleischmann had always had a reputation for telling a person what he wanted to hear to get rid of him. In the case of Green, he seemed to be telling him what he *didn't* want to hear to get rid of him.

The stage was set for another confrontation when Fleischmann told Green that he was putting his son Stephen on the board of directors. Stephen, since his departure a year earlier, had worked as assistant treasurer of New World Computers. Green was floored, but it was clear from the way Fleischmann presented the news that there was no point in arguing. The decision was final. Stephen would be nominated at the February 22 board meeting.

In the meantime Philip Messinger, more frustrated than ever by the lack of communication between *New Yorker* directors and management, phoned George Green. He said that he and Bill Eiseman had been discussing the gaps in their knowledge about the business and wanted to set up an informal meeting with Green. Perhaps they could chat over dinner. Eiseman recalls the approach somewhat differently. He remembers contacting Green on behalf of Walter Curley and himself. In any case, the result was the same.

Green thought the request—whoever originated it—was reasonable, and he agreed to schedule a dinner. Unknown to the outside directors, Green invited Peter Fleischmann to participate. (Green's recollection is that the directors invited Fleischmann's participation.) The chairman disliked the idea, but grudgingly agreed to attend. A dinner in a private room at the Sky Club was arranged for February 21, 1984.

Eiseman recalls walking into the room that night and feeling dismay upon noting Fleischmann's presence. The evening seemed doomed to be unproductive. It was much worse than that.

It began pleasantly enough. The men exchanged pleasant chit-chat at the cocktail hour. When they sat to dine, Green made some welcoming remarks. There was some general discussion about the magazine. Phil Messinger gave an informal presentation on the subject of saving family ownership of *The New Yorker*. He suggested that there were ways in which the company could avoid a future fight for control. He cited another company, Citizens Utilities, which had divided its stock into A shares, with full voting privileges, and B shares, with only a limited vote.

Peter Fleischmann said that someone else had mentioned such a possibility. Messinger said it was one means the Fleischmanns could use to protect themselves from raiders.

Fleischmann remarked, "Very interesting. Let's look into it."

It was soon after that cordial exchange that the evening took an ugly turn. Green began to discuss the business. He told his fellow directors that *The New Yorker* had to face some harsh realities—namely, that the magazine world in which the publication now operated was very different from that which had existed a decade or two earlier. Twenty years before, *The New Yorker* had stood alone as a virtual icon of elitism, a journal that emphasized quality, not mass appeal. Its readers were well educated, well read, and financially well endowed. Their spending power made *The New Yorker* most appealing to advertisers.

Over the past decade, though, the magazine had been bombarded with competition in its category—call it "upscale" or "upmarket" or "high demographic" or any of the other buzz phrases. Other publishers had caught on to the beauty and profit of luring affluent snob-appeal advertisers, and had gone after them by either changing existing publications or starting new ones. He cited *Town & Country, Connoisseur, New York, House & Garden,* airline magazines, and city magazines among the many that were courting the affluent. At the same time, traditional upscale *New Yorker* advertisers, notably the liquor companies, were slashing ad budgets.

"The real world," Green told his audience, "is that we have to gear ourselves to face not only competition, but the cycles of our industry as well."

As Green spoke, Fleischmann's impatience with the proceedings became apparent. He shifted restlessly in his chair, sighed profoundly, coughed frequently, and tapped his voice box on the table. Then, abruptly and unexpectedly, he hurled a preemptive strike.

"You don't know what the fuck you're talking about!" he told Green.

The room was stunned into silence. The directors looked from Green to Fleischmann and back again, then down at their plates in embarrassment. Green paused briefly, then, ignoring the chairman, tried to mask the awkwardness by continuing his remarks. He began to tell the directors about the company's diversification strategy, which was aimed at creating a well-rounded entity that was resistant to cycles. When one business was weak, it was hoped, the others would be strong. He wanted to emphasize that *The New Yorker* magazine would remain the jewel in the crown, that it would be cushioned by the other endeavors. Their financial strength would help shelter *The New Yorker* from any demands of commerce that might prove detrimental to its character.

But Green didn't get very far, because he was cut off again by Fleischmann.

"You're full of shit, George!" the chairman told him. Fleischmann was just getting started. He kept up a stream of what one director calls "inane comments," ridiculing Green, and attempting to quash any foolish notions Green might have that he was in charge.

He told his president, a director recalls, "I run this thing and I own this company! The Fleischmanns started this. We always determined what was best for our interests, and neither you, George, nor anyone else, will tell us what to do!"

With that, Green retreated into silence. Phil Messinger tried to salvage the proceedings. He asked whether *The New Yorker* was considering buying other media properties or magazines. He specifically mentioned *Architectural Digest,* which was rumored to be for sale.

"Stop it right there!" Fleischmann exclaimed. "There's no way we're going into that!"

Someone tried floating a query on the continually nagging question of who would succeed Shawn. It got so tiresome to constantly be asked the question and not have a clue as to the answer. But Fleischmann was in no mood for answers. He took the floor and held it.

"This is bullshit!" one of the directors recalls his saying. "Everyone is sitting around here talking about the real world! The real world this, the real world that! You don't know what the real world is!"

His words were difficult to decipher, especially to those unused to the robot sounds that his machine emitted. He seemed, though, to be returning to a refrain quite familiar to those who knew him well. The real world was 1944, the Battle of the Bulge, being separated from your troops with Germans all around shooting at you.

It was difficult to know what prompted Fleischmann's behavior. It would have been easy to dismiss it as the influence of alcohol. Everyone knew that Fleischmann "liked his liquid," as his friend Curley put it. That particular day, he had indulged in a long drinking lunch, gone home to nap for a few hours, and returned to the Sky Club for more of the same. But no one attributed his remarks that night to drunkenness. All believed them to be deliberate. Fleischmann had simply had it with Green. He was tired of the constant push and pull of their relationship.

There were a few more sallies put forth, but it was hopeless. The dinner ended awkwardly. Someone, maybe everyone, ventured, "Why don't we call it a night?" The men retrieved their coats and straggled out, exchanging noncontroversial, self-conscious remarks. Fleischmann and Curley stepped into a waiting car and pulled away. Eiseman, Messinger, and Green walked north together, up Park Avenue, Eiseman toward a Morgan Guaranty corporate apartment, Messinger and Green toward their Upper East Side apartments. They only briefly and casually discussed what had happened. Eiseman and Messinger were embarrassed for Green. As they headed further north, the men separated, and Green trudged alone, the evening's events replaying in his head. He was mortified. He was not a man given to displays of emotion. If he erred, it was on the side of control. He was disturbed at the outbursts the directors had been forced to endure. But more than that, he was frustrated at his inability to communicate his message. "I am the captain of the ship," he was fond of saying. "If something goes wrong, it is my fault." He felt he had failed. He wondered what more he could achieve at *The New Yorker*. Only two months earlier, he had received an overture from Gil Maurer, president of Hearst Magazines, about moving to Hearst. He hadn't been interested. Now he wondered if he should be.

Philip Messinger returned to his apartment that night and sat for a while, thinking about the future. The stock price of *The New Yorker* had soared, his investment was worth many times what he had paid for it. It had risen so much compared with anything else he owned that it now accounted for 90 percent of his wealth. He believed in George Green, but something told him that Green was not long for *The New Yorker*. Messinger was worried. He had too much invested to gamble. His instincts told him that the evening would not be without its consequences.

The evening proved to be a turning point for Green, and so did the morning that followed, because February 22 was the day of the board meeting at which Stephen Fleischmann would be nominated as a director. Green had spent weeks agonizing over how he would react when Stephen's name was put up for a vote by the board. The events of the preceding night made him even more confused.

When he entered the boardroom the morning of February 22, he still had not decided how to vote. At 10:30, the meeting was called to order, the minutes quickly dispensed with.

Walter Curley then proposed that Stephen Fleischmann be nominated for a seat on the board of *The New Yorker*. Sam Spoto motioned to elect Stephen, and Elaine Matteo seconded the nomination. Someone said, "All those in favor say 'aye,'" and while the directors began to utter the word, several pairs of eyes twitched nervously in Green's direction. Green's voice held little conviction as, after hesitating only briefly, he said "aye." The motion to elect Stephen Fleischmann was carried unanimously. The notes of the meeting bore the legend: "Resolved: that Stephen G. Fleischmann be and he hereby is elected a director of the corporation."

It was asking a lot of Peter Fleischmann to deny his son a place on the board. *The New Yorker* was a Fleischmann family company, and Peter Fleischmann was not only mortal, he was human. He wanted to know that when he was gone, the Fleischmann name would carry on at *The New Yorker*. It was asking too much of a father to deny his son his birthright, and his family its natural succession. After all, his own father had placed him on the board while he was still young and still a broker at Smith Barney, not an officer of *The New Yorker*.

Green didn't see it that way. He took Stephen's presence on the board as a personal and professional affront. After the meeting, he returned to his office and phoned Gil Maurer, the president of Hearst Magazines. He told Maurer that he would like to meet to discuss the job offer Maurer had previously made him. They had lunch to discuss what specific role Green might play at Hearst, and in the days that followed they negotiated briefly, then came to terms. Green accepted the title of executive vice president of Hearst, in charge of six magazines: *House Beautiful*, *Harper's Bazaar*, *Town & Country*, *Connoisseur*, *Colonial Homes*, and *Motor Boating & Sailing*. It was a collection known as "the Hearst Gold Buy," a grouping of its most affluent magazines.

On February 27, George Green and Peter Fleischmann had lunch at the Sky Club. Green told Fleischmann about his offer from Hearst. He had not yet signed an employment contract, and while he intended to do so, at the back of his mind was the thought that maybe Fleischmann would talk him out of it. Maybe the chairman would persuade him to stay.

At the lunch, Green reminded Fleischmann of several conversations the two of them had had about Green's future at *The New Yorker*, when Green was worried about what might happen to him when Fleischmann died. He told Fleischmann that he never intended to get into an argument or a debate with either Peter or his family, and that certainly he could not give Peter any ultimatums about choosing between him and Stephen. He said he knew he owed the chairman a substantial debt of loyalty for championing him through the years. "I know I am a product of your interests," he said. But over the previous months, several concerns had been nagging at him. He felt that he had gotten too close to the *New Yorker* employees and too close to the magazine, that perhaps he wasn't the one who could carry out and enforce the kinds of internal changes that were needed in a company that, to his way of thinking, had grown sloppy. He reminded Fleischmann of the disagreement over the computer advertorial. He said he felt strongly that the advertisement had been appropriate to *The New Yorker*, that it was "the way publishers ought to go," and that he had not pushed the subject because he did not want to fight with Peter.

He told Fleischmann that he believed that Peter had appointed Stephen to the board because he had in mind more of a family business than a public company. Stephen, he said, was unqualified to be an outside director. It would have been far more prudent to bring in an investment banker who could provide acquisition expertise. He said that he had refrained from voting against Stephen out of his personal loyalty to Peter, but admitted he had not made his final decision until the morning of the board meeting. He said that over the years, he had received overtures from other companies, but that he found it easy to deflect them. He loved *The New Yorker*. The developments of the past year had made it more difficult not to be receptive when Hearst came along with a unique offer to oversee six magazines. He said that for several months he had been talking with Hearst, and he described the job to Fleischmann.

Green said, "They made me a substantial offer that I might well accept." The tentative language left room for the chairman to dissuade him. Fleischmann did not.

The monologue lasted forty-five minutes. Throughout, Fleischmann sat passively, listening without emotion. He asked a couple of interested questions about what exactly Green would be doing at Hearst. He then stilled any hopes Green might have clung to when he turned to the practical topic of Green's replacement. "Is there someone inside *The New Yorker* you would recommend to take your place?" he asked. Green replied that he did not believe that anyone currently employed at the magazine was qualified. He suggested that a headhunter be put to the task of finding someone on the outside. He added that there were many people in magazine publishing who would apply for the position, once they knew it was available.

Fleischmann said, "You and Shawn are conspiring against me." It was meant humorously. Throughout the lunch, the chairman was cool, in control, unflappable. The only emotion he seemed to be experiencing was relief. It was as if he welcomed Green's decision.

Fleischmann asked Green to keep his resignation confidential for the time being. Green agreed, but said he did not want to delay too long before joining Hearst. Fleischmann requested that he stay to run the annual meeting, which was a month away.

A few days later, Fleischmann himself called Philip Messinger to tell him that Green had resigned. It was the first and last time the chairman ever phoned Messinger. The director had trouble deciphering Fleischmann's remarks and had to repeat everything back to him to make sure he had heard it correctly. In a later conversation, Elaine Matteo told Messinger that Green would be replaced by Ken Bosee. Matteo would replace Bosee as treasurer. Messinger's immediate unspoken reaction was that with Green gone, it might be time to end his own involvement.

Green himself called Donald Pels. Pels and Green were by now friends. Pels was concerned about Green's future. "Is it a good career move, George?" he asked. Green assured him it was. They discussed the *New Yorker*'s business prospects. Green didn't go into much detail, but it was clear he foresaw major difficulties.

Bill Reik learned of the resignation while sitting in his Paine Webber office, surrounded by his Johnny Bench and Pete Rose posters and jars of Smucker's jams. The news flashed across the screen of his Quotron machine. "I became hysterical," he says. "Absolutely hysterical." His instinctive reaction was that of a stockbroker: He reached for the phone and called Green.

"What the hell are you doing?" he asked. Green stated the obvious. He was leaving *The New Yorker* to take a job at Hearst. He invited Reik to his office to chat. Reik trekked uptown to Forty-third Street and met with Green, who told him of the problems he had had, the deterioration in his relationship with Fleischmann.

"How could you *do* this?" Reik demanded. He felt abandoned, and nervous. The value of his stock in *The New Yorker* had risen sixteenfold since Green took over, and Reik didn't regard that as a coincidence. He gave most of the credit to Green. *Now* what?

At *The New Yorker* there was a mixed reaction to the news. The event went all but unrecorded in editorial. Green was just another businessman, not even a Fleischmann. What did it matter?

Business reaction was divided into two camps. Janet Muir recalls that she and Green were passing in the hall when he, lacking in sensitivity, stopped her and told her the news. She had been on her way to the lobby to greet a visitor. Instead, she pushed past Green, walked into the library, and burst into tears. Among younger salespeople, it was, says one, "the end of the world." But some among the old guard found the news cause for celebration, and were openly jubilant, filled with a kind of "ding-dong the witch is dead" euphoria. It was the same story, the old versus the new, the Green camp versus the traditional *New Yorker*.

Green signed the contract with Hearst on March 15. The following morning, he presided over a *New Yorker* annual meeting that was uneventful, save for the news that Green had resigned. Neither Fleischmann nor anyone else in a position to do so made polite remarks thanking Green for his contributions and nineteen years of service. The lapse irked a lot of interested onlookers.

After the meeting, Green made a point of introducing Phil

Messinger and Bill Reik to one another. "You two have interests in common," he told them. The men straggled out of the hall. On the street, in front of the Morgan Guaranty building, Green, Reik, Messinger, and Pels chatted briefly, then exchanged parting pleasantries: "Good to see you." "Let's have lunch." Green trundled off down the street, carrying his "briefcase," a small navy duffel bag with a picture of Eustace Tilley on the side. Reik thought it was a very sad sight.

11

The following night, March 28, Bill Reik and Philip Messinger met for dinner at the Jockey Club restaurant on Central Park South, to get better acquainted and to discuss their mutual predicament.

Reik was uncomfortable when unexpected news disrupted his normal investment patterns. *The New Yorker* under George Green had fit neatly into his market philosophy. He liked to buy a stock that looked promising, place it in his and his clients' accounts, and then stick with it forever. He might add to the position from time to time, but he wouldn't *fret* short-term, if he could help it. He was an investor, not a trader. *The New Yorker*, he says, was an investment he was "totally sure of. Like everything else in life, you've got different levels of sure. Different levels of strength in your convictions. When I look at all my companies I know which ones I think are inevitable. To me *The New Yorker* was inevitable—with George there. I had it totally tucked away in my mind and put to sleep."

Messinger, too, would rather that Green had stayed. He approved of the way Green ran the company. On the infrequent occasions when he disapproved of a decision, he would discuss it with Green, and, he says, after hearing Green's reasons for having done something, he rarely continued to disagree. Further, he naturally appreciated the fact that his stock had soared during Green's tenure. As discomfited as he was by Green's departure, Messinger was equally upset by his replacement—Ken Bosee. Messinger didn't believe that Green was irreplaceable, but he was not happy about the choice of Bosee as successor. While he liked him personally, he simply didn't believe that he was qualified to run the company. Bosee blames Green for Messinger's attitude. As Bosee sees it, "George Green had Messinger convinced that he was the white knight and the rest of us were a bunch of klutzes." Messinger says that his opinion of Bosee was based on years of observation. "He had no depth or understanding of business," he insists.

In a general sense, George Green had influenced not only Messinger but Reik as well. He was their pipeline into *The New Yorker*. Neither man had previous experience with magazines, so it was natural to accept Green's wisdom on the way the business should be run as well as on the competency of other executives and employees, including Bosee and Stephen Fleischmann. But then, Reik and Messinger were both sophisticated investors, perfectly capable of evaluating a situation and arriving at their own conclusions. They could have dismissed Green as a high-level disgruntled former employee or a less-than-objective source, but they didn't. They believed him.

Reik had been unnerved by Green's accounts of life at *The New Yorker*, and now here he sat, with his elbows propped on a restaurant table, listening intently aghast to Messinger's litany of doom. Messinger, unlike Reik, had front-line experience at *The New Yorker*—he was on the board. Messinger told Reik that Ken Bosee and the other management directors served as "yes-men" for Peter Fleischmann. He said the magazine was in disarray. Bosee and Fleischmann didn't have a good grasp of the business, nor did anyone else there. Green had groomed no successor. He mentioned the fact that Fleischmann did not seem to be around on a day-to-day basis. Often, when Messinger had visited Green, he had borrowed the phone in Fleischmann's habitually unoccupied office. "What are we going to do?" asked Reik. "This isn't funny. You've got 12 percent of The New Yorker and I've got 14 percent, so here we sit with 26 percent of the company, and the entire management just walked out yesterday!"

Messinger said, "We have to sell it."

Reik's notion couldn't have been more different. "I want to *buy* it," he said. "I want to own it. I've *always* wanted *The New Yorker*. Let's buy the whole thing."

Messinger told him he was crazy. The magazine had lost its niche. The business was going sour. The stock market had not yet grasped that fact. The shares had not so much as shuddered at the Green departure. But when the real business difficulties it was encountering became apparent, the stock would plummet. *The New Yorker*, he told Reik, accounted for 90 percent of his entire net worth. He had to protect the investment.

Reik persisted in his campaign: "We'll buy it and we'll bring George back to run it," he said. "We'll never be able to replace George. He knows everything about the magazine."

"That's ridiculous," said Messinger. "Nobody's irreplaceable." But even so, he didn't want to be involved. "You're young," he told Reik. "I'm not. That's the sort of thing that would appeal to you. I can understand why it would. I'm trying to get out and disengage in life; you're trying to get further in, make more money. It's perfectly logical that you should want to do that, but it doesn't fit my program."

The dinner was friendly, but Reik and Messinger parted without agreeing on strategy. Each promised to consider the other's position carefully. Messinger did have a number of discussions with Green about bidding for the company, but Green said his contract with Hearst forbade his getting involved for two years. Messinger also doubted they could raise the funds for a leveraged buyout.

At *The New Yorker*, Ken Bosee moved into the seventeenth-floor office formerly occupied by Green. Bosee was thrilled to hold the title he had lost to Green a decade earlier, but he was sixty-three now, just two years short of the business department's mandatory retirement age. (The rule had once applied to editorial as well, but was dispensed with there when Shawn neared the mark.) Indeed, Bosee even looked forward to retiring—he had been at *The New Yorker* for thirty-six years. He had planned to leave by late 1985, and he intended to stick to his timetable. Peter Fleischmann appointed Bosee president with the understanding that he would serve on an interim basis. That, of course, meant that he had to set to work immediately to find a replacement. Fleischmann brought his son Stephen back into the business to work as an assistant to new treasurer Elaine Matteo.

It was widely believed internally that with Green out of the way, Stephen now had a clear path to the presidency, but it didn't work out that way. Green's had only been the loudest voice crying in the wilderness. With him gone, many more were heard. Stephen got almost unanimously bad grades from other executives, including Elaine Matteo, who was often heard to exclaim in frustration, "If that kid weren't Peter's son I'd fire him!"

Stuart Jason, the comptroller, says, "Every time I think of Stephen I think of someone walking through water in slow motion. He just never seemed to get enthusiastic about things." If Stephen did not like an assignment a boss gave him, he might simply ignore it. Elaine Matteo assigned him the task of overseeing a new contract with the printer. It should have taken weeks. Months later, he hadn't done it. Yet at other times, he would invent the most unlikely tasks and pounce on them. For instance, he mounted a crusade when he learned that a *New Yorker* messenger had put in a chit for a couple of dollars for transportation he had not taken. (A fellow messenger had turned him in.)

"Stephen spent *weeks* on that," recalls an executive. "He was on the case and he was going to hunt his man down." It turned out that Fleischmann was right, the messenger *had* filed a phony report: He was fired. Stephen seemed proud of his victory, but other employees were confused, resentful, and sad. Why couldn't Stephen put that kind of energy into the assignments he was given? And would his concern over such a piddling amount perhaps owe to the fact that he regarded *The New Yorker* as *his* company? His arrogant attitude rankled.

"There was an air about Raoul and an air about Peter," says Elaine Matteo. "They could win you over with their personalities. Stephen did not inherit that charm. They are not comparable human beings. They share the same last name, but they are not alike at all." Ill will toward Stephen escalated when he took to whiling away the afternoon hours sleeping on the couch in his father's office. He denies he did this, but other employees report having witnessed it frequently. Once, when Bosee was trying to find Stephen, he turned out to be sleeping on Sam Spoto's couch.

Both Elaine Matteo and Ken Bosee were forthright people, and they did not shrink from expressing their pronounced reservations about Stephen to his father. So for all of his wishful thinking about Stephen's prospects, Peter Fleischmann could not dismiss the constant buzzing in his ear. He himself began to display ambivalence about Stephen's prospects. In conversations with other executives he would waver. One day he would say that he believed Stephen would learn, and the next day he would seem discouraged. People whose judgment he trusted doubted that Stephen would ever be up to the task. If Stephen did not take over, it would represent the end of an era. At Peter Fleischmann's death, *The New Yorker* would be left without a Fleischmann in command. It must have been a depressing thought for a man with as sure a sense of family history as Peter Fleischmann possessed.

Fleischmann postponed any decisions about his son. Instead, he and Bosee jointly decided to seek another executive to succeed Bosee. Stephen could serve as that man's "understudy," and perhaps assume control at a later date. Fleischmann and Bosee first considered the in-house possibilities, but they concluded, as George Green had, that there was no one on the staff who could fill the job. They retained the executive search firm of Farrell & Phin to headhunt suitable candidates. Bosee would remain president until the successful conclusion of the search. They did not inform the board that a search was under way.

The *New Yorker* staff greeted Ken Bosee's promotion, interim or not, with mixed emotions. Everyone liked Bosee, and so they wished him well. There was a certain coziness to his settling into the president's chair. He was well over six feet tall, and with his bashful smile and large mustache, he resembled an elongated Don Ameche or a Disney character. His genial manner inspired trust not unlike that provoked by a country doctor with a pleasing bedside manner. Ken Bosee, everyone agreed, was a *nice* man.

What's more, his style was more traditional, more "New Yorkerly" than that of George Green. He was not brash and headstrong, but soft-spoken and contemplative. He surely wouldn't march around waving banners the way some of the more tenured *New Yorker* employees thought Green had. In fact, on assuming the presidency, Bosee called his staff together to assure them that he would pursue "business as usual." They could expect nothing radical from him.

William Shawn, by some accounts, was pleased by the change in executives. Ken Bosee believes that Green and Shawn had a strained relationship. Green didn't feel that way, but Bosee observed it. Bosee believed that anyone succeeding Green would have been warmly greeted by Shawn, not because Green had been difficult, but because he had effected change that was distasteful to Shawn. In any case, Bosee did not strike the editors and writers as a meddlesome man. And besides, as one writer puts it, "We never really noticed who was in the business department, as long as they left us alone."

But on the business side, doubts abounded about Bosee's abilities. One executive says that the appointment of Bosee was "further evidence of Peter's unerring instinct for picking the wrong man for the wrong job." (The same executive, it should be noted, had deplored the choice of Green, nearly a decade earlier.) One former executive feels that Bosee would have been an excellent choice ten years earlier, when Green got the job instead, but that he was not a magazine executive for the eighties, and the more competitive nature of the business.

Nearly everyone who worked for him appreciated the fact that Bosee left them to their appointed tasks, a relief after what seemed to some Green's intrusions. Executive Pete Spelman recalls that Bosee told him, "You know advertising and you know communications. I don't. So go out and do it." Spelman was elated: "I hadn't heard those words in ten years." But executives wondered if Bosee knew enough to know what he *didn't* know. It was one thing to give free rein to someone doing a good job, quite another to grant total independence to one who was incompetent. Bosee had meaningful experience in only one area of the business—the treasurer's office. If there was trouble in a department whose workings were unfamiliar to him, would he notice? If he noticed, would he know how to react?

"As a boss," says a former executive, "you can't be George Green and you can't be Ken Bosee. You have to be somewhere in the middle. You have to let people do their jobs, but you also have to have a firm grip on the wheel."

Janet Muir, who became Bosee's assistant after Green's departure, believes that the new president's management style had the immediate effect that bright, capable people began to grow and blossom, in a way that some had been stifled from doing in the Green era. But at the same time, she says, others' lack of talent, formerly obscured, now was apparent. Also, in her view, politics began to brew. Fiefdoms sprang up as executives competed for territory. Bosee, unlike Green, was not strong enough to control that.

Some on the staff found Bosee exasperating. He was not known for quick decisions. "I don't have all day to give to a conversation," one executive grumbled. Another describes Bosee as "so good-hearted, so lovely, but unbelievably disorganized. His office was incredibly backlogged. It was like a Roach Motel. Stuff checked in but it didn't check out!"

Bosee had his champions, among them comptroller Stuart Jason and treasurer Elaine Matteo. Matteo had started working for *The New Yorker* twenty-four years earlier, at the age of seventeen. She attended school at night after days spent stashed away in the fulfillment department on Forty-fifth Street, punching labels from stencils. She was plucked from there to serve as a temporary secretary to Bosee, at that time director of market research. She stayed on to become his secretary of twelve years, and he, in turn, became her mentor, taking her with him to the treasurer's office, guiding her career as she became assistant to the treasurer, corporate secretary, and a director, and now treasurer. To her, Bosee was a man given to impromptu displays of kindness. When she was about to leave on her first trip to Europe, he put in a surprise appearance at Kennedy Airport to see her off. He was the person she most often turned to for advice, because he cared, and because he looked at problems in ways that nobody else did. "He could see things I would never pick up," she says. "He was thoughtful. He could play devil's advocate.

"I know all the jokes," says Matteo. "Don't ask Ken what time it is because by the time he tells you, it's an hour later. But Ken is very bright. He should work in a think tank. He's an egghead. George probably felt that Ken needed a bomb under him because he tends to be very methodical and careful. He's not a hip shooter at all. But he is extremely bright. *Extraordinarily* bright." Matteo thought that Green and Bosee had made a good team, that they complemented each other. Where Green would rush headlong into new pursuits, Bosee was a tempering force.

Green thought Bosee was capable as long as problems fit neatly into categories that were black-and-white. When situations entered the gray area, it seemed to him, Bosee had a problem. Furthermore, he didn't distinguish between the importance of matters. He would devote the same time to a trifle as he did to a major issue.

In a way, Bosee was perhaps too *nice* to be president. He could be taken advantage of. His dealings with "Mr. Shawn" were always cordial, but Bosee soon proved less successful in controlling the editor than his predecessor had been. For instance, Bosee told Shawn in early 1984 that despite the fact that ad pages were declining, he would not whittle editorial space. He believed that the magazine had an unwritten agreement with its readers to keep a constant supply of words flowing. Green, while president, had considered that approach foolhardy. If there was not enough advertising to support the editorial pages, the profits would be squeezed. There had to be some give-and-take, though even under Green, the magazine never ran less than sixty-four pages, no matter how few ad pages there might be.

When Bosee told the editor he would not subtract space, he added, "But I don't think that you should *increase* your pages." Shawn replied that he *had* to have more space. He had commitments to writers. Bosee's resolve quickly collapsed. He acquiesced, but not without warning Shawn that he would have to limit himself the following year. Shawn agreed, but the following year the editor came back to Bosee for even more columns, and once again Bosee granted them.

Bosee was also unsuccessful when, at the urging of William Eiseman, he, too, tried to persuade Shawn to allow grants of stock to "key" editorial employees. Bosee was optimistic that he could succeed where Green had failed, because he thought that he and Shawn communicated better than Shawn and Green had. But when Bosee made the same elevator trek to Shawn's corner office, he was greeted with the same reply: There were no key editorial employees. Shawn would not pick and choose among editors and writers.

Bosee was upset at the rejection, which he termed ridiculous. Shawn did not *pay* everyone the same, so how could he logically argue that all were equal? The board again discussed the matter and once more debated bypassing Shawn and selecting grant beneficiaries. Fleischmann quashed the proposal. Editorial was Shawn's domain.

Bosee was in philosophical agreement with his predecessor, Green, on acquisitions: He agreed that well-selected outside investments could provide a financial cushion for *The New Yorker*. He had not always agreed on specifics. He approved of the investments in Raven Books and *Cook's* magazine, but not the one in *Horticulture*. He believed that more people were interested in cooking than in gardening. (Even if true, it begged the question of how many more magazines were competing for cooks' attention than for gardeners'.) The deal he most disapproved was the American *Elle*, the joint venture with the French Hachette Publications. He termed it "pretty far out" as an investment for *The New Yorker*, and therefore was less than enthusiastic when, he says, "*Elle* was put in my lap when George resigned." Bosee had an ally in Shawn, who "was clearly no fan of *Elle*'s," says Bosee. The editor continued to voice his opposition to the publication throughout the life of the deal. According to Bosee, the more the *New Yorker* contingent learned about Hachette chief Daniel Filipacchi, his executives, and his magazines, the more they were convinced that they were not compatible with *The New Yorker*.

Filipacchi's stable of publications ranged from the news-feature weekly *Paris-Match*, France's largest-selling magazine, to the French version of *Penthouse* and other soft-porn magazines. It was the latter category that offended Shawn and Bosee, who branded the publications "sleazy." Also, Filipacchi himself seemed a bit on the vulgar side. His office on the Champs Élysées was filled with pictures and sculptures of women's derrières.

Nor did Bosee and Shawn, or Matteo and Fleischmann, need to conjure up guilt-by-association objections to the deal. They disliked *Elle* for its own sake. According to Elaine Matteo, the prevailing sentiment was that it was discordant with the style of *The New Yorker*. Janet Muir, a champion of *Elle*, puts it differently: "It was French and racy and it had style. It was exactly what *The New Yorker* was not."

Despite the opposition, Green had pushed *Elle* through. The first issue hit the stands in late March 1984, just before Green left.

The debut was editorially inauspicious. The magazine was printed in France and shipped to the States. The reproduction was poor. Color was not true, and photos and type were blurred. It was fraught with typographical errors and misspellings. The middle third of the book was not paginated, so the notation "Continued on page ____" could not be followed. The editing was sloppy. A "knit it yourself" instruction specifying three buttonholes was accompanied by a photograph showing four. The names of two sisters were reversed halfway through a story. The translation was uneven, at times embarrassingly bad, pidgin English. Adding insult to incompetence, the editorial thrust was slighting of American women. Some of the "how to's" on love and related matters more than implied that American women should take lessons from their French counterparts.

Elle's overall editorial policy reflected a sensibility that young American women had rejected fifteen years earlier. An article called "Make Me a Baby and Get Out," titillating as it sounded, was a radical feminist manifesto in headline only. In text, it turned out to be the sad saga of women who are seduced and abandoned. Janet Muir surveyed readers, including co-workers at *The New Yorker*, and found that they detested that piece, as well as another one about French lovers, deeming them too "Cosmo" (*Cosmopolitan* magazine) in presentation.

But *Elle* showed glimmers of promise. Its fetching cover featured the actress Isabelle Adjani, and there were some intriguing graphics. Nor was it a business flop. By the standards of new magazines, eight out of ten of which fold in the first year of publication, it could even be deemed a success, an improbability given the casual and inexpensive way in which it was run. At times *Elle* staffers imagined themselves at a student newspaper, instead of a national magazine. Manpower was minimal, and titles nearly meaningless since everyone assumed multiple duties.

The advertising department consisted solely of ad director Sunny Bates, a friend of Muir's who was hired from the trade publication *Folio*. She, Muir, and publisher Didier Guerin sold all of the space. Muir sat up many a late night at her apartment in front of her Kaypro computer, working up promotion lists. *Elle* hired Muir's actor-husband's out-of-work actor friends to stuff and address envelopes. The endeavor was undertaken with a sort of Andy Hardy jauntiness: "Hey kids, let's put out a magazine!"

The first issue carried eighty pages of paid advertising, a quite respectable sum for a maiden effort. Many advertisers had at least a nodding acquaintance with *Elle* because the French version had been one of its homeland's most popular women's magazines for decades. That gave it a head start. The *New Yorker* connection helped too. It turned out that 60 percent of the initial *Elle* advertisers had bought at least one page of advertising in *The New Yorker* the previous year. In a preliminary business plan, that figure had been estimated at 25 percent. *Elle*, naturally, charged much lower ad rates than were being collected by the magazines with which it expected to compete. Its four-color, one-page tag was $5900 compared with around $22,000 for Condé Nast's *Vogue* and Hearst's *Harper's Bazaar*, and $20,590 for Condé Nast's *Mademoiselle*. But that is not to detract from the selling success of the first issue of *Elle*, because few magazines are launched as fat with ads as this one was, no matter what the rate. It is quite common, in fact, for fledgling magazines to give ads away. *Elle* didn't have to.

A bonus was that circulation exceeded expectations. Women actually went out and bought it. It sold out on many stands. Even Green was surprised. When he made the deal to publish *Elle*, he privately wondered whether the world needed another fashion magazine. The risk had been an inexpensive one, and he had taken it. As it turned out, the world might not have *needed Elle*, but it wanted it, and reader and advertiser response was warm enough to impel *The New Yorker* and Hachette to forge ahead with a second trial issue.

Muir's enthusiasm was dampened, though, when she learned from Didier Guerin that Daniel Filipacchi was very upset about George Green's resignation. The French boss had exchanged a handshake with Green only months earlier. He considered the contact and even the contract to be personal between him and Green. Yet he had learned of Green's departure only when the public announcement was made. The clear implication from Guerin was that Filipacchi was reconsidering the deal. Muir asked Green, in his final days at *The New Yorker*, to call Filipacchi and to try to unruffle the French feathers. Green phoned the other publisher and was greeted with anger. The Frenchman was furious that Green had quit without telling him.

Green got off the phone and called Muir. "You're going to lose the *Elle* deal," she recalls his telling her.

The words inspired controlled panic in Muir, but she could not elicit any similar emotions from her superiors. *Elle* was not a priority. Fleischmann was rarely in the office, and so was not involved. Bosee wanted *Elle* to go away, and he largely ignored it.

"For the next six months," says Muir, "it was like shadow puppets. Sunny Bates and I tried to pretend that all of these people at *The New Yorker* were involved in this, but it was really just us." In her view, Bosee and Fleischmann had "no sense of survival or growth. No sense of what was happening."

The first major setback to the partnership came in early April. A meeting between *New Yorker* and Hachette officials was scheduled for the ninth and tenth of that month. Hachette executives were flying in from Paris for a two-day session to hash out plans for the second issue. Muir considered it vital that *The New Yorker* present a united front, that the top executives, minus Fleischmann, appear, and that everyone at least *pretend* to be 100 percent behind the venture. If *The New Yorker* could summon up enough enthusiasm, maybe it would prove contagious. It seemed the best hope for salvaging the partnership.

But as it happened, Ken Bosee had planned a vacation to Hawaii that week. He wanted some time off before throwing himself into his new job as president. Muir pleaded with him to change his plans. "It's really important that you be there," she told him. The Filipacchi people were already nervous. It would only make the situation worse if Bosee didn't show up to greet them. But Bosee was not moved by her pleas, nor did he share her priorities. He went to Hawaii, and later wished he hadn't, not because of what happened to *Elle* but because he came down with pneumonia as soon as he arrived.

At the meeting, seven executives from Hachette were greeted by eight from *The New Yorker*—what Muir categorizes as the "second tier." In addition to Muir and Bates, *The New Yorker* was represented by production chief Sam Spoto, treasurer Elaine Matteo, ad director Robert Young, comptroller Stuart Jason, circulation director Douglas Florenzie, and the retail ad director, Louis Farrelly. *Elle* publisher Didier Guerin, Hachette "international publisher" Robert Gutwillig, and fashion editor Nicole Crassat, among others, represented the French publisher.

Muir thought the meeting went badly. She says she and Bates "tried to do a song and dance about how everything was still going forward, but it was obvious to the French that the people sitting there were not really involved. I tried to prep everyone in advance. I told them everything that was going on, so at least they could act knowledgeable. But they asked too many questions and they acted too neutral. They weren't 'Gee! Let's jump up and do this thing!'"

Stuart Jason recalls the event differently. He thought it ran smoothly. He was not aware of any particular tension. There were a lot of questions asked, he remarks, but he was under the impression that they were there to learn. Muir's and Bate's anxieties were no doubt heightened by the fact that it was *their* production, they were ambitious for it, and they were consumed by the fear that it was doomed. They stuffed a folder with statistics about the U.S. magazine market and the *New Yorker*'s place in it, defensively intent on proving that *Elle* was receiving the support of *The New Yorker* and that, indeed, *The New Yorker* was the right partner in the deal. One exhibit detailed the *New Yorker*'s standing among the kinds of advertisers *Elle* would most likely seek out. In 1983, for instance, *The New Yorker* ranked third among all consumer magazines in number of pages sold to retail advertisers, after *Los Angeles* magazine and *Vogue*. It was eleventh in fragrance and fourteenth in cosmetics after a list constituted largely of strictly women's magazines, and tenth in women's apparel, all of which rankings were more than respectable considering that *The New Yorker* was a general-interest, not a fashion, magazine. The point they tried to make was that the kinds of advertisers *Elle* wanted were ones that *The New Yorker* already had. But a conflict arose over who would sell the ads.

The Hachette executives thought the *New Yorker* sales staff would do it, in addition to their duties selling *The New Yorker*. By piggybacking that way, they figured, they could more quickly and efficiently reach the kinds of glossy advertisers *The New Yorker* had. Unfortuantely, everyone at *The New Yorker* rejected that plan, and all disclaimed any prior knowledge of it. *The New Yorker* would be corrupted if its sales force tried to serve two masters. They envisioned having a separate ad department for *Elle*, and flatly refused to lend their in-house reps. Hachette executives were confused and displeased.

The confusion owed to the fact that George Green had intended to involve the *New Yorker* sales force, at least to the extent of shepherding the Hachette contingent in the general direction of the affluent American market. He even leaned toward allowing the staff to sell directly, thinking that aggressive sales representatives would be delighted, because there would be extra money in it for them. But when he left, the idea left with him. So, says Janet Muir, "Sunny Bates and I spent a lot of time pretending we had all sorts of other resources to rely on."

In May there was another meeting, which Muir came to regard as the fatal blow to the deal. The French had not given up on somehow utilizing the *New Yorker* ad department expertise, if not personnel. *Elle* publisher Didier Guerin met with Muir and *New Yorker* ad director Bob Young to pursue it further. But at the session, Bob Young showed such a lack of knowledge about *Elle* that it was obvious he hadn't gotten involved with it and, what's more, didn't care to get involved. Unknown to Muir, Filipacchi and Didier Guerin quietly began shopping for a new partner.

12

Following George Green's departure, there was a marked change in Philip Messinger's attitude toward his fellow boardmembers, and in his behavior at meetings, according to other directors. If Messinger was unhappy with the way the company was being run, it showed.

Messinger had always been an *interested* director, asking questions and voicing strong opinions. But after Green left, other directors perceived that Messinger stepped across a line into rancor. Ken Bosee says that his fellow director "went from passive to active antagonism" toward management. According to Elaine Matteo, there was a heightened animosity by Messinger toward Peter Fleischmann. "If Peter had a spot on his tie," says Matteo, "you had a feeling you would hear about it from Philip." Matteo says Messinger seemed to blame Fleischmann for Green's departure, and the reasons for his dismay at the parting seemed clear: He had made a fortune in *New Yorker* stock in the Green years. Says Matteo: "Phil Messinger had a multi-million-dollar axe to grind."

Walter Curley grants that Messinger was within his rights to demand accountability. But Curley objected to the way Messinger voiced his objections, calling him "accusatorial" and "negative." Fleischmann, for his part, made his displeasure with Messinger abundantly clear by his shifting and tapping and sighing at meetings. Messinger frequently committed two unpardonable sins: He sought information that was none of his business, and perhaps even more heinous, he caused meetings to last longer.

But Messinger had his defenders. Comptroller Stuart Jason, while not a director, always sat in on board meetings. He saw nothing untoward about Messinger's behavior. He says Messinger spoke in a quiet voice and asked businesslike questions. Advertising chief Bob Young, who was a director, says that Messinger was the only director who asked "real director"–type questions.

Messinger has no regrets about the way he conducted himself. He was trying to behave like a professional businessman dealing with a management that he regarded as dangerously amateurish. He interested himself in all aspects of the business. Ironically, many of the practices he found wanting dated back to the Green years. Since 1982, for instance, he had been trying to persuade management to change the New Yorker's method of dealing with inventories, a fancy accounting word for, in this case, unpublished manuscripts. His campaign was founded on figures in the annual report plus a chance encounter.

At a party, Messinger met author and New Yorker writer Nat Hentoff. The two men discussed The New Yorker, and Hentoff expressed his exasperation at how difficult it was to get published in its pages. The magazine paid him for stories he had written, but they hadn't published one in ten years. It was nice to receive a check, but it would be nicer still to see the prose in print occasionally. The conversation was light and even humorous, but it riled Messinger. He knew that writers were paid for stories that were not published. Worse, he knew that some were allowed to draw a paycheck week after week even though they never wrote a word. All of that bothered him, but there had been an abstractness to the stories in the past. Now, here was a firsthand account, an immediate, in-the-flesh description of payment without publishing. In Hentoff's case, it wasn't that the writer didn't produce but, rather, that Shawn paid for stories he never ran. As far as Messinger could determine, Shawn was accountable to no one.

Messinger repeatedly broached the subject in front of the board and at audit committee meetings. In 1984, *The New Yorker*, in its financial filings, valued unpublished articles and art at $3.7 million. Messinger wanted to know how they arrived at that figure, and how they kept track of what was likely to be published and what wasn't. In response to his persistent questioning, he received a letter from Stuart Jason:

Dear Phil,

... You raised the question of controls on manuscript inventory pertaining to purchase, whether or not a piece is run in the magazine, "kills" (removed from inventory), etc. In response to these questions, what follows is an outline of our procedures for purchasing manuscripts, inventory, publishing, killing, etc.

Generally, manuscripts are purchased only with the approval of the Editor, William Shawn, frequently on recommendations from our other editors. The price to be paid is based on predetermined rates. Expenses incurred in relation to the piece are documented by the author, reimbursed by us, and added to the inventory value of the manuscript. Mr. Shawn determines the scheduling of material. Again, this may be with the advice of his associates. Once a year, Milton Greenstein meets with Mr. Shawn, and they survey the material on hand. Based on their best estimates and experience, specific writings may be killed or retained in inventory.

With respect to art work, Mr. Shawn meets with the Art

Editor. The decisions are purely of an editorial nature, and we have found that no "financial"-type controls can be effectively exercised here to replace the editorial judgment. I do not believe that a third party, not in the editorial department, could have any idea as to the merit or worth or timeliness that is inherent in a manuscript. We have continued to rely on this procedure because it works well for us. In addition to the kills, we fully reserve for any items over four years old.

I hope this answers your questions.

It didn't. Messinger was not satisfied. The companies he knew best were ones with quantifiable inventories. General Motors could tell you how many cars were shipped, or sitting on a back lot, or scheduled to come off an assembly line, and it could arrive at a reasonable valuation of those. It was mathematical. *The New Yorker* didn't operate that way. It was a place where art, not steel, happened. Messinger argued that, in his words, "if you say for five years that something is going to be printed and it's not, by the sixth year it certainly becomes doubtful whether you're going to print it or not. Most publications adopt a rule that says that anything that's over a year old, you write off a certain amount; over two years, another; by three years everything is written down to zero. It doesn't matter whether you're going to print it or not. But for accounting purposes, it's written down to zero."

Messinger wrote fellow audit committee member William Eiseman that Stuart Jason's reply to his questions "indicates an inadequate trail and control of... payments." He proposed a "perpetual inventory record" to better track works and payments. It would classify works by author and artist, date bought, amount paid, and subsequent disposition. His suggested record looked like this:

Date Purchased	#Assigned - Title Identification of Piece	Amount Paid	DISPOSITION YEAR					
			1978	1979	1980	1981	1982	1983

Messinger's opinion was that the prevailing system left too much room for abuse by Shawn. "The reason for the proposed record-keeping," he wrote Eiseman, "is that no one knows the history by person so that payments could be made for many years with no item ever published. Since I personally am aware that this has actually happened and no one could supply me the information, I am not sure how prevalent this practice has been. My suggestion includes that the year's inventory be prepared with the backing of author/artist records as previously outlined."

Messinger's proposal was not adopted. Treasurer Elaine Matteo resented a campaign that to her mind was based on one chance encounter Messinger had with one author. She resented still more Messinger's implication that *The New Yorker* was wasting *his* money. Bosee and Jason both believed that the accounting methods employed were adequate. George Green claims that *The New Yorker* conformed to the accounting profession's "Generally Accepted Accounting Standards." Unpublished works were written down to zero for accounting purposes after four years. (Messinger "strenuously" disagrees with Green that this is true.) That did not preclude Shawn's resurrecting a story and running it twenty years later, if he so desired.

Further, according to Green, all of the inventory was traceable by author and subject. Messinger claims that Shawn never gave the business department enough information to allow them to *begin* to sort out what manuscript was how old or how dead, or what had been paid for it. He says that an ill-sorted batch of three-by-five cards controlled by Shawn was all the documentation that existed.

His argument about Hentoff, he says, fell on deaf ears. "They could not know if twenty other writers were treated the same because no one traced payments of articles."

Actually, Fleischmann, Green, and later Bosee were given a copy of each week's issue that was notated, by Milton Greenstein, with the payments made to each contributor for each story or art work. That, of course, told them who had been paid what for publishing, but not who had been paid what for *not* publishing.

Claims Messinger, "Paying for articles that didn't run or weren't even written was a means for Shawn to be loved by starving writers or by friends."

In all of the fuss, Messinger's real point was lost. He was not simply posing an accounting question, he was challenging the *New Yorker's* own singular definition of editorial independence. Shawn was free to pay what he wished to whom he wished. He would run the result when he wanted. It had always been that way. To try to upset so entrenched a system with new accounting methods was futile. Philip Messinger was treading perilously close to editorial territory.

Messinger forayed into another editorial stronghold. The audit committee, when formed in 1982, was charged with overseeing the compensation of officers and executives. Peter Fleischmann, George Green (while still president), Ken Bosee, and other top executives all fell under its purview. But the committee was prohibited from passing on William Shawn's salary. Messinger tried several times to obtain a copy of the editor's contract, but he was ignored. He thought it was peculiar that Shawn should escape the scrutiny of the independent committee. As editor, he was not only among the highest-ranked "executives," he was also, Messinger believed, the highest paid.

"Nobody had any idea what the terms of his contract were,"

says Messinger. "Whether it had a termination date, what the length was, what his salary was, what his obligations were. And here he was, vetoing things to go to the board of directors, and nobody was even able to read his contract!" Messinger never did get a copy of the contract, and he was not told the editor's salary. He did hear from George Green that it was well into the hundreds of thousands of dollars, and that Shawn was paid more than anyone else at the magazine, including Fleischmann, Green, Bosee, or any other executive.

Nor were the outside directors given any information on who would succeed Shawn, and that bothered all of them. They could not help but notice the constant speculation in the press. There were always rumors that Shawn had named a successor, then changed his mind, then planned to quit, then decided to stay. The directors did not know that years earlier, Fleischmann had considered firing Shawn. On the contrary, it seemed to some of them that Fleischmann regarded the editor as irreplaceable. Thus, his leaving and his replacement could have material consequences, and the board wanted to be prepared for them.

Walter Curley recalls that at one meeting, the directors placed on the agenda for the subsequent meeting the topic of Shawn's successor. But by the time the meeting took place, the subject had been removed from the agenda. Fleischmann said it was not worth discussing because Shawn was not leaving.

A director spoke up and said, "Wait a minute. This man is in his seventies. We *have* to discuss it!" But they never did. According to Curley, the board was left with a "vague impression" that the successor would be fiction editor Chip McGrath or fact editor John Bennett.

In 1984, the lack of discussion took on added meaning when Shawn made an unprecedented announcement. In response to rumors, he publicly admitted that he had appointed two co-managing editors: McGrath and Bennett. They had become the new "focuses of the experiment," in the parlance of the editorial department. He said that one or both of the men would likely succeed him. The outside directors learned of the appointments at the same time that the general public did: when they read it in the papers.

To Messinger, it was further proof that the outside directors were victims of a kind of corporate news blackout. At meetings, it seemed to him, nothing was ever discussed in depth, and what's more, no one ever disagreed with Peter Fleischmann. He recalls advising Elaine Matteo that the management directors, like her, owed it to the shareholders occasionally to take independent stands, to disagree with Fleischmann. He recalls Matteo's telling him, "We all express our dissatisfactions before the meetings." The reply rankled Messinger still more, because it meant that pertinent topics were being discussed out of his hearing.

Messinger frequently spoke on the phone or had lunch with Matteo, who, in addition to being treasurer, was corporate secretary, charged with sending notifications to the directors as well as recording and disseminating minutes of meetings. Messinger recalls taking Matteo aside following a board meeting and offering a caution that was not intended to be ominous, though history has made it so. He said that he felt he was the only boardmember who defended the rights of shareholders who were not there to speak for themselves. He said he thought she should be more vocal. He recalls saying that the day would come when "the present prevailing management might not be the same." In that case, he warned, it would be important for her "to have been true to no one, but to be independent as a boardmember."

He recalls pushing the point: "If this company ever goes away from Peter, then you have cut all your ties to this company because you have not been loyal to anybody else."

Messinger says that Matteo replied that she would seriously consider his remarks. Matteo, for her part, does not recall the conversation. She says that at one or more lunches with Messinger, the subject of directors' responsibilities arose, but that never did Messinger mention control moving from Fleischmann hands.

Messinger did not consider Ken Bosee receptive to his queries. That the two men were at cross-purposes is illustrated by the fact that Bosee recalls that Messinger never approached him. Bosee's feelings were hurt by what he perceived as a snub. He would happily have talked to Messinger, had he only phoned. As for Fleischmann, he and Messinger had never set up lines of communication. From Fleischmann's standpoint, Messinger was Green's idea, not his.

Messinger pinned few hopes on swaying others to his way of thinking. The way he viewed it, the management directors were too intent on acting like "good soldiers—they didn't want to embarrass Peter by bringing up a negative at a meeting." He didn't expect Ken Bosee to incite any riots, because Bosee's paycheck was dependent on Fleischmann. Conversely, reasoned Messinger, "Bosee could disagree with me easily because I didn't draw his paycheck."

Bosee, in contrary fashion, contends that the management directors disagreed with Fleischmann *more* often than the outside ones did. But those disagreements did not take place in Messinger's presence.

As Messinger agitated, his conversations with Reik continued. Reik still wanted to buy *The New Yorker*. Every two weeks or so, he would call George Green and ask him to return. "I'll get financing, George," he would say. "We can buy it. You can run it. It will be great." Green would reply that he had signed a two-year contract with Hearst and therefore was unavailable. Reik would counter that contracts could be broken. He asked Green,

"How much time do I have to get you to change your mind? I like tasks that are very difficult." Green said, "Talk to me in two years." Reik's remonstrations, ego-building as they were, could not override Green's belief that *The New Yorker* could not be bought.

Messinger believed that the magazine could be bought. He had studied the list of shareholders—there were fewer than eight hundred—and toted the stock of Fleischmann family members and friends. Search as he might, he could not see how they controlled more than 30 percent of the vote. Peter Fleischmann and the Fleischmann family trusts controlled around 25 percent. Messinger figured that assorted friends and relations held another 4 percent, at most. Together, they did not have a majority, which meant that theoretically, it was possible to buy *The New Yorker* out from under the Fleischmanns. Still, Messinger didn't believe that Reik could summon up the money to accomplish that objective.

Messinger himself had not arrived at any clear course of action. His instincts told him that he would have to sell his stock, but he was not yet ready to preclude other options. He considered drawing in another investor—a strong partner. It was a notion Reik found appealing as well. An institution with publishing expertise could buy a lot of stock and use the position as leverage to obtain a seat on the *New Yorker* board. Some knowledgeable executive could then sit as a director and serve as an overseer, to ensure that *The New Yorker* was professionally managed. Reik thought of LIN Broadcasting. The company owned 5 percent of *The New Yorker*'s stock. Peter Fleischmann had known its chairman, Don Pels, for twenty-five years; he seemed to like him. If Pels, Messinger, and Reik banded together, Reik reasoned, they would have what he called "a legitimate platform from which to discuss matters with management." More crassly put, they would have a strong position from which to bargain. Together they represented more than 30 percent of the stock. Oddly enough, though, two and two didn't make four where *The New Yorker* was concerned.

The Fleischmann family had always done a superb job of convincing the world that *The New Yorker* wasn't *really* a public company, but instead a privately held family concern, and therefore, that it couldn't be bought. George Green, who had run the company and was well acquainted with its financial constitution, didn't believe it was possible to buy it. Elaine Matteo still believes it couldn't be done. She says that she could have picked up the phone and within hours culled enough support from Fleischmann friends, relatives, and employees to put their voting power at over 50 percent of the total shares. And indeed, while Messinger figured that Fleischmann friends and family controlled only 4 percent on top of the 25 percent listed in proxies, the Fleischmanns put their total family holdings at 32 percent.

No would-be purchaser was willing to take the chance that the calculation was incorrect. The suitors that had called on *The New Yorker* over the years had stepped softly, bearing soft words and pleasant promises, not proxy battles and (shudder) lawyers. There was a new generation of gladiators on Wall Street, men called "greenmailers" or corporate raiders, who saved sentiments about delicacy for the collections of Chinese porcelain or the Rubens paintings they had amassed with their spoils. They had left *The New Yorker* alone. This institution had always moved forward on quirkiness and gentility. It might bruise with rough handling.

But even Bill Reik, who understood the nuances of *The New Yorker*, laughed at depictions of the organization as frail. Only one year earlier, he had owned shares in Sotheby's, an institution that had much in common with *The New Yorker:* They both had great prestige in their fields which led to a certain arrogance on the part of their employees, who tended to regard themselves as irreplaceable. At *The New Yorker*, writers were paid even if they didn't produce. At Sotheby's, the employees wallowed in extravagant expense accounts. At both establishments, the staffs were relatively unconcerned about the fact that business prospects seemed to be dimming.

Two businessmen, Marshall Cogan and Stephen Swid, had offered to buy Sotheby's, only to be greeted with disdain by the Sotheby's employees, who called them "rug dealers," a slighting reference to the industry in which Cogan and Swid had amassed much of their wealth. The notion of the two gentlemen from New Jersey owning Sotheby's was repellent. The in-house "experts"—the men and women who appraised art objects—tilted their fine-boned noses toward the skies and threatened to find employment elsewhere should such an unpleasant event come to pass. The threats had caused Bill Reik no end of merriment.

"Quit!" he would exclaim to Sotheby's president John Marion. "Where would they go?! To set up orthopedic practice at New York Hospital?! Let's put this thing in perspective! We're talking here about people who know what a vase is worth!"

The experts didn't quit, because a white knight galloped in in the person of real estate magnate Alfred Taubman. The end result was that Taubman bought Sotheby's, Reik and his clients made a killing, and the experts stayed on.

Now, a year later, Reik figured that the *New Yorker* writers were in a similar fix. There wasn't that much call for ninety-page stories, either. Where would they go?

Nor was Reik (or Messinger, for that matter) convinced that Shawn possessed either popish infallibility or immortality. Reik told Messinger that it was "sick" for the world to believe that *après* Shawn, the deluge. He said, "Replace him and watch the magazine come out next week. It won't be long before everyone realizes that *The New Yorker* can run without Shawn."

Reik, like Messinger, was restless. He and Messinger had, by late spring, had several worried conversations, but neither of them had reached any conclusions. With the exception of Donald Pels, Reik had been the principal purchaser over the preceding years. They did not know of anyone else who was interested in buying. If they decided to sell, it was unlikely they would unload such large positions in the market, because to do so would be to greatly depress the price of the stock. They would have to place the shares with one or two interested partners, perhaps a company intent on acquiring the whole.

Whether he decided to sell or not, Reik was still intent on gaining the involvement of another knowledgeable investor. He decided to test the waters with a call to Donald Pels. Pels had been a relatively passive investor. Reik wanted to make him more active. In mid-May, Reik phoned Pels.

"You have told me repeatedly," Reik said, "that you're interested in buying more of The New Yorker. But you said you only wanted to buy big pieces."

"That's right," said Pels.

"Well," said Reik, "I think you should get more involved. You should be on the board. And you should own more stock. I'll offer you another 5 percent of the company. That's a big piece, right?"

Pels agreed that it was. "How long do I have to decide?" he asked.

"How long do you need?"

Pels said that he wanted to have lunch with Peter Fleischmann before he made any decisions.

"Do you want me to go with you?" Reik asked.

Pels said no; he would go alone and report back.

Reik had not planted in Pels's brain any notion that hadn't already taken root. Pels was friendly with George Green.

"When George Green left The New Yorker," Pels told this writer, "we concluded that we should either be more involved with the company or that we should sell our investment."

Pels and Peter Fleischmann shared a cordial lunch at which Pels offered to buy The New Yorker. He assured Fleischmann that it was a friendly offer, that he would give the magazine a good home and run it in a way befitting its history and dignity. Fleischmann was not ready to sell.

A couple of days later, Pels called Fleischmann and said that he had decided to sell LIN's New Yorker stock. He didn't want to do it, though, without first offering it to The New Yorker. Would the company be interested? Messinger recalls that Pels placed on it a price tag of $140 a share, higher than the current market bid of $127. Fleischmann told him no, they weren't interested; he thought the stock price was too high. On two subsequent occasions, Pels again offered The New Yorker his block. Twice more Fleischmann declined. Pels phoned Bill Reik.

"A week ago you offered to sell me 5 percent of The New Yorker," Pels said.

"Right," said Reik.

"Well, I'm refusing," said Pels. "I'm now offering to sell you 5 percent."

Reik was not surprised. "How much time do I have?" he asked.

"How much time do you need?" Pels replied. It was a Xerox copy of their previous conversation.

"What happened at lunch?" Reik wondered. "I take it it didn't go too well. Did you tell him he's going to lose his company?"

"I did," said Pels.

"Did he believe you?"

"No."

Pels told Reik that he was no longer comfortable sitting with

the block. He had offered to buy *The New Yorker*, but Fleischmann had turned him down. Nor did Fleischmann want to buy
the LIN position, so Pels was now offering it to Reik. Reik said
that he would consider buying it, but that if he didn't, he would
at least place it for Pels—in effect, broker the deal. He needed
some time. Pels authorized Reik to handle the sale, and asked
him to move quickly.

13

At a board meeting on May 24, 1984, the already strained relations between Messinger and the *New Yorker* management took a turn for the worse. The meeting was called to order at 10:30 A.M. in the small boardroom attached to the conference room on the sixteenth floor. The rote preliminaries were quickly dispensed with: the approval of the minutes of the previous meeting, a brief discussion of the balance sheet, a vote to approve the dividend. Next on the agenda was a discussion of raises for Fleischmann, Bosee, and Matteo, and it was on that subject that controversy arose. William Eiseman reported that the compensation committee had agreed to recommend salary hikes for the three retroactive to January 1. The vote was a formality, since the raises were already in effect.

Further, the committee urged board approval of additional increases to those executives, and a raise as well to ad director Bob Young, to reflect what the committee report called "new responsibilities due to the changes in management following the resignation of George Green."

Peter Fleischmann, whose compensation was raised by $8000,

to $118,000, retroactive to January, would receive another $12,000, for a total of $130,000, before bonuses. Ken Bosee's salary was increased by $8000, to $118,000, and then by another $22,000 to $140,000, before bonuses and stock grants. (Fleischmann was not eligible for grants.) Elaine Matteo received an extra $5000 effective January, then another $10,000, for a total of $85,000. Bob Young received no raise in January because ad sales had slipped, but was now given an additional $5000 a year for a total of $125,000.

The recommendations had not been unanimously endorsed by the outside directors at their compensation committee meeting. Philip Messinger had dissented. First, he didn't understand any raise to Fleischmann that was based on "new responsibilities." Fleischmann had been chairman before Green left and he was chairman still. His poor health prevented him from resuming a full schedule, and, according to Messinger's sources, he still did not spend many hours at work, nor did he seem very involved in operations. The only direct action he had personally taken, as far as Messinger could determine, was to approve a renewal of the ban on cigarette advertising.

Eiseman had initially expressed reservations about the raise to Fleischmann, but he had dropped the subject—it seemed to him too small an issue to debate. Eiseman favored the hikes to Matteo and Bosee, because they had clear new titles and increased responsibilities. Messinger opposed those as well. He said that Matteo had essentially been doing the treasurer's job before. He understood that Bosee had a loftier title, but he didn't rate the prospects for Bosee's success in the post very highly. Messinger had suggested skipping the interim raises and instead voting year-end bonuses if warranted by performance. But Messinger was overruled when the rest of the directors all cast their votes in favor of the raises. Messinger recalls that he abstained.

That piece of business behind them, Bosee provided status reports on Boulder Enterprises, *Horticulture*, *Cook's*, Teleram,

Raven Press, Terre Haute Newspapers, and Elle international. The presentation was too brief and sketchy to suit Messinger. Bosee next informed his fellow boardmembers of a *fait accompli.* He had made his first investment as president, purchasing for *The New Yorker* a 15.8 percent stake in a Boulder, Colorado, office furniture manufacturer called Drever Business Systems. That news sent a ripple of shock through all the outside directors—it was the first any of them had heard of it. Bosee distributed around the table copies of the contract as well as related financial data. Messinger had never before entered a board meeting without being prepared to discuss the business at hand. George Green never dumped something like this on the directors' laps without advance warning. Messinger began to do a slow burn.

Bosee had been approached by a man named John Davis. Formerly chief financial officer of Boulder Enterprises, Davis quit to join the start-up furniture concern, and he asked Bosee for seed money. Bosee had mentioned the Drever deal to Fleischmann and Elaine Matteo, as well as to Janet Muir. Muir wrote her boss a memo in which she advised against advancing the funds. She noted that at the March annual meeting, only two months earlier, George Green, in response to a question, had told shareholders that *The New Yorker* would continue to seek out new investments, concentrating in the communications field, their area of expertise. The company had learned an inexpensive but real lesson when it forayed into Teleram Computers. Muir pointed out that *The New Yorker* knew nothing about the furniture business and had no way of evaluating Drever's potential success. Bosee ignored the advise; $200,000 was not that much to risk.

Messinger knew none of the background, only that he had not been consulted. He was angry at the "case-closed" manner in which the deal was presented. After flipping through the financial material, he says, he objected to the deal on three grounds:

Bosee had used company funds to make an investment without first consulting the board; it was "inappropriate" for *The New Yorker* to become involved in the furniture business, especially since George Green had told shareholders they would confine their acquisitions to media companies; and the deal was too small.

Nor were the other directors enthusiastic. "You could tell from the remarks around the table that everyone had the feeling that this was a piece of crap," says Messinger. Even Fleischmann seemed to smile with approval when the other directors challenged Bosee on Drever.

Bosee had a ready reply to the first objection. In 1981, he reminded his fellow directors, the board had authorized the chairman and president to advance sums under $300,000 for investments without consulting the board. The resolution was passed, at Elaine Matteo's suggestion, when George Green was in the final stages of negotiating the Teleram and *Horticulture* deals. It seemed silly to Matteo that she, as assistant treasurer, could buy or sell millions of dollars worth of bonds at will, while the president and chairman were prohibited from spending a couple of hundred thousand dollars. Messinger's recollection was that the resolution applied only to those two deals, and indeed, after the *Horticulture* and Teleram deals were done, Green had not again invoked the privilege. Messinger thought that in Bosee's hands, discretionary powers were dangerous. If he strung together enough marginal $200,000 deals, it could wind up costing millions.

Nor was Bosee contrite about investing in a business outside of magazines. He said that Drever produced beautiful, high-quality furniture, and that the investment would surely pay off.

A year later, Drever filed for bankruptcy.

In retrospect, Bosee regards Drever as a bad investment because "it was too small. It didn't really mean anything." He adds, though, that it served to transmit to the world a signal that *The New Yorker*, even without George Green, "had not stopped expanding."

There were more revelations to come at the board meeting.

Peter Fleischmann told the directors that he had had lunch with Donald Pels, the chairman of LIN Broadcasting, and that Pels had offered to sell his *New Yorker* stock back to the company. Fleischmann related that he had told Pels that he thought the price was too high. The issue was not that Pels was asking too much, but rather that the stock price had simply become over-inflated. According to Bosee, management thought *The New Yorker* was worth around $90 a share.

Fleischmann further informed the board that William Reik of Paine Webber would probably be authorized to sell the stock if *The New Yorker* didn't want it.

Messinger was again taken aback. He had not spoken to Reik lately and knew nothing of what had transpired between him and Pels. Messinger spoke up and urged that the board seriously consider the purchase.

Ken Bosee opposed the suggestion. The asking price was close to $6 million; the company couldn't afford it. Someone else wondered about the legality of paying Pels more than the market price. At the very least, other shareholders would probably complain.

Someone ventured the suggestion that they offer Pels $75 a share, far below the $132 that was the bid price in the market. Messinger scoffed at the suggestion. Pels might negotiate, he might even accept a lower-than-market bid, but it was unrealistic to think he would sell at a price that was just over half of what he was asking. Pels could find a buyer at far more than $75.

Messinger recalls beseeching the board to at least arrange for the placement of the shares, rather than allowing them to be shopped around. If they were adrift for an extended period, they would acquire a "damaged goods" stigma. That could tarnish the company's image and lower the value of the rest of the stock. Worse still, the shares might fall into the wrong hands.

"In this day of the corporate raiders," Messinger recalls saying,

THE LAST DAYS OF THE NEW YORKER

"of Ivan Boesky and Carl Icahn, it is very, very important that blocks of stock of this magnitude not be floating around Wall Street. There's not a company in America that would let five percent of their stock just float around without placing it in friendly hands."

Walter Curley was inclined toward that position as well. After the meeting he took Fleischmann aside and offered to place the shares for him. Fleischmann politely refused the offer.

Messinger remembers that at the meeting, Milton Greenstein asked with what, in hindsight, seems like prescience, "Did Pels offer to buy the whole company?" Neither Matteo nor Bosee recalls the question's being asked. But everyone agrees that at some point in the discussion, Fleischmann told the board, "Pels might have said something in a joking manner" about buying *The New Yorker*. But what Pels really wanted, Fleischmann told the board, was to sell his stock.

Messinger requested a recess in the meeting and asked Robert Winge, the company's counsel from Winthrop Stimson, to accompany him to the outside corridor. The men repaired to the hall, where Messinger told Winge that he might be interested in buying some or all of the LIN shares. "Do you envision any potential conflict of interests?" he asked the lawyer.

Winge thought for a moment, then replied that such a purchase would present no particular problem. When they returned to the boardroom, Winge announced that Messinger had told him that, depending upon price, availability, and his ability to raise the money, he might buy the stock. The news went unremarked. The meeting had dragged on far too long to suit Peter Fleischmann, and it was adjourned.

Messinger's anger did not end when he walked out the door that afternoon. There were several subjects he didn't intend to drop. One regarded the discretionary funds that Bosee had used to invest in Drever.

Messinger protested in separate conversations with Elaine Matteo and Robert Winge that the $300,000 allowance had applied to only two acquisitions—Teleram and *Horticulture*. By way of reply, Winge sent Messinger a copy of the resolution that had been adopted at the August 1981 board meeting.

> Resolved, that the Chairman of the Board and the President, and either of them... is authorized and empowered to negotiate, execute, deliver and perform any and all agreements, instruments and documents and to take any other actions, for or on behalf of the corporation... including... agreements, instruments and documents relating to... entry into or dissolution of a joint venture or partnership... [and]... purchases, sales or leases of real or personal property... provided, however, that this resolution shall not authorize any action... which involves payment or the incurring of liability by the corporation exceeding $300,000....

Messinger was not appeased and shot back a copy of the minutes of that meeting. They detailed "Mr. Green's" reports on a possible reorganization of Teleram and acquisition of *Horticulture*. "In connection with the aforementioned reports," the minutes read, "there was a discussion to expand the authority of the chairman and the president with respect to investments." Messinger pounced on the phrase that began "in connection with" to make his case that that resolution had referred only to Teleram and *Horticulture*.

The funds diminished somewhat in importance following a conversation Messinger had with Reik in the week following the board meeting. Messinger told Reik that his name had come up in connection with a potential sale of LIN's stock. Reik said that selling the stock had been Pels's *second* choice. He would have much preferred to buy the company. Reik explained that Pels offered to buy *The New Yorker*, but that Fleischmann had turned him down.

Messinger was stunned. His recollection of the board meeting was that Greenstein had specifically asked whether Pels wanted to buy *The New Yorker*, and that Fleischmann had responded that Pels had made a joking remark to that effect. Messinger was furious at what he saw as a lie and a breach of fiduciary responsibility. The chairman was legally obligated to bring all purchase offers to the board, he believed. Messinger had long suspected that Fleischmann rebuffed offers without consulting his board. Now there was proof.

Messinger phoned Don Pels and requested a meeting. On June 12, he visited Pels at his office at the headquarters of LIN on the Avenue of the Americas. In a forty-five-minute conversation, Pels confirmed that he had recently met with Fleischmann and offered to buy *The New Yorker*. It was just one of several such overtures he had made over the years, he explained, but Fleischmann always turned him down. That revelation, of course, only served to fan Messinger's flames. He asked Pels if he had made the recent offer in a joking manner. He recalls that Pels said, "I'm not much of a comedian and I don't make jokes about business. The offer was serious."

Messinger urged Pels to return to Fleischmann and be more insistent, *persuade* him to sell. Pels said that he was not interested in a fight. He didn't want to get involved in any situation that was not conducive to a good corporate relationship. Pels says, "It was always a question of a friendly offer or none at all. Peter expressed no interest in additional involvement by LIN." He adds that there were no specifics discussed, and no negotiations. "I would have been surprised if Peter had thought that our conversations had gotten to the point where it might have been appropriate for discussion with his Board."

Pels told Messinger that he felt he had no choice but to sell. Since *The New Yorker* didn't want the stock, he had authorized Bill Reik to sell it.

Messinger left Pels's office and began to debate his own options. Should he buy the LIN stock? Should he sell his own position? He had to be careful. He didn't want to flood the market with stock. If he and LIN both tried to sell in the open market it would surely depress the price. Messinger was sitting on more than 80,000 shares of The New Yorker. Every time the price dropped a point, he lost $80,000. If it dove ten points, he was out $800,000. In addition to math, there was psychology to consider. If two large blocks were put up for sale simultaneously, people might start to wonder what was wrong at The New Yorker. Why did two men with an inside track want out? Negative guesses might even lead to a run, which would *really* slam the price.

Angry as he was at Fleischmann, Messinger was also emboldened. There was vindication in knowing that his suspicions were verified. Messinger did not immediately move to confront Fleischmann. He was not one to indulge in spontaneous outbursts. He would wait for the appropriate forum in which to voice his displeasure

On July 12, Elaine Matteo sent each director a draft of the minutes of the May meeting. They would be approved at the next regularly scheduled session on August 16. It was a formality: No one had ever found fault with the content of the minutes. That precedent was about to be overturned.

It is common in the business world for a four-hour board meeting to be summarized in two pages of minutes. By law, the minutes must report on action taken. If, for example, the board votes in favor of a dividend hike, the minutes must record the fact. Past that legal minimum, substance of minutes is left to the discretion of the corporation. At The New Yorker, according to Elaine Matteo, who wrote the minutes, the policy was to provide details only if a resolution did not describe the action taken. For example, if the board slashed the dividend, the minutes would carry a paragraph explaining the reason for the move, as discussed by the board. If the dividend was simply maintained, the action would be noted without further elucidation. Matteo says that the

New Yorker minutes were carefully reviewed by lawyer Robert Winge before being distributed to the directors.

Nevertheless, Messinger found the written record of the May session wanting. On July 16, he dispatched to Matteo a two-page missive outlining his objections. It read:

Dear Elaine:

Significant omissions from the minutes of the meeting of May 24 are as follows:

1. I believe I abstained re the salary increases.

2. Investment in Drever Business systems was done upon Mr. Bosee's use of what he described as discretionary funds. Some directors, including myself, were critical of the investment because:

   1) It is not in the communications area, in which the Company stated their acquisitions would be targeted at the last annual meeting.

   2) There were no consultations with the Board or the Company's attorneys as to the purchase agreement.

   3) As Mr. Messinger read the Purchase Agreement, he felt it could be difficult to sell the investment because certain rights and conditions customarily granted to the buyer were not in this agreement.

   4) The business plan was deficient as it did not show monthly projections of cash flow and net income for the next several years.

   5) The venture capital firm which was a coinvestor is small, and invests in penny stock deals out of Denver. Thus it does not represent the "deep pockets" or management assistant usually looked to in a local venture investor.

3. The other material omission was the following set of facts relating to LIN Broadcasting:

    1) The Chairman had met with Don Pelz [*sic*], Chairman and CEO of LIN at which time Mr. Pelz offered to sell the 42,600 shares of New Yorker back to the Company. He offered the shares at 140. If the company did not purchase these shares, Bill Reik would probably handle it.

    2) Mr. Messinger called for a brief recess and asked to consult with Robert Winge, Company outside counsel.

    3) Upon returning to the meeting, Mr. Winge reported that Mr. Messinger informed him that he may directly or indirectly acquire all or part of the shares.

    4) A discussion was held and to a question by Mr. Greenstein, the Chairman answered Mr. Pelz had not made any offer to buy additional shares of the Company and just indicated he wished to sell. The Board decided to pass on the purchase and Mr. Messinger abstained.

These are material omissions which should be included in the minutes in order to accurately report the meeting. Please advise.

Very truly yours,
Philip Messinger

Messinger refrained from commenting on what he had learned about the Pels-Fleischmann discussion. The letter served to lay the groundwork for a confrontation that would be a month in coming.

14

In mid-July, Janet Muir and Sonny Bates flew to Paris. The city abandoned itself to the boisterous merrymaking of Bastille Day, the French celebration of independence from the shackles of monarchy. Bates and Muir toiled in the offices of Hachette, on the Champs Élysées, in the shadow of the Arc de Triomphe, feverishly racing the closing deadline on the second issue of *Elle.*

Little of portent had passed since the two meetings of April that Bates and Muir considered disastrous. The second issue had sold fewer advertising pages than the first—sixty pages compared with eighty—but that was to be expected. Advertisers were waiting to see how effective a selling tool *Elle* would prove to be.

Muir and Bates were nevertheless worried. The calm had too much weight. Curiously, the Hachette executives made no remarks about the future. It was like being engaged to someone who never mentioned marriage. Occasionally, a Hachette executive would pose a seemingly casual question about George Green. Was Muir in contact with him? She would reply equally casually that she and Green were friends, and sometimes had lunch or chatted on the phone. She thought the questions odd.

One afternoon, recalls Muir, Didier Guerin and Robert Gutwillig of Hachette "hauled Sonny and me into a private dining room and started grilling us." Again they wanted to know if Muir had spoken to Green. "I didn't know if I was *supposed* to be talking to George or *not* supposed to be talking to George," she says. So again, she hedged her answer. But nothing she and Bates said seemed to satisfy the Frenchmen. "I knew then that it was over," she recalls. She and Bates figured that Hachette must have another partner lined up.

It was not until a year later that Muir learned from a magazine article that Hachette had begun searching for a replacement for *The New Yorker* immediately after Green left the company. Didier Guerin, *Elle*'s publisher, explained that *The New Yorker* was never an appropriate sponsor for *Elle*. Hachette approached several big publishers but met with rejection. Everyone thought that the women's magazine field was already too crowded. It was some months before they seized upon the idea of Rupert Murdoch, the Australian-American press lord who had built a fortune on sensationalist "killer bee" journalism. Entering the eighties, Murdoch had begun to splurge on more prestigious properties, most notably the *Times* of London. Also, as noted earlier, he had purchased *New York* magazine. Still, Murdoch did not enter Hachette's corporate consciousness until he purchased the magazine *New Woman* out from under Daniel Filipacchi, who was also bidding on it. Murdoch suddenly became a likely candidate.

While Muir and Bates worked in Paris putting the second edition of *Elle* to bed, Murdoch and Filipacchi met an ocean away, at Murdoch's office at the *New York Post* on South Street in lower Manhattan. Hachette had supplied Murdoch with files full of facts and figures on costs per thousand, projected ad revenues, and potential share of market. Murdoch had thrown them barely a glance. Murdoch and Filipacchi were like-minded men when it came to business. They knew that statistics could tell you everything and nothing. They preferred to move on instinct. Murdoch's instincts told him to give *Elle* a go. Standing in Murdoch's office, in the shadow of the Brooklyn Bridge that loomed outside the window, the two titans of international publishing shook hands on a deal. Their companies would jointly produce *Elle*; costs and profits would be equally split.

On August 10, Didier Guerin, Ken Bosee, and Janet Muir met in Bosee's office. In a cordial session, Guerin informed the others that Filipacchi did not feel *The New Yorker* and Hachette were compatible. Hachette preferred to find a new partner. They were severing their ties.

Two days later, with the coffin on the old deal barely sealed, Murdoch and Filipacchi issued a press release that was a study in international cooperation: The media empires of Rupert Murdoch, the Australian, and Daniel Filipacchi, the Frenchman, together would publish the American *Elle*.

With the third issue, dated September 1985, *Elle* became a monthly. After its halting start, it would prove one of the most successful launches in American publishing history. It was lauded for a design that was young, bold, and sassy, and best of all, *different* from that which prevailed at other women's publications. Even the *Wall Street Journal* became giddy describing the competitive chill running up the fashionable spines at *Vogue* and *Harper's Bazaar*. *Elle* was soon chubby with ads. Ad rates were hiked from the initial $5900 level for a four-color page to $19,000 by 1987. Circulation soared to 851,152 in 1987. *The New Yorker*, of course, did not partake of the success, because by the time *Elle* took off, their investment had ended. Ken Bosee had no regrets. He never grew fond of the project that he had inherited. "If Hachette hadn't fired us," he says, "we would have fired them."

At around the same time that the *Elle* deal was ending, it appeared that the *New Yorker*'s association with Raven Press would do the same, but on happier terms. The 38.6 percent of Raven had been George Green's second investment as president. It proved a good one. It had carved out a strong position for itself in its field, and sales and profits were growing. With favorable results and even better prospects, it is not surprising that it caught the corporate attention of Macmillan, a large New York publisher that specialized in textbooks. Macmillan made an offer to buy Raven for $10 million. Raven executives were pleased with the offer, and *The New Yorker* saw no reason not to be pleased along with them. *The New Yorker* would net $3.8 million, or nearly four times the $1 million investment it had made just four years earlier. After consulting with boardmembers, Bosee agreed to sell. Lawyers were put to work drawing up contracts. But at the final hour, the deal fell through. Investors, including Reik and Messinger, could not learn why it collapsed.

On August 13, in response to an invitation from Ken Bosee, Bill Reik met Bosee and Peter Fleischmann for lunch at the Sky Club. Bosee, who was late in arriving, wore a worried expression when he greeted the others at the bar. Bosee ordered a drink, then said to Reik, "Mr. Reik, there are some things that happened at the office today that I have to discuss with Peter. I hope you don't mind if we do it in front of you."

Reik replied that he didn't mind at all.

Bosee told Fleischmann, "I've got bad news on the Raven thing. The deal has fallen through."

Bosee was clearly upset and shaken. There had been no hint that the deal might collapse. Macmillan had pulled out without providing an explanation.

Reik was unnerved by the drama unfolding before him. It worried him that a $10 million deal had evaporated and management did not know why. The lunch represented his first lengthy encounter with Bosee and Fleischmann. Since George Green had left, Reik's line into the magazine was Elaine Matteo. He phoned her when he noticed sudden upward blips in the price of the stock to ask if there was any fundamental reason for the rise. She would invariably say there was none that she knew of, and that was the end of the conversation. The only other person with whom he communicated was Messinger. He was surprised, then, when Bosee extended an unsolicited invitation to lunch. Reik guessed that management's newfound interest in him had something to do with the fact that "Phil had started popping off at board meetings by then." Perhaps Bosee and Fleischmann "were putting two and two together and figuring out that Phil was really angry, worried, nervous—whatever—and that he might try to do something." Perhaps the *New Yorker* executives were trying to find an ally in Reik.

Bosee says he called because Reik was a major investor and deserved to be kept abreast of developments. Bosee recalls that he and Reik always enjoyed a pleasant, communicative relationship.

But the get-together did not heighten Reik's confidence. On the contrary, he was dismayed by what he regarded as Bosee's and Fleischmann's lack of basic knowledge about the business. After the lunch he intensified what to date had been an unsuccessful search for a buyer for the LIN stock. Messinger helped Reik in the quest, since he himself wanted to see the shares resting peacefully in friendly hands. He called Fred Wilpon, an acquaintance who was a real estate developer and a part owner of the New York Mets baseball team. Messinger didn't think it likely that Wilpon himself would be interested in *The New Yorker*, but he believed his partner in the Mets might be. That was Doubleday & Co., the giant book publisher and retailer. Wilpon was particularly friendly with executive and family member Nelson Doubleday. Messinger asked Wilpon if he thought Doubleday might consider buying a stake in *The New Yorker*. Wilpon said he doubted it because Doubleday was not in the magazine business. At the time, also, the Doubleday family was embroiled in an internal war that would culminate with the sale of the publishing arm of the company to a German conglomerate and of the Mets to Wilpon and Nelson Doubleday. But Wilpon said he would look into it and get back to Messinger.

Within twenty-four hours, Wilpon phoned Messinger with an alternative recommendation. He suggested that his friend Mortimer Zuckerman might consider buying *The New Yorker*. Zuckerman was a real estate developer active in Boston, New York, and Washington who had branched out into publishing with the 1981 purchase of the *Atlantic Monthly* magazine and book press. He added to his publishing holdings when, in 1983, he bought the Washington-based weekly magazine *U.S. News and World Report*. Zuckerman had more than a passing acquaintance with *The New Yorker*. In addition to being a self-described longtime admirer, he had, as mentioned earlier, hired one of the *New Yorker's* top editors, William Whitworth, to edit the *Atlantic*. He had once attempted to hire George Green to run his magazine ventures.

Wilpon said that he would consult Zuckerman and report back, but Messinger never heard from him again. He figured that Zuckerman was not interested. Actually, Zuckerman briefly considered buying *The New Yorker* with a group of investors that included Wilpon. Zuckerman says he gave serious thought to the problem of changing it, but he eventually concluded that he was too busy with his other publishing properties to take on the "maelstrom" that was *The New Yorker*.

Oddly, Zuckerman believed that he could buy all of the stock of *The New Yorker*—that the company was actually for sale. It wasn't.

One of the more unlikely potential buyers to come along was Ivan Boesky. Boesky has since caused the word "arbitrageur" to become synonymous with "crook" in many minds. In 1984 he was merely notorious, and even grudgingly admired as a ruthless yet canny financial whiz, not yet having emerged as the main attraction in the government's investigation into insider trading on Wall Street, and not yet having gone to jail. His reputation was less than savory even in 1984, though. He was a "corporate raider," a romantic name bestowed upon an unglamorous but extremely rich lot of men who made hostile advances on a company's stock, not necessarily, or even usually, because they believed in that company and wanted to be a part of its growth, but because they could use their positions to manipulate managements into buying them out at a higher price. Failing that, they might lunge for the whole and obtain it, only to sell it off again in pieces at a profit.

Boesky was a Central Casting ideal for the part of the avaricious acquirer. He did not look like a potential publisher of the refined and stately *New Yorker*. And indeed, his was not a name that had occurred to either Messinger or Reik. It came up quite by accident.

Coincident with his and Reik's discussions about *The New Yorker*, Messinger was thinking about entering the business of merchant banking and money management. In Palm Beach, where he owned an apartment, he had a neighbor named Joel Lutz who was a business associate of Ivan Boesky. He called Lutz and asked him for a copy of Boesky's partnership papers in his managed funds so that he could get an idea how such partnerships operated. Lutz agreed to send him the papers. Lutz then added, "Maybe you should meet Boesky. I think he has an interest in media companies and you are involved with The New Yorker." At the time, Boesky was considering founding a media empire, a not uncommon pursuit of men who have grown rich through other means and now seek prestige and a different kind of power. Messinger agreed to meet with Boesky. He says that his intention was never to solicit Boesky, but he adds that he would not have refused the right offer, though he doubted there would be one. As it turned out, there was not even a meeting, perhaps owing to a conversation Boesky had with George Green.

Boesky and Green had a mutual acquaintance—Richard Press, president, and grandson of the founder, of J. Press, a men's clothing manufacturer and retailer. Press phoned Green and told him that Boesky was toying with the idea of buying *The New Yorker*. He asked Green to meet with the arbitrageur to talk about the company. Green said he would and traveled with Press downtown to Boesky's Wall Street office. In a meeting that was punctuated by the arbitrageur's frequent exits from his office into the adjoining trading room, Green offered Boesky his tepid opinions on the *New Yorker's* prospects. He also described the company's management structure—the Fleischmanns ran the place. Within a week of the meeting, Boesky had decided against buying the LIN block. Green heard that Boesky—later to be dubbed "Ivan the Terrible" by the tabloids—feared that his raider reputation would not sit well with the corporate culture at *The New Yorker*.

Possibly, too, Boesky was nervous at the prospect of leaping at a company whose shares were not readily marketable. He tended to go for sure deals. He would take a position in a company that other traders were after as well. Then still more traders, betting that Boesky would drive up the price, would enter the fray. All engaged in a competition to see who could sell before the shares tumbled again, and who could get the highest price. *The New Yorker* was not the kind of stock that you could move swiftly in and out of. It was not that easy to unload even 5 percent, as Messinger and Reik were quickly learning.

Reik still wanted to find a buyer with expertise in the publishing field. His thoughts turned to the Los Angeles–based Times-Mirror Company, parent to the *Los Angeles Times*, as well as other newspapers, television and radio stations, and, in a small way, magazines. *The New Yorker* and Times-Mirror seemed to be a logical fit. Both had a reputation for quality. Both were controlled by families—the California Chandlers dominated Times-Mirror. Finally, it was well known in publishing that Times-Mirror wanted to build its magazine business, preferably through acquisitions. The division was based in Manhattan, not far from the *New Yorker* offices.

Reik called a Times-Mirror acquaintance and told him about the LIN stock. It represented only 5.1 percent of the company, Reik explained, but he believed that other large shareholders might be willing to sell too, and Times-Mirror might be able to build a controlling interest. The acquaintance agreed to approach Times-Mirror's top management with the idea. But Times-Mirror was not in a hurry, which was unfortunate for Reik, because Donald Pels was.

Once he had made the intellectual decision to sell, Pels was eager to follow it with physical action. Thomas Unterberg, a partner in the investment firm of Rothschild Unterberg Towbin, was a director of LIN Broadcasting. At the August 1984 board meeting, Pels mentioned that he was going to sell LIN's holdings in *The New Yorker*. He said that he had authorized Bill Reik at Paine Webber to sell it, but that to date he had been unsuccessful.

Unterberg told Pels that Rothschild could dispose of the stock quickly, painlessly, and profitably. Pels replied he would be grateful for the help and took Unterberg up on the offer. Bill Reik learned what had happened only after a Rothschild investment banker phoned a Paine Webber counterpart and asked for advice on handling the sale. Reik was livid.

"They called somebody in our firm and asked for ideas!" he exclaims, amazement still in his voice well after the fact. "They came through somebody to get to me! In the first place, they couldn't sell it. They had no idea how to sell *The New Yorker*. And they told Pels they *could*, which is what really upset me!"

Reik phoned Pels to protest. "You're doing this all wrong,"

he told him. "You're reducing the quality of your block." Reik tried to convince Pels that potential investors would be scared off if they thought the stock was being frantically shopped.

Pels appreciated Reik's point, but he was nevertheless anxious to sell. He didn't want to be the cardplayer left holding the Old Maid.

Reik said, "Look, one way or the other, I'll place the stock. Just give me some time." Pels acceded to the request, but he made it clear Reik didn't have a lot of time. Reik was in a difficult position. His best hope, Times-Mirror, was still mulling.

Phil Messinger, too, continued to search, but to no avail. As he did so, he did not rule out arranging the sale of his own stock along with LIN's. He became further inclined in that direction as a result of the *New Yorker* board meeting of August 16.

Elaine Matteo, as corporate secretary, had sent copies of Messinger's two-page letter of objections to the minutes of the May meeting to each boardmember. The directors arrived at the subsequent session prepared to debate Messinger's exceptions. Messinger noticed that Bill Eiseman was not at the meeting. It was too bad, because Eiseman was his best hope for an ally. Messinger's letter was debated early in the session. The directors dismissed each of his objections in turn. Messinger insisted that he had abstained from voting on salary increases. Bosee and Matteo countered that he might have refrained from voting, but that he had not actually abstained.

"I don't read lips, Philip," Matteo said flatly. It was a confusing discussion, because even if Messinger did not vote, it still didn't explain why he was counted as part of a unanimous "yes" vote.

A lengthy exchange followed on the Drever furniture company acquisition. Messinger had listed in his letter five reasons why directors, including himself, had criticized the investment at the May meeting. His fellow directors did not recall the points' being raised. They agreed that Drever had been discussed, but not in remotely the detail that Messinger described. They saw no reason to record in the minutes a conversation that hadn't occurred. The board turned its attention to the LIN stock. Again, nobody else recalled that the discussion was as replete with detail as Messinger claimed. They then arrived at his final and most controversial point. Messinger had written: "A discussion was held and to a question by Mr. Greenstein, the Chairman answered [that] Mr. Pelz [sic] had not made any offer to buy additional shares of the Company and just indicated he wished to sell."

Messinger turned his gaze on Peter Fleischmann. "Your reply," he told the chairman quietly, "was lacking in candor."

He was aware of a sharp collective intake of breath around the table. Messinger had become openly confrontational. Messinger was not deterred. He told the board that the LIN chairman *had* made an offer. Pels himself had testified to the fact. Only Fleischmann seemed unfazed by Messinger's boldness. He repeated his earlier statement that Pels might have said something in a joking manner. Messinger countered that Pels had assured him it was *not* a joke.

A brief, awkward silence fell over the room. Bosee quickly filled it. He motioned that the minutes of the May meeting be approved as originally submitted. He did not need to utter the phrase "minus Messinger's proposed changes." Production chief Sam Spoto seconded the motion, and it was carried by the affirmative vote of all of the directors except Messinger, who opposed it in a clear voice so that Matteo did not have to read his lips. The board turned its attention to other business.

Bosee informed the board that the Raven/Macmillan merger had been "delayed." He didn't know when, or even if, it would proceed. He further reported that *The New Yorker* was "terminating its relationship with Edi Sept" for the joint publication of

American *Elle*, effective with the soon-to-be released Fall 1984 issue. Bosee spoke with poise and aplomb, as if the messy little business at the beginning of the meeting had never occurred. "He's very good at that sort of thing," says Elaine Matteo.

Messinger achieved one victory. The board discussed the 1981 resolution that allowed the chairman and the president to use up to $300,000 of company funds at their own discretion. They decided that the language of the act should be narrower. Lawyer Bob Winge was asked to draft a new resolution limiting the authority to cases where board approval was impractical.

Bosee assured the board that he would not again make an investment without first consulting them. Messinger thought the president sounded contrite. The new resolution was later approved because, according to Matteo, Messinger "caused such a stink." Clearly, though, other directors saw merit in it as well. It could even be interpreted as a slap on the wrists of management.

15

The summer of 1984 passed into fall; Bill Reik still had not found a buyer for the LIN stock. In September, he approached Donald Marron, the chairman of Paine Webber and his ultimate boss, and requested that the firm buy LIN's *New Yorker* shares and hold them until he could find a suitable purchaser. It was an unusual request, and Marron was hesitant. He thought it was risky. (Donald Marron, in conversation with this writer, said that he recalls almost none of the details of the events surrounding the sale of *The New Yorker* or Paine Webber's part in the transaction. He says it was just another deal. This account is based on firsthand reports from others who were involved.)

Paine Webber was used to committing large sums of capital to the purchase of securities. As is the practice at other major brokerage firms, its block desk uses firm funds to take large positions on a daily basis. The objective is to sell quickly and profitably.

The best turnaround is a fast one. Many block desk buy-and-sell transactions are carried out almost simultaneously. To hold a block is to risk a loss. If the *New Yorker* stock price dropped, Paine Webber incurred a loss. The amount involved wasn't that great by the standards of block desks. Pels had agreed to lower his asking price to $123.25 a share, for a total of $5.3 million. Nevertheless, Paine Webber was not in business to lose money. Also, the deal would place Paine Webber in the unusual position of owning a large portion of another company's stock. But Reik convinced Marron that the risk was not that great. *The New Yorker* was a valuable property. He felt certain he would soon find a buyer for the shares, probably at a profit to Paine Webber. Marron acceded to the request, with one major condition: Move the block fast.

On September 25, Paine Webber purchased 28,100 of the shares. At the same time, Phil Messinger had already bought 6250, his family and one close associate bought 1750, and Reik bought a few thousand more for himself and twenty discretionary accounts. Messinger says he was not aware at the time that Reik had been given a mandate to sell fast. He says that had he known, he would not have bought, because he wanted to be a part of a friendly and permanent home for *The New Yorker*. Now it was no longer Pels with an intense interest in whether Reik had found a buyer, but Donald Marron. The dogs of pressure hadn't been called off, they had simply found a new master.

Donald Marron is a tall, gangly man with a controversial personality. He was not universally loved by his employees. He could exude charm when he so desired, but he could also be cold, arrogant, and abrasive. At the same time, Reik was known around the office as someone with an occasionally explosive temper. "He's a Dr. Jekyll and Mr. Hyde," says an associate.

According to Reik, Marron began to phone him "periodically to inquire as to the availability and any activity on the block."

Another eyewitness Marron describes as calling Reik on an almost daily basis, as if he had penciled the activity onto a notepad headed "Things to Do." According to that version, Marron always asked the same question: "Have you sold your stock yet?" with emphasis on the word "your." Reik says that Marron would ask, "Do we still own that stock?" Reik says he was sensitive to the fact that Marron had committed capital on his recommendation. He says that gave him a heightened sense of responsibility. (It is worth noting here that Reik is still employed at Paine Webber, and that Marron is chairman of a mutual fund he created. It is not in Reik's best interests to alienate the boss. Close associates of the two men claim that their relationship was characterized by extreme rancor throughout the New Yorker dealings.)

Philip Messinger, too, was feeling increasingly "insecure," as he puts it, about his investment. He had gotten only one concession from management as a result of his letter and the follow-up board meeting. If anything, he was now more alienated from the company. He could see no cause for hope on the horizon. It was his understanding that the company was not even searching for a new president to succeed Bosee. That thought was terrifying. Bosee was due to retire in a year, there was no one inside who could fill the job, and they were not looking outside. Unknown to Messinger, the search firm of Farrell & Phin had produced a number of presidential candidates. According to Ken Bosee, by the fall of 1984, he and Fleischmann had entered into serious negotiations with two of them. Incredibly, though, neither Bosee nor Fleischmann informed the board or even other top executives of that fact. Had Messinger known, it might have alleviated some of his concerns.

Messinger broadened his hunt for a buyer by approaching the investment firm of Lazard Frères. He explained to a partner there that he owned a large portion of The New Yorker that he might sell. He said that Bill Reik, an investment manager at Paine

Webber, represented another big block, and while Messinger hastened to add that he could not speak for Reik, he believed that Reik might be willing to sell as well. If someone were to purchase both blocks, they would be in an excellent position to seek control of the whole company. He said that he doubted that a takeover of *The New Yorker* could be accomplished in a friendly manner. "To my mind," he said, "Peter Fleischmann is not a willing seller of these shares."

Lazard agreed to help find a buyer, and to explore the possibilities of either a hostile or a friendly takeover. Messinger suggested that Lazard consult Bill Reik about his intentions. Lazard investment bankers phoned Reik on repeated occasions, but he did not return the calls. An annoyed Lazard partner called Donald Marron to complain.

Marron passed the message on to Reik, but he did not try to influence his behavior. Paine Webber would lose potentially large fees should Lazard effect a deal before they did. Phil Messinger, however, was annoyed at Reik's seeming lack of cooperation. "Reik was delaying everybody because of Times-Mirror," he says. "They had been thinking for three or four months. He didn't want to take it away from Times-Mirror."

But Reik's behavior was motivated as well by his own ambivalence. He wanted to sell the LIN block, but he wasn't sure he wanted to dispose of his and his clients' shares. Clearly, though, that was what Lazard was after. Lazard was Messinger's idea, not his. If Messinger wanted to deal with them, that was his prerogative. But Reik didn't see any reason why he had to.

"I was so emotional through this whole thing," Reik recalled later. "I was worried about the company, but at the same time, I didn't want to lose it. I was just trying to maintain it. I was calling George every week asking if he was ready to come back. I thought we could get him back." Reik escalated his crusade to bring Messinger's thinking more in line with his own. He asked

Messinger, "Phil, why don't we go to Citibank and borrow the money and take out Fleischmann? Why wouldn't they give us the money? They could give us the money they give to Bolivia. Hell, they give money to *anybody!*"

"Go find something else to get attached to," Messinger replied.

"Phil was aware that *The New Yorker* was an emotional thing with me," says Reik.

In late September, the Lazard Frères partner told Messinger that his firm had located a potential buyer, a large German company that wanted some American publishing properties. He was not at liberty to divulge the corporation's name. However, the Germans were willing to make the corporation's identity known and enter into serious negotiations, under one condition: that they were the only company with whom Reik and Messinger were dealing. If anyone else was allowed to consider the purchase while negotiations were under way, they weren't interested. Messinger called Reik, who told him that Times-Mirror was still considering the purchase. Messinger told Lazard that for now, he could not promise the Germans exclusivity.

Messinger was irritated at Times-Mirror. Either they wanted the stock or they didn't. He didn't see why it was taking so long to decide. He put pressure on Reik, who phoned Herb Schnall, chief of the Times-Mirror magazine division, and requested a meeting. Messinger, Reik, and Schnall met in Schnall's office. Messinger got the distinct impression that Times-Mirror hadn't really mulled the purchase at all. A frustratingly large segment of the meal was spent with Reik and Messinger trying to explain what to Messinger seemed a simple concept. Reik, his clients, and Paine Webber owned more than 17 percent of *The New Yorker*. Messinger held 13 percent. Together they controlled 30 percent, which was about the same amount as the Fleischmann family owned. Times-Mirror could buy the LIN stock, and then add to its position by buying in the open market. Eventually, Reik, Messinger, Schnall, and the organizations they represented could boast of 40 or 50 percent of the stock, the amount Messinger figured would represent control. Schnall seemed unconvinced. Reik suggested that he meet with George Green, who, said Reik, "knows everything there is to know about *The New Yorker*." With that recommendation, the deal was doomed.

Schnall called Green and invited him to lunch at the Swiss Pavilion. The two men had often met at publishing functions, and the invitation seemed a casual one. Green did not know until much later that the call was initiated at Reik's behest. The subject of *The New Yorker* "came up," says Green, and he was "candid" in describing the potential pitfalls facing the magazine. Within a week, Schnall told Reik that Times-Mirror was not interested.

"George really made it hard on Phil and me," Reik recalled later. "It's pretty devastating when you're analyzing whether to buy a magazine, you're sitting down with a publisher, and he's telling you, 'There's only two things wrong with *The New Yorker*. They're selling less ads and less magazines every year.' You immediately start wondering what it is that Reik is trying to get you involved in."

But even if Green had printed a prettier picture, publishers would have been put off. The gloomy business prospects were not sufficient to drive them away. There were egos to spare in publishing, people who thought they could surmount the problems. *The New Yorker* was still the most prestigious publishing property around. It would have made a handsome addition to anyone's library of publications. What discouraged would-be owners was that they could only be assured of buying a *minority* interest. When Reik and Messinger tried to market the *New Yorker* stock, they were first greeted with a burst of enthusiasm, but it was short-lived. "What would we want with 4 percent?" publishers invariably asked. They weren't even sure what 30 percent would get them. The follow-up question was so frequently asked that Reik and Messinger could guess it was coming. "Can you get us fifty percent?" publishers would wonder. Reik and Messinger were compelled to reply, "Not without a fight." No one was willing to fight.

Neither Reik nor Messinger told *New Yorker* executives that they were considering selling, but it seemed inevitable that word would eventually filter back to the staff. It was Janet Muir who had a chance encounter. She was at a business luncheon in downtown Manhattan, seated next to a man who worked for the investment firm of Warburg Pincus. They had not previously met. They chatted about, among other things, their jobs. Before the lunch was over, the man said to Muir, "By the way, you people at *The New Yorker* had better watch out for Philip Messinger. He's not a loyal director." Muir asked him what he meant by that statement. He said that he would not be surprised to see Messinger's stock sold along with the LIN block.

After lunch, Muir hurried back to Ken Bosee's office to tell him what she had heard. Bosee didn't seem interested. "He looked at me like I was a crazy person," says Muir. She urged him to have a talk with Messinger, but he didn't deem it necessary. He never mentioned it again. "It was just a total lack of aggression," says Muir.

In October, Messinger left for an extended vacation to Europe, leaving behind him three unresolved business situations. Parallel Computer, a small computer company he owned, was shaky and in need of a capital infusion. (Previous investors in the company had included George Green.) The rental building in which he lived was on the brink of conversion into a cooperative, and he wanted to buy his apartment. And last, his *New Yorker* shares were for sale, maybe. He gave his lawyer power of attorney to deal with the computer firm and the apartment, but asked to be kept informed of developments regarding *The New Yorker*.

He flew to Rome, stayed there a few days, then rented a car and wended his way north to Venice, then to the south of France, and finally to Paris, where he turned in the car and boarded a train to Brussels. He was in frequent contact, by phone or Telex, with his lawyers regarding his apartment and Parallel Computer. He was not, he says, anxious about *The New Yorker* on that trip, though Reik called him several times to discuss progress or lack thereof. It was inevitable that after months of attempts to find a partner or a buyer, it would be while Messinger was away that one would suddenly materialize. Reik called Messinger in Brussels to tell him that he thought he had found a buyer who wanted all of the shares Paine Webber managed or controlled—the position on the block desk, Reik's clients' stock, and Reik's own. Reik thought the buyer would probably want Messinger's as well.

After all of the pressured and restless searching of the previous six months, it was ironic that the sale of *The New Yorker* came about as the result of a casual question over a bacon, lettuce, and tomato sandwich.

Reik had an associate at Paine Webber named Charlie Perlitz. Perlitz had made some early unsuccessful attempts to help sell the LIN stock, but selling was not on his mind when he met a friend, William Furth, for lunch one October day. Furth was an oil analyst for Bear Stearns. (Perlitz spoke to me. But Furth, when phoned, said, "I have no interest in discussing this subject," then slammed the receiver down.) They met at Wolf's, a large delicatessen restaurant on lower Broadway in the financial district which they frequented with ritualistic fervor.

Two weeks before the Furth-Perlitz lunch, on October 5, Paine Webber had filed with the SEC a required "13 D form" reporting that it held 42,400 shares of *The New Yorker* in its own and some discretionary brokerage accounts. Included in the figure were 28,100 shares purchased on September 25 as part of the firm's "general broker/dealer activities."

Paine Webber "expects that such securities will, in due course, be resold by it as a broker or dealer," the filing read. It further recorded that another 102,459 shares were held in the nondiscretionary accounts of certain clients. The transactions were noted without comment in the *New York Times* on October 6 and in the *Wall Street Journal* on October 9. It was from the papers that Furth learned of it.

"What does Paine Webber want with all of that *New Yorker* stock?" he asked his friend Perlitz at lunch.

"I don't really know," said Perlitz, "but I think we might sell it." They discussed the possibilities.

Furth said, "I think I know someone who would be interested."

After lunch, Furth returned to his office and phoned Abe Blinder, an acquaintance who worked as a "finder" of properties in the magazine business. He was most closely identified, in that capacity, with Samuel Irving Newhouse, Jr., who, with his brother, Donald, ran one of the world's largest and most successful media empires. Furth told Blinder about the conversation at lunch, and asked if he thought that "S. I." (pronounced "sigh") might be interested in buying the *New Yorker* stock. Blinder thought he might. Within twenty-four hours, Blinder phoned Furth, Furth phoned Perlitz, and Perlitz phoned Reik. Each relayed the same message: S. I. was interested.

16

S. I. Newhouse was a man who had everything. Ignore, even, for the moment, his status as one of the richest men in America. Skip the trappings of wealth—the East Side town house, the house in Palm Beach, the world-famed art collection, the limousines. Forget, too, the emblems of societal acceptance—the seat on the board of the Museum of Modern Art, the power-profile table at the Four Seasons, the stacks of invitations to the most expensive parties. Concentrate, instead, on a company called Advance Publications.

Advance Publications? What was that? In the waning months of 1984, it was a name on no one's lips. It had an address that was highly improbable, to say nothing of inelegant: Fingerboard Road, Staten Island, New York. Who had ever been there? Certainly not most of the publishers who inhabited Park and Madison Avenues. And hardly anyone from *The New Yorker*. Staten Island was a borough that was out *there* somewhere, in every way.

But then explore beyond the name and location. Simply put, Advance, which owned more than an estimated $3 billion of media properties, was one of the largest, most prosperous, most intensely private companies in America. *Advertising Age* ranked it fifth in size among all U.S. media companies, after ABC, CBS, Time Inc., and RCA.

Advance was founded by Newhouse's father, S. I., Sr., who was born in 1895, the son of Eastern European Jewish immigrants, in a tenement on New York's Lower East Side. The neighborhood was a synonym for immigrant hardship and poverty, teeming, then, with new arrivals from old worlds, displaced people in search of a fresh start.

His family moved to Bayonne, New Jersey, where, at the age of fourteen, S. I. went to work for a lawyer at a salary of two dollars a week. When one of the lawyer's clients defaulted on a note, the lawyer took over the man's business, the *Bayonne Times* newspaper, and put S. I. in charge of it. The teenager ran the ailing newspaper into profitability.

S. I. was too ambitious a young man to remain content working for others, so in 1922, at the age of twenty-seven, he bought his own paper, the *Staten Island Advance.* He parlayed his stake in the *Advance* into a media empire, spending the next half century pursuing ever-larger media targets. Unlike, for instance, Time Inc., he never started newspapers or magazines, he simply acquired them, and in obtaining and running them he developed a reputation for being ruthless. He was a merciless union buster, and seemed obsessed with driving competitors out of business. Yet some who knew him and worked for him recall that, especially in his later years, he was a sweet, benevolent man, a little man, a diamond in the rough, who remembered your name when you ran into him at a local movie theater.

Following Newhouse's death in 1979, his sons, Donald, then forty-nine, and S. I., Jr., then fifty-one, carried the company forward successfully, building it still larger by following their father's policy of aggressive acquisition. The publishing and business genes were not diluted in theirs, the second generation. What is Advance Publications? A company best described by what it owns: a slew of media properties.

Through a subsidiary, Condé Nast Publications, Advance today publishes eleven consumer magazines: *Vogue, HG* (formerly *House & Garden*), *Mademoiselle, Glamour, Bride's, Vanity Fair, Gentlemen's Quarterly, Self, Condé Nast Traveler, Gourmet,* and *Details*. In addition, there are French, Italian, Australian, German, British, Mexican, and Brazilian versions of *Vogue*, and American, British, and French editions of *House & Garden*. Condé Nast also owns the British magazines *Tatler* and *World of Interiors*. S. I., Sr., had bought Condé Nast because his wife, Mitzi, loved *Vogue*, and he wanted to give it to her as a present. While all of the publications mentioned were not yet in the Condé Nast stable at the time that Newhouse bought it, several were. "When I set out to buy *Vogue*," Newhouse was fond of saying, "how the hell was I supposed to know that all those other magazines were going to come with it!"

Also in the Advance lineup is *Parade*, distributed as a Sunday supplement in 314 newspapers to a massive 64.8 million people. Advance owns twenty-nine newspapers, including the *Newark Star Ledger*, the *Cleveland Plain Dealer*, and the *New Orleans Times-Picayune*. It is parent, too, to a brood of book publishers—Random House, Alfred A. Knopf, Pantheon, New York Times Books, Ballantine, Fawcett, and Villard. There are also television and radio stations and one of the country's largest cable TV systems.

So, then, by many definitions, S. I. Newhouse *was* a man who had everything. But there was something he didn't have: *The New Yorker*. According to Harold Evans, a former London Sunday *Times* editor now working for Condé Nast, Newhouse *always* wanted it. He told him so. His father before him had coveted it as well. Advance had approached *The New Yorker* many years earlier, but encountered the mannerly rebuff.

It was not surprising, then, that Newhouse was immediately receptive—eager, even—when Abe Blinder phoned to tell him about the available *New Yorker* stock. Newhouse authorized Blinder to act as his agent and to find out what the company's reaction to the purchase might be. Would Peter Fleischmann sell as well? Blinder paid a call on Fleischmann. He told him that Newhouse was interested in buying *The New Yorker*. Fleischmann said the magazine was not for sale. Fleischmann was not aware that Newhouse was within grabbing distance of a larger block of the stock than he himself controlled.

The Paine Webber shares had found their way to Newhouse through the coincidence of a deli lunch. The add-on coincidence was that they were at the door of perhaps the only American publisher who might put up a fight to buy *The New Yorker*. For the first time in decades, someone had come along who might not take "no" for an answer. Newhouse, like most buyers, would prefer to buy on friendly terms, but if that was not possible, then he would consider other routes. For now, he would move on what could be easily obtained.

The LIN stock was available for the bidding. Bill Reik had lost his control over that the day it went on the Paine Webber block desk. But Reik still had his own shares, and he oversaw large blocks in his clients' accounts. Even with a nearly certain sale in prospect, Reik was torn over how to proceed. He *still* hankered to buy *The New Yorker* outright, though after his next meeting with management, he grew more nervous about holding onto what he had.

In late October, Ken Bosee had again called Reik to extend a second unsolicited invitation to have lunch with Peter Fleischmann and himself. Reik, who had absorbed Messinger's assorted tales of woe about management's nonresponsiveness, was again taken aback. He told Bosee that he was flattered to be invited, but demurred because he realized that Peter Fleischmann's health was not the best. He didn't want Fleischmann to "race around town" on his behalf. "I never pressure my companies," Reik explained to the *New Yorker* president. But Bosee was full of gracious insistence, and Reik accepted the invitation. When the call came, Newhouse had not yet entered the picture. By November 1, the date of the lunch, he had.

Before meeting with Bosee and Fleischmann, Reik called George Green. Reik had gotten in the habit of consulting Green before most conversations with management. He would ask Green for informed questions to ask *them*. Green said that the latest Audit Bureau of Circulations data showed that circulation was down. Why not ask them about that?

Reik, across a Sky Club table from Bosee and Fleischmann, asked why circulation was down. Bosee replied, "Well, our circulation manager says that it's because we raised the price of a subscription from twenty-eight to thirty-two dollars a year."

Reik was floored by the answer. "You're kidding!" he said.

Bosee said no, that was the answer he was given.

Reik said, "The circulation manager thinks because you raised *The New Yorker* four dollars a year you're losing readers?"

Bosee said yes.

Fleischmann picked up his microphone and held it to his throat. "I'm not entirely satisfied with that answer," he said. But he seemed at a loss for an answer of his own.

Reik's heart sank.

"That was the chairman and the president of this company," Reik later recalled. "When I realized that they knew *less* about it than I did, it really shook me up. When you raise the price to thirty-two bucks you're really not going to hurt a lot of people. This is the most upscale audience in publishing!"

Also at that lunch, Reik, reacting in part to strong behind-the-scenes urging from Messinger, asked to be put on the *New Yorker* board. He was told there were no vacancies. The lunch

went a long way toward persuading Reik of the futility of hang-
ing onto *The New Yorker*. Assuming that he could not get Green
to return, and assuming that he would not get financing to buy
the magazine outright, and assuming he could not get a place
on the board, all of which were good assumptions, then Reik
had to face facts. Under present management, how viable was
his investment? The lunch provided a rude awakening.

The following morning, Friday, November 2, Reik picked
up the phone to one of the ubiquitous calls from Donald Marron,
expecting from his boss the usual greeting: "Do we still have that
stock?" (A reliable source, again, says that the standard greeting
was "Have you sold *your* stock yet?") Reik was bowled over by a
change in the script.

Marron's voice was brimming with good cheer. "Well, I've
sold our company!" came the opening line. (Note the change
from "your" to "our.")

"Really?" replied Reik. "Which company is that?" He thought
the remark humorous, but Marron didn't.

"*The New Yorker*," said Marron.

"*The New Yorker!*" Reik exclaimed. "I sold that *days* ago!"

Was Marron trying to take Reik's deal away? Marron related
that he had attended an art auction the night before at Sotheby's,
and happened to bump into S. I. Newhouse. (The two men were
formerly acquainted. Marron, like Newhouse, collects contemporary art, and he, too, serves on the board of the Museum of Modern Art.) Newhouse had remarked that he heard Paine Webber
had some *New Yorker* stock it might be willing to sell. Marron
was only too familiar with the shares languishing on the block
desk. He casually replied that yes, Paine Webber did own a percentage of *The New Yorker*. (Marron was too seasoned a Wall
Street player to let a note of urgency creep into his voice.)
Newhouse said he might be interested. Marron said Paine Webber
would be more than happy to pursue the matter.

When Marron relayed the news to Reik, Reik told him that a contact had already been made. Reik recalls that Marron's reply was, "I'll handle it from here." That afternoon, Marron called Newhouse to say he would like to continue the conversation of the previous evening. The men agreed to meet over the weekend.

On a chilly early November Saturday, Marron and Newhouse convened in front of a fire in Marron's Park Avenue apartment, and Marron spent several hours "whipping up S. I." as a business acquaintance later described it, talking animatedly about what a great property The New Yorker was. It was not being managed to its full potential, the men agreed. There was plenty of opportunity to make it better and more profitable. Newhouse didn't really require much inciting. He didn't need Wall Street to tell him what to want. Newhouse had near perfect pitch when it came to publishing. Besides, he had always wanted The New Yorker.

The meeting was perhaps more beneficial to Marron, who got some business for his firm out of it. Newhouse agreed to let Paine Webber handle the investment banking side of the deal. For all of his protestations that he recalls little of the New Yorker deal, sources close to Marron say that the New Yorker transaction was important to him, because at the time he was fighting an uphill battle to build the firm's investment banking division. (And indeed, in a later interview in a financial publication, Marron singled out the New Yorker deal as one of which he was particularly proud. He also took credit for it.) In 1980, in an attempt to become a presence in that field, then Paine Webber chairman James Davant bought the old-line investment banking firm of Blyth Eastman Dillon. Before closing the deal, Davant consulted with the head of his back office to make sure that the department and its computers were equipped to handle the processing of Blyth's trades and transactions in addition to their own. The officer said yes. The reality was that they could not.

After the acquisition, Paine Webber's back office was in turmoil for two years because it proved unable to consistently fulfill necessary and legally required functions, such as sending confirmation slips to customers who had traded a stock. So serious were its problems that the SEC considered shutting the firm down. Donald Marron, when he became chairman, spent the better part of two years repairing the damage. It was time he would rather have devoted to building up his investment banking department. The irony was that Blyth's most talented investment bankers quit the firm when it was acquired by Paine Webber, so the purpose for which Blyth had been bought was voided, and at great cost. Paine Webber had to start from nearly scratch establishing itself in investment banking. Marron hired Peter Slusser, who had recently retired from another firm, to head up mergers and acquisitions at Paine Webber. When the *New Yorker* deal came along, Paine Webber still did not rank as an investment banking powerhouse (actually, to this day it does not), and every deal counted. Further, in investment banking, one deal could lead to another. The sale of the LIN block could lead to the sale of Reik's and Messinger's shares, and that in turn to the sale of *The New Yorker.*

The New Yorker was not a large company. The fees that Paine Webber could extract were pin money, by the standards of a big investment bank like Goldman Sachs or Morgan Stanley. However, it was possible that the transaction could gain Paine Webber future Advance Publications investment banking business. Advance was not likely to go public. It was so resolutely private that Newhouse once termed any prospect of its public ownership "nonexistent." Lest anyone harbor doubts, he added, "There is no possibility of it." However, Paine Webber might be able to aid it in the purchase of other properties. Also, the *New Yorker* transaction would be highly visible, since both *The New Yorker* and Newhouse garnered a lot of publicity with every action, and it would be prestigious. These characteristics could only benefit

Marron's attempts to plant the Paine Webber flag firmly on mergers and acquisitions ground.

On Sunday, November 4, the day after Marron and Newhouse met to talk about *The New Yorker*, Phil Messinger, a thrifty man who flew first class only on a frequent-flyer upgrade, sat in a coach seat on a Sabena charter flight somewhere over the Atlantic Ocean. He knew nothing of the most recent events, yet his investment was much on his mind. His time away had given him new perspective. His instincts told him he did not have a future with *The New Yorker*. As his fellow director William Eiseman puts it: "Messinger and Fleischmann had reached an impasse." There was no treaty in sight.

The next morning, Bill Reik woke a jet-lagged Messinger with a phone call. He invited him to attend a meeting with Newhouse lawyers that afternoon at five. Reik figured he would sell his stock at the session, and said that Messinger could probably do the same. Messinger promised to attend.

They convened at the Blyth Eastman Dillon offices on the Avenue of the Americas. Peter Slusser ran the meeting. Philip Messinger came with his lawyer from the firm of Kronish, Lieb, Weiner & Hellman. Bill Reik attended, along with Samuel Butler, the top partner of the Wall Street law firm Cravath, Swaine & Moore, which represented Paine Webber. A late arrival was Donald Marron.

S. I. Newhouse did not attend. Newhouse was a man who seemed to find safety in large numbers of attorneys, and the vast financial resources at his disposal made him adept at moving mountains of them around. Rather than handle the transaction with Reik and Paine Webber personally, Newhouse put three law firms on the job. He was represented by Sabin, Bermant & Blau, which was located in the Condé Nast Building at 350 Madison Avenue, and which existed as a quasi-in-house firm for Advance; Wall Street firm Sullivan & Cromwell; and takeover specialists

Wachtell Lipton. All three firms had at least one principal present that day.

There was not a soul in the room who did not understand what the final outcome of the conversation would be. S. I. Newhouse would own *The New Yorker*. Maybe not that day, or that month, but certainly in a year or two. Newhouse was not the sort to bide his time sitting with a big block of another publisher's stock. When he wanted something, he went after it until he got it. He was willing to pay handsomely. No one ever called him cheap, but they did call him tenacious.

The room rocked with details, with terms and prices and percentages, as the participants paved the way for the termination of sixty years of family ownership of *The New Yorker*. There was something sad about the scene. In decorator modern offices, businessmen used cold, hard mathematics to determine the fate of *The New Yorker*. Just five blocks away, in shabby surroundings that no investment banker would deem fit for habitation, editors edited and ad staff sold, peacefully unaware of their own impending doom. Had they known, they would have reacted with horror.

The Newhouse lawyers seemed to Messinger to be quite solicitous. They explained to the group that their client wanted all the *New Yorker* stock he could get. Four distinct blocks were represented in the room. The first, comprising 28,100 shares, represented the bulk of the former LIN position that now belonged to Paine Webber. Reik had facetiously taken to calling it "Marron's stock." The second block was Messinger's. He and his family had 109,340 shares, or around 13 percent of the total. Reik and his discretionary clients—those for whom he was authorized to act without prior consultation—owned 14,300 shares, or nearly 2 percent of the company. Finally, 12 percent of *The New Yorker*, or 102,459 shares, rested in 118 nondiscretionary accounts.

Newhouse was willing to pay $160 a share, a price he considered fair in light of the fact that the bid price over the counter was $135. Messinger spoke up and said he thought the price was too low. It was very difficult to assemble a block that size. After that one session, if all went well, Newhouse would find himself in possession of 30 percent of *The New Yorker*. You had to pay up to amass such a total. Furthermore, said Messinger, he had done some math, and according to his calculations, *The New Yorker* was worth $200 a share in a hostile acquisition. It would be worth even more, he figured, in a friendly takeover, because that would entail fewer legal hassles, and fewer employees would threaten to evacuate the premises.

Messinger produced a sheet of paper which he had covered with his detailed analysis. He added to the company's current cash position the potential liquidation value of its properties, including *Cook's*, *Horticulture*, and Boulder Enterprises. (Messinger assumed that Newhouse coveted only *The New Yorker*, not its poorer relations.) He divided the total by the number of shares outstanding and came up with a value of $200 a share.

Messinger contended that a price of $160 a share might invite a bidding war as other companies got wind of the fact that buying *The New Yorker* was a possibility. (Such a contest *might* work to his financial advantage, but then again, the deal could fall through, because *The New Yorker* would have time to prepare a defense. Besides, it was difficult to guess how long it might all take. Messinger felt more comfortable selling his shares quietly, privately, and quickly.)

Messinger was outspoken at the meeting, but Bill Reik was uncharacteristically subdued. Reik was not a man who often went unnoticed. His physical presence was commanding, as was his manner. As Messinger put it, when Reik was in a room, you knew it. This man had no trouble filling gaps in conversations. Reik occasionally quipped that he loved teaching because it meant that a roomful of people was forced to sit and listen to him for an hour. Reik *liked* to talk. Yet that day, Messinger had to press

Reik to answer questions. Reik's replies came in the form of mono-syllables, or mere changes in facial expression. The only expla-nation Messinger could divine was that Marron was a dampening influence. Before Marron's late arrival, Reik had been his usual self. When Marron appeared, he clammed up.

Reik was squeezed awkwardly in the middle of an emerging conflict of interests. On one side was Donald Marron, as a proxy, of sorts, for his firm. Marron, according to associates, was in-tensely interested in Paine Webber's representing Newhouse as an investment banker, and for reasons previously mentioned, he was equally concerned that the job be done well. Simply put, part of doing it well was to obtain for the client, Advance Pub-lications, the lowest possible purchase price.

On the other side, yet under the same corporate umbrella, was Bill Reik, an investment manager whose prime responsibil-ity was to protect his clients and to procure for them the *highest* possible price. Reik was not obliged to sell to Newhouse. Indeed, he could withhold his customers' shares if he decided that the transaction was not in the clients' best interests. So it could turn out that the needs of Newhouse, a Paine Webber client, and Reik's customers, also clients, could diverge dramatically. It would have been difficult for William Reik *not* to have felt pressure, real or imagined, from Marron.

Even Marron recalls that Reik was in "a complicated posi-tion." Says Marron: "His role was representing his clients. My role was to make sure that S. I. was properly represented in buy-ing as much of *The New Yorker* as possible." Marron says that it is "normal" to have differing interests within the same firm in-volved in the same transaction. His view is not one that is widely held in the investment banking community, and Paine Webber's own lawyer, Sam Butler, was perturbed enough to write a letter to Newhouse's lawyers cautioning about the emerging conflict of interests. According to Butler, Paine Webber's role as adviser was greatly reduced. Marron recalls no such reduction of responsibility.

The negotiations dragged on for hours. The Newhouse team was not motivated by Messinger's fancy figurings to raise its price. They repeated that Newhouse considered $160 a share to be a fair price. Eventually, a tentative agreement was reached at $160, but Messinger placed a condition on the sale. Until the deal was closed, he would retain the right to find a higher bidder. If he did so, the deal with Newhouse was off. The Newhouse lawyers were unhinged by the prospect. They would have preferred to leave the room with a firm commitment in their pocket, but they agreed to consult with their client.

The Advance lawyers also cut a deal for the LIN/Paine Webber stock, but by the time the next meeting arrived, the parties could not agree on what had been decided. Reik, Messinger, and a Newhouse lawyer recall that Newhouse agreed to buy the former LIN block as well as the shares in Reik's discretionary accounts. Those together represented less than 6 percent. They diverge on whether and how Newhouse agreed to buy the shares in Reik's nondiscretionary accounts, which constituted a hefty 12 percent of the total.

Messinger believes that the Newhouse contingent agreed to purchase those too, but that instead of buying the shares outright, Advance would extend a tender offer to all holders of the stock to sell their shares. Reik remembers that the Newhouse clan agreed to buy everything—discretionary, nondiscretionary, and LIN—outright. It turned out that Newhouse wasn't thinking along either of those lines.

The following afternoon, November 6, S. I. Newhouse made a house call at Peter Fleischmann's apartment on the Upper East Side. Newhouse might have considered it proper and expeditious to send a gaggle of lawyers after Reik's and Messinger's stock, but he made a personal appearance in front of Fleischmann. Perhaps he was less motivated by an awareness of the delicacy of the situation than he was by the fact that sending an emissary, Abe Blinder, hadn't worked. Newhouse came alone. Fleischmann was joined by Merrell E. "Ted" Clark, Jr., a partner in Winthrop Stimson Putnam & Roberts and a trustee of the Fleischmann family trusts. (The other trustees were Peter Fleischmann, Gardner Botsford, and Milton Greenstein.) Clark was a close and trusted adviser.

S. I. Newhouse and Peter Fleischmann were both sons of the founders of their companies, yet they inhabited their roles quite differently. Peter Fleischmann was dedicated to preserving his father's legacy more or less historically intact, almost frozen in time. Like his father, he cared more for the magazine than for the corporation. Also like his father, he was hesitant about branching out. Aggressive was not a word that would have described the Fleischmanns.

"Aggressive" went a long way toward defining the Newhouses, father and sons. S. I. and his brother, Donald, had taken a large company and made it bigger in ways that their father would likely have approved. So in his own way, S. I. Newhouse, too, was preserving the past, but his past was based on action, not the nurturing of literary landmarks. Even the room they sat in that afternoon spoke volumes about the differences in style. Peter and Jeanne Fleischmann surrounded themselves with old and traditional comforts. They lived in a Gothic-style building erected at the turn of the century. Their walls were paneled with the richest woods, the upholstery was deep and cozy, the furniture antique.

Newhouse lived in a contemporary town house that bespoke today, adorned with paintings of the modern kind, abstracts that left many less sophisticated tastes bewildered.

S. I. Newhouse was a wheeler-dealer, a brusque man who

didn't pause for niceties. Fleischmann was dignified, a consummate gentleman, a man who would never wittingly take advantage of another. S. I. Newhouse and Peter Fleischmann sat across from one another, each very much his father's son, each quite different from the other.

Newhouse told Fleischmann that he had learned that a sizable block of *New Yorker* stock was available. He was interested in purchasing it. He had always admired *The New Yorker*, he said, and had the utmost respect for the Fleischmann family and for the magazine. He would like to be a part of it. He assured Fleischmann that he wanted the stock for investment purposes only; he had no plans to try to buy the company. He wondered if Fleischmann would mind having him as an investor in his company.

Few casual acquaintances attribute to Peter Fleischmann any particular shrewdness. Those close to him know better. Shrewdness is a trait he exhibited that afternoon. It cannot have been clear to Fleischmann what block Newhouse was referring to. The LIN stock, perhaps, but would he ask permission to buy that? Doubtful. It had to be a much larger stake. But what? From all accounts, Fleischmann still had no inkling that Messinger was close to selling, or that Reik was willing to dispose of the shares in his accounts. If only 4 or 5 percent were involved, Fleischmann perhaps would not have minded, but it was much more. Fleischmann listened politely, as he had to similar entreaties that had come his way over the years, but his reply to Newhouse was swift and clear: "Yes," said Fleischmann. "I would mind." Fleischmann knew that Newhouse would not be happy with *some* stock, but instead would eventually want it all. Fleischmann later gathered his executives around him and explained: "I just didn't want him fishing in my pond."

Newhouse made no follow-up comment. At no point did he vow to buy only with Fleischmann's approval. When he left, the parting exchanges were cordial. As Fleischmann watched the other publisher leave, he couldn't help but hope that he would *really* go away. But Newhouse was not derailed for long. The following day he called Fleischmann to say that he had bought the stock. That would not have been news to the assorted lawyers and businessmen who had negotiated the purchase the previous day. Newhouse in essence had already done what he had asked Fleischmann's permission to do. He had agreed to buy. Fleischmann didn't happen to be one of the many people who were privy to that particular piece of information. In the phone call to Fleischmann, say sources close to the transaction, Newhouse promised Fleischmann that he would limit his investment in *The New Yorker* to 25 percent of the stock.

Two days after the initial meeting, a Newhouse lawyer phoned Messinger's attorney with a new proposal. Newhouse was not keen on any provision that would allow Messinger to continue to shop his shares. He was willing to raise his offer by $20 a share to $180 if Messinger would cut a deal now. It was typical of the Newhouse approach to acquisitions. He did not inch the price up by $5 increments, but instead anted up another hefty $20 in order to get the deal done quickly. Messinger was more receptive now.

In a November 8 session at the Paine Webber offices, Messinger and his lawyer met with the Newhouse lawyers to hammer out the details. The lawyers agonized for interminable hours over the language of the contract. An exasperated Messinger agreed to accept some of the phrases his lawyer wrangled over because, as he saw it, either the deal was going to go through or it wasn't, and in any case, a couple of stray words weren't going to make the difference.

One of the terms Newhouse imposed was a three-day blackout period during which Messinger was restrained from disclosing the transaction to anyone, including Peter Fleischmann. Typically, such a term is imposed so that the buyer can quietly buy more stock in the open market before word of a possible acquisition begins to push the price up. Messinger agreed to the provision, but he asked to be allowed to be the first to inform Fleischmann of the sale when the blackout period expired. The Newhouse lawyers verbally acceded to that request; there was nothing in writing. Messinger insisted on, and won, a price protection clause. If Newhouse were, in the next twelve months, to buy shares from other sellers at a price that exceeded $180, he would have to make good to Messinger the difference.

In an office next door to where Messinger sat, Reik, too, came to terms with the Newhouse forces. Reik did not sell his own shares to Newhouse. Instead, Newhouse cut a deal with Reik and Paine Webber to buy the former LIN block and the shares in Reik's discretionary accounts at $180. Reik's clients and Paine Webber also obtained price protection. The Advance Publications lawyers told Reik that Newhouse had decided not to buy the nondiscretionary shares "at this time."

Under the requirements of the Hart-Scott-Rodino Antitrust Improvements Act of 1976, Newhouse had to wait sixty days for the justice department to clear the deal. It was a formality.

With 17 percent of *The New Yorker* in hand, S. I. Newhouse placed a call to Peter Fleischmann and told him what he had done. According to a source close to Fleischmann, the chairman's response was, incredibly enough, "Good. I like strong shareholders." If that is true, perhaps it was because he trusted Newhouse's pledge to limit himself to 25 percent. Or perhaps he was happy to exchange Messinger for Newhouse.

Fleischmann and other *New Yorker* executives were furious that Messinger had not told them in advance that he was selling. The first they heard of it was when Newhouse informed Fleischmann. Newhouse did not honor the pledge his lawyers had made to allow

Messinger to break the news to Fleischmann. But it was a moot point, who told whom first. To the *New Yorker* executives, it was unthinkable that a director should unload his shares without offering them first to the company, or at least telling management about the sale. Messinger disagrees. The directors, he points out, had rejected all other offers of stock that came their way. Clearly they would have rejected his as well. Further, Fleischmann had ignored Pels's warning that he would lose the company. (And, unknown to Messinger, Bosee had disregarded Janet Muir's intelligence about Messinger's stock going with the LIN block.) Parties on the other side counter that Messinger ignored the fact that had management been informed, they could have been prepared. But if management had time to think, Messinger might have lost the opportunity to act. Nor did Messinger, who felt betrayed himself, feel any particular residual loyalty to management. *The New Yorker* and Messinger were at cross-purposes. Messinger stepped out of the role of director and into that of investor.

Peter Fleischmann believed that S. I. Newhouse would honor his pledge to limit his *New Yorker* stock to 25 percent, a faith he shared with Ken Bosee. Bosee admits now that he and Fleischmann were lulled into complacency by previous experience. In the past, unwanted buyers had disappeared. No one had gone after *The New Yorker* in a pushy, unfriendly manner. Why should Newhouse be different? But others, like Janet Muir, Elaine Matteo, and Pete Spelman, among many, were stunned at the naïveté of the chief executives. Muir remembers how she first learned of the purchase. Bosee stopped her in the hall and said, with what she describes as the utmost casualness, "Oh, by the way, Newhouse just bought 17 percent of the company." Muir was dumbfounded. Her reaction was immediate: How could anyone possibly believe that Newhouse would stop there? She also was furious that Bosee had not taken action earlier when she told him that Messinger reportedly was not loyal.

Muir and other staff members launched a campaign to persuade Bosee to hire an investment banking firm to ward off the inevitable further advances by Newhouse. Matteo and Muir, who often did not get along, banded together on this. They all but begged Bosee, but he was not moved. There was really no danger, he assured them. Newhouse had given his word. And besides, if they hired an investment banking firm, Newhouse could take it as a hostile act, a call to arms, and it might incite him to go after the whole company.

Bosee's argument seemed silly to the executives, but it was not without historical merit. In 1976, the Newhouses collected 25 percent of the stock of Booth Newspapers, an eighty-four-year-old Michigan publishing concern, and claimed they were content to hold there. But when nervous directors sought out the Times-Mirror Company as a white knight, Newhouse swooped down and bought the whole company. Of course, chances are he would have bought it eventually anyway.

The *New Yorker* staff's pleas thudded at Bosee's feet. If Peter Fleischmann was open to suggestion, no one could tell. He had been sick again, and wasn't often in the office. (In addition to all of his other illnesses, he had undergone eye surgery.) It never occurred to anyone to seek the support of Peter's son Stephen. Or if it did, the notion was quickly dismissed.

In the editorial department, as usual, the news first surfaced as rumor. Washington-based writer John Newhouse (no relation to S. I.) first heard of the sale at lunch with an investment banker acquaintance. The man told him, "S. I. Newhouse is going to buy *The New Yorker*." He added that he thought it would be good for the magazine.

In the editorial offices in New York, the news traveled raggedly around. No one was exactly sure what the details were until November 13. That day, *The New Yorker* and Advance Publications issued a joint press release that was most unusual in content, considering that less than two weeks earlier, Peter Fleischmann had politely asked S. I. Newhouse to disappear. The missive read:

Advance Publications, Inc. will acquire from investors approximately 142,000 shares of common stock of The New Yorker Magazine Inc., representing 17% of the company's shares, it was announced today by S. I. Newhouse, chairman of Advance Publications, Inc. Peter F. Fleischmann, chairman of The New Yorker Magazine, and his family continue to own approximately 32% of the outstanding shares. The acquisition price of the Newhouse investment is $180 a share.

Mr. Newhouse said that Advance Publications, whose subsidiaries include Condé Nast Publications and Random House, is pleased to be an investor in The New Yorker. "Under Mr. Fleischmann's management and William Shawn's editorial direction," he said, "The New Yorker sets the standards of quality and leadership in its field and is one of the most respected publications in the nation. Our entire corporate history has been devoted to the publishing and communications industry. Our investment in The New Yorker is consistent with that history, and we are honored by this association." Mr. Newhouse said that there were no plans to seek control of The New Yorker or to influence its management.

Mr. Fleischmann, when reached, stated, "I am pleased to welcome Advance Publications as an investor and look forward to the relationship with such a distinguished publishing group."

There was nary a hint that the *New Yorker* management had not welcomed the intrusion. Ken Bosee says that the release was aimed at "putting on our best face for employees" in order to stem panic. It was not successful in that.

With an intent that went unnoticed by most readers, some *New Yorker* writers, mainly Lawrence Weschler and Jonathan Schell, took to using the Notes and Comments section of Talk of the Town to vent their feelings about the Newhouse invasion, albeit in disguised form. Incredibly, Talk reporters managed to equate their plight with those of Poland, Iran, the American Founding Fathers, and some buildings being torn down on Forty-fourth Street. Only *New Yorker* writers could have placed the import of their travails so high among those that befell the world at large. The customarily recalcitrant reporters readily offer that several pieces were intended for double interpretation, and they encourage the reader to let his or her imagination run amok.

"The world is notorious for blithely forgetting even the recent past," reads one essay. "Just before invading Poland, in 1939, Adolf Hitler is reported to have told his associates that since public opinion soon ignored the genocidal slaughter of the Americans by the Turks during the First World War the same public would also ignore the obliteration of other peoples by the Germans during the coming war." The intended interpretation was that Newhouse thought he could get away with it, that the flurry of negative opinion would soon give way to apathy.

That article went on to note that "news of recent Bahai executions continues to consist of two-inch items on back pages of the world press." No such fate would befall *The New Yorker!*

Here's a pointed line from another offering: "Several commentators in recent years have been struck by the extraordinary convergence of talent, grace, genius and wisdom in the current generation contesting for legitimacy in Poland. How is it possible, these observers wonder, for a single generation in a relatively small, relatively isolated country in the middle of Eastern Europe to have produced such a host of great-souled men and women. . . ?"

The writers were comparing themselves to other great-souled patriots. No one ever accused *New Yorker* writers of undue modesty.

Where there's a patriot, there is inevitably a traitor, and in this case, it was Messinger. Or so thought Fleischmann and Bosee. Neither man minded that Newhouse had barged in despite their objections. They did mind Messinger's methods. Following the sale of Messinger's stock, Fleischmann called a special meeting of the board. As it turned out, Fleischmann was ill and did not attend. No one else missed it.

Before the meeting, there was a lot of conjecturing and even a little giggling among the management directors over whether or not Messinger would have the nerve to appear. At 10:10 A.M., twenty minutes before the meeting was scheduled to start, Bob Young went to the sixteenth floor and poked his head into the conference room. Messinger was there!

Young raced back up to seventeen with the news. "You're not going to believe it!" he told Matteo. "Messinger is the first one there!"

Messinger stood alone in the room until the others began to straggle in. He began to greet Matteo. She brushed past him, a bundle of earthy feistiness. Ken Bosee offered a curt, cold hello, as did Bob Young. Walter Curley said nothing, nor did Sam Spoto. The last to arrive was Stephen Fleischmann. He spotted Messinger, strode across the room, and stuck out his hand. "Nice to see you!" he said. Messinger thought he heard relief in Stephen's voice. Maybe Stephen realized the end was in sight, he thought, and maybe he was glad.

The meeting was not pleasant. Two events stand out in the memories of those who were there. Walter Curley, nearly always the genial ambassadorial presence, turned to Messinger and with raised voice said: "You have no right being here. I for one don't want to serve with someone like you." And with that he stalked from the room.

Then Ken Bosee, with the utmost poise, asked Messinger for his resignation from the board. Since Messinger was no longer a major shareholder, he said, it seemed appropriate.

Messinger said, "I'll think about it." He added that his resignation was not on the agenda for that meeting.

The others were stunned by the reply but, in true club fashion, got through the meeting with no further reference to Messinger, the sale, or any other unpleasantness. The board could have voted him off right then and there. Instead, they waited for his resignation. His letter of resignation was a month in coming.

Messinger had to "repatriate" to *The New Yorker* the $431,507 in pre-tax profit he would have made on the *New Yorker* shares he had recently bought from LIN. Directors are not allowed by law to benefit from swings in the price of a company's stock they have held for less than six months. The funds went into the *New Yorker* treasury, which is to say that eventually they would go to Newhouse.

17

In December, S. I. Newhouse returned for more of Bill Reik's stock. The Newhouse team had never explained to Reik why they had previously reversed their decision to buy. A Newhouse lawyer says that the reversal came because at the initial meeting, they learned something that made them nervous. They had originally guessed that Reik had ten or twenty discretionary accounts under management. In fact, they learned, he had over one hundred, and that made the situation far more complicated.

Reik, as a lawyer, former securities law professor, and investment manager, was well aware that he had to adhere to SEC regulations. But sometimes even securities lawyers were unclear about the conclusions of a pertinent, precedent-setting case—the 1977 attempted acquisition of drug company Becton Dickinson by Sun Oil. Typically, in a tender offer, a company extends to all shareholders, via the *Wall Street Journal* or other newspapers, an offer to purchase shares. Sun Oil, instead, mailed individual letters of solicitation to Becton Dickinson shareholders using phrases aimed at imparting a sense of urgency. Becton

Dickinson accused Sun Oil of violating the tender laws, and the SEC tended to side with the drug concern. Sun Oil was forced to sign a consent decree, a regulatory slap frequently defined this way: "We didn't do it but we promise we won't do it again." Consent decrees are not considered overly enlightening as a means of interpreting the law.

Did Sun Oil err with the urgent language of its letters? Or had it gone astray by *not* making a sweeping offer to all shareholders simultaneously? Reik's interpretation led him to believe that to approach his clients on an individual basis would be to violate the law.

While he was considering it all, Reik's clients began to call. Many newspapers had carried detail-filled accounts of Newhouse's purchase of 17 percent of *The New Yorker*. Some clients who had not been offered the opportunity to sell phoned Reik and demanded to know why their stock was worth only $140 in the market while other shareholders had sold their *New Yorker* stock at $180. Why hadn't Reik sold theirs as well? Reik explained that he had sold only the stock in discretionary accounts. He could not legally solicit his other clients on an individual basis. It would constitute a violation of the tender rules. The clients were not interested in the tender rules. They were worried that if they didn't sell *now*, they might never live to see $180. Reik could offer them no blanket assurances. He had no way of knowing if Newhouse would pay $180 for the remaining shares.

Then on December 12, Reik and his son William J. Reik III, known as "Trey," and lawyer Sam Butler met with the usual plumped-up platoon of Newhouse lawyers at the Mitchell Hutchins offices at 140 Broadway. (They have since moved uptown to Avenue of the Americas.) The message with which they were greeted made it clear that the Newhouse contingent was wary of breaking the law. The attorneys informed Reik that Newhouse wanted to buy some, but not necessarily all, of the *New Yorker* shares in Reik's nondiscretionary accounts. Specifically, he wanted to purchase shares only from Reik's customers who had expressed interest in selling, and he didn't necessarily want all of theirs. He intended to limit himself to 25 percent.

The figure was meaningful on two counts. First, Newhouse had promised Fleischmann that he would limit his ownership to 25 percent. Second, it gave Newhouse control of the same percentage of *New Yorker* stock that Peter Fleischmann and the Fleischmann family trusts owned. But if the number was convenient for Newhouse, it was less so for Reik. It placed him in the position of having to choose among clients who wished to sell. Furthermore, Reik knew that the more he allowed Newhouse to whittle his block down, the less bargaining power he retained. With 12 percent, Reik was a potent force. If that position was substantially cut, Newhouse could call the shots. He might never offer $180 for the rest of the stock. He might wait twenty years. He could afford to do that. Reik decided to stall.

He told the gathered attorneys that they were going about their purchase all wrong. They didn't understand that it was a delicate situation; you couldn't barnstorm in on Peter Fleischmann. He said, "This is a very fragile man. He looks at *The New Yorker* as his family. It's his whole life. I think you're reading the situation wrong."

"That's just conjecture," snapped Patricia Vlahakis, a young associate from Wachtell Lipton. "We don't deal in conjecture."

Reik shot her a look of disgust. "Have you been over to see Peter Fleischmann?" he demanded. "Do you know him? What do you think of him? How do you think you'll be able to do this?"

"No, we haven't met him," she said. "We don't have to worry about that. We've been through a lot of these before."

Reik exploded. "You've never been in anything like this before!" he said. "You have no idea what you're talking about!" Reik seemed to resent the notion that any deal involving *The New Yorker* was just another deal.

Butler tried, with only mild success, to restore calm, "to keep it from breaking out into a fistfight," as Reik recalls.

According to others in the room, Vlahakis proceeded to lecture the gathering on securities law, to the annoyance of all. Sam Butler, who had been in the legal profession three decades longer than she had and who had risen to the top of it, told her calmly, "We don't need you to educate us on securities law."

Someone from the Newhouse team reiterated the offer to buy the stock of the clients who had expressed interest in selling, but again, to a limit of 25 percent of the company. Reik said that he would not split up the stock.

"If you want the stock," he said, "tender for it. It's a perfectly normal thing to do. You already own 17 percent, tender for the other 83 percent. And when I see the tender in the newspaper, I'll react to it. I may tender all of it, I may tender none of it. But don't tell me you want to buy *some*."

A lawyer said, "We don't want to tender."

"Then you're not going to buy any of my stock," Reik snapped.

One of the Newhouse lawyers explained that they didn't want to tender because it would mean going after the whole company, and that might upset Peter Fleischmann. They wanted to do this thing *quietly*.

Reik said, "I'm not going to get involved in any situation where we're breaking up nondiscretionary pieces. It would be perceived as a securities violation."

A lawyer said, "You can always argue it."

Reik told him, "I don't want to be in a position where I'm arguing it. Who wants to be in that position, sitting in Washington, explaining why they did something?" Reik wondered how a lawyer and securities professor like himself might go about explaining to the SEC that he didn't understand securities law.

Several of the lawyers took the position that it was within the law to sell the stock of the clients who so requested. Reik didn't want to be the one to test that contention. He also didn't want to have to face the wrath of clients who called later, only to be told the offer was closed. And he didn't want to call *them*, because that would put him in the position of choosing among clients. Who would he pick? And what about the law? Round and round it went—lawyers talking and Reik brooding. Reik didn't like the lawyers. He resented Newhouse's sending this *gang* of them. He began to wonder about Newhouse.

Then he began to ponder what he had unleashed on Peter Fleischmann. "What are they going to do when they get their hands on *him?*" he wondered. "Fleischmann is frail, he is sick, he is weak, he can't talk, he can't walk. These guys are pushing me around off the walls. Wait until they get hold of him. They'll kill him!"

Reik was steaming, too, at what he perceived as a condescending attitude on the part of the lawyers. "They really must have thought I was some country bumpkin," he later recalled. "Like, 'Here's this bozo who doesn't know what he's doing. He bought all this stupid magazine stock. He has no idea what's going on in the world. God knows how he found his way to the office this morning. But he seems to be here, so we'll just tell him what we want done and he'll obviously do it because we're these big-name midtown law firms and we work for S. I. Newhouse.' And that just sailed right by me."

To a large extent, of course, Reik was posturing. Beneath his heap of heaving emotions was a hard, cold financial calculation. Newhouse was eventually going to have to pay dearly to get Peter Fleischmann out of the way, and if you were in with Peter, you were going to get paid dearly as well.

So Reik explained his quandary one more time. "How can I justify breaking up my clients' stock?" he said. "How can I sell for one and not another? Who would I pick? Why didn't I pick who I didn't pick? This puts me in a very bad position with my clients. I can't choose between my clients."

Reik recalls that Loeber Landau, a partner from Sullivan & Cromwell, replied with level voice: "Mr. Reik, your clients are really no concern of ours." (Mr. Landau, a pleasant voice on the telephone, declined to speak to me, on instructions from Advance.)

That was all it took. Trey Reik, watching his father, noticed that he began to shake. "He looked like he was going to cry," Trey recalled later. Reik rose from his seat. "I don't like anything about this," he exclaimed. "I don't like the meeting. I'm perfectly happy with my stock. I love the company. I'll sit there until hell freezes over. Hell, I might buy more!" And with that he stormed from the room.

Reik returned to his office, picked up the phone, and called Phil Messinger to tell him what had happened. Reik told Messinger, "I'm going to keep my *New Yorker* stock forever."

Messinger, by then out himself, cautioned Reik to "proceed at your own risk."

Reik said, "I am. I'll just sit here. *The New Yorker* will be owned by Peter Fleischmann, Bill Reik and his clients, and S. I. Newhouse. I'll just sit here for the next hundred years."

Messinger applauded Reik's stand. He told him that if he held off, "You know you're going to get a higher price." (That meant that Messinger, with his price protection, would get a higher price too.) The risk, Messinger said, was that Newhouse could outwait Reik. Newhouse had a billion dollars and could sit forever.

"Fine," said Reik. "I'll sit forever too."

If it was true, as Reik suspected, that the Newhouse lawyers thought of him as an eminently pliable hick, they thought wrong. Reik knew that his chip wasn't the largest, but at the moment, it was the only large one still in play. In a sense, Reik had Newhouse blocked. Says Reik: "They had to tender or do something. What could they do? They were sitting there with this piece of stock and they couldn't get more. If I wasn't going to sell to them and Peter wasn't going to sell to them, they had a very bad investment."

Reik told Sam Butler that he was upset about the meeting and appalled by the Newhouse attorneys.

Reik recalls Butler's saying, "We see things like that all the time."

Reik said, "I can't believe it."

Butler said, "You sit there in your ivory tower, you choose the kind of people you deal with. We deal with people like this all the time."

"I wouldn't walk in a room with those people," said Reik. "I really wouldn't."

Reik recalls that toward the end of the stormy session, lawyer Loeber Landau said, "I'll be in Arizona on vacation next week, but you can proceed with my partner over here. He'll handle all the details." As if there was no question that the purchase would go through in the form the Newhouse team envisioned. When Landau returned from his Western sojourn, he was appalled to learn that no shares had changed hands. He called Sam Butler to express his profound shock. Butler told him that Reik had reacted poorly to the lawyers, and suggested that S. I. Newhouse get involved, maybe even call Reik and apologize.

For of all that annoyed Reik, what made him the crankiest was the fact that Newhouse had not bothered to come in person. Instead, recalls Reik, "He sent this whole raft of used-car salesmen to my office to threaten me. To bang me up against the wall and tell me that I have to do something." The outcome might have been very different, says Reik, if Newhouse had taken a more personal approach. "All he would have had to do was pick up the phone and come to see me. Or invite me to lunch and say, 'I understand you're very sensitive about *The New Yorker*. I understand you're very sensitive about ever selling it. I understand you're very sensitive about Peter Fleischmann. Here's what I would like to do. How do you think I should do it?'"

According to Reik, "It would have changed the whole equation."

Reik figured that Newhouse must be out of touch with the realities of the everyday world: "When you're worth a billion and you're chauffeured around town with an entourage and you send a large group of lawyers to a very simple negotiating meeting, and you go to the office at four in the morning, you go home in the afternoon, you take a nap, you go to a black-tie supper, you go home, go to bed, get up to be in the office at four o'clock in the morning.... How real is he? He might not know how he comes off." Reik had read numerous profiles of Newhouse that described his daily routine. He says he "could not comprehend how his reportedly rigid schedule would not permit his attendance at a meeting of such magnitude."

Newhouse never did apologize, but he called Donald Marron and asked him to intervene on his behalf. Marron contacted Reik and told him that Newhouse would like to meet with him. A date was arranged.

At *The New Yorker*, executives toiled in ignorance of the proceedings. There were only occasional gusts of information. But even so, they knew that Reik had not sold all of his stock, and Reik thought it odd that neither Peter Fleischmann nor Ken Bosee contacted him to ask what he was going to do with the rest of it.

Former director William Eiseman recalls that after Newhouse bought his initial stake, panic set in on the board and among officers. The directors discussed what action to take, with a couple of them urging management to look into some antiacquisition defenses before it was too late. But he says that Fleischmann seemed riveted into inaction on the advice of Milton Greenstein, who convinced him that Newhouse had Reik's stock all sewn up, that the end was near and there was nothing he could do about it.

On the seventeenth floor, Elaine Matteo, Janet Muir, and Pete Spelman continued to hammer at Ken Bosee to consult an investment banker. It was sheer folly not to have some contingency plan in the event Newhouse had further designs on the company. Certainly there was no harm in preparing.

Bosee continued to resist. He still didn't want to antagonize Newhouse. His approach was friendly. He even took Newhouse out to lunch a couple of times, "to talk to him as I would to any major stockholder." What's more, Fleischmann was adamantly opposed to the use of offensive tactics.

Says Bosee: "At the time, people were telling me, we've got to do this or got to do that [to avert] a takeover. I knew that. That was a given. At the same time, I had to go with what the chairman wanted."

Eventually Fleischmann agreed to allow Bosee to contact an investment banker. He imposed one condition: It had to be Smith Barney. Smith Barney was the kind of brokerage firm referred to on Wall Street as "brown shoe." Peter Fleischmann had worked there briefly after graduating from college, and felt comfortable with the people and the reputation. Smith Barney, in brokering, stood for many of the same things that *The New Yorker* did in publishing—gentility, tradition. It was for Smith Barney that the actor John Houseman flashed across TV screens, imprinting upon America's consciousness the slogan "At Smith Barney, we make money the old-fashioned way. We *earn* it." There was nothing wrong with Smith Barney as a firm, but it was not a logical choice in this case because it was not exactly in the forefront of takeover defense. Nor did it pretend to be. Janet Muir, for one, railed against the selection. She suggested contacting First Boston, which combined combative skills with a particular expertise in media companies. Ken Bosee himself admits that Smith Barney was "not

an A-1 selection" to handle the business at hand. But Fleischmann was adamant.

Bosee scheduled a meeting with Smith Barney, the content
of which was to be kept so secret that only Bosee and Stephen
Fleischmann would attend. Peter Fleischmann would not. He
said he had a conflict of interest based on his large stock holdings and his trustee status. Arguably, since he was a beneficiary
of the Fleischmann family trusts, Stephen Fleischmann, too, had
a conflict. But in any case, Stephen was the delegate.

The morning of the meeting dawned. But *where* was Stephen?
Nine o'clock, no Stephen. Nine-thirty, still no Stephen. Nine-
forty-five, the same. The Smith Barney contingent was due at
ten. Elaine Matteo was frantic. Ken Bosee was furious.

It is possible that the meeting might have proved a turning
point. Perhaps Smith Barney could arrive at a way to keep control
of *The New Yorker* in Fleischmann family hands, to stop it from
slipping into the hands of an outsider. Perhaps, at the very least,
they could see to it that events did not just *overtake* the magazine
and the company. That *The New Yorker* could control its own
fate, by deciding to sell or not to sell, and if to sell, then to whom.
The New Yorker might have been placed instead of auctioned to
the first (albeit very high) bidder. But we will never know what
might have come of it, because Stephen didn't appear.

At ten o'clock Elaine Matteo instructed her secretary to phone
Stephen at home and find out "where the hell he is." After several rings, a groggy Stephen answered. The secretary was nervous and embarrassed; clearly, she had roused young Fleischmann
from sleep. The word spread quickly through the office: Stephen
had overslept.

Bosee alone met with the Smith Barney bankers, but nothing came of it. No one felt any urgency to act.

18

Bill Reik did not miss his scheduled meeting with S. I. Newhouse. Reik, Butler, Newhouse, and assorted lawyers met in another session dominated by the attorneys. Newhouse was quiet. He seemed almost timid, a perceived characteristic that may owe in part to his diminutive size and "mousy," some say, appearance. He spoke early in the session to tell Reik that he really wanted to buy *The New Yorker*. He said he thought that he could get it, but he needed Reik's stock.

Then the lawyers took over, and once more the old topics arose, the old ground was covered. Advance did not want to tender for the stock. They wanted to buy stock from clients who had expressed interest in selling, but only to a limit of 25 percent. They told Reik not to worry about the tender rules.

Reik said, "You guys are great to say that. You know when the SEC calls, you're not gonna have to go." ("Lawyers are funny when they're giving you advice," Reik later mused. "They tell you what they think's going to happen, but if they're wrong, you're the one who's dead.") But the session was far more amicable than

THE LAST DAYS OF THE NEW YORKER

that which had preceded it. It ended when Reik agreed to re-think delivering just part of the stock, not in a tender, but in a direct sale.

When he sat in the room, he says, it all seemed quite logi-cal. But when he left and began to think about it, the familiar qualms overtook him. He didn't want to let go of *The New Yorker* altogether. He might violate the tender rules. How could he break up his clients' stock? What would it do to Peter Fleischmann? Perhaps most compelling, though least expressed, was the instinct that if he waited for Fleischmann to sell, he could get more money. It was a perfectly appropriate motivation for an invest-ment manager.

Sam Butler, a pragmatic person with a sophisticated grasp of business, was sympathetic to Reik's priorities. Reik, in turn, had great admiration for Sam Butler, one of the most highly regarded and best-liked men in his profession. Reik had said, after the first meeting with the Newhouse battalion, "They can send all the lawyers they want, but as long as I have Sam Butler, I'm ahead in lawyers."

Butler worked out a script for Reik that he could use in his approach to customers. Butler had previously advised Reik to keep a log of customers who had called him about selling. Now, Reik was to call them and say that a buyer had authorized Paine Webber to contact clients who owned *New Yorker* stock and of-fer them $180 a share for it. If the client was interested, Paine Webber would forward a purchase agreement. Reik was to as-sure them that there was no deadline for signing.

Reik said to Butler, "If I do this, can you promise me that the SEC won't drag me down to Washington to testify?"

Butler said, "No. But I can promise you we'll win."

It wasn't the answer Reik wanted to hear.

Donald Marron also was growing irritated over Reik's inac-tion. Marron had some sympathy for Reik's dilemma, but nevertheless, he didn't want to look foolish in front of Newhouse with his inability to get Reik to deliver the stock. Their differences over the whole *New Yorker* saga eventually flared into very heated "discussions" behind closed doors, according to colleagues who could not help but overhear. According to one report, Marron once demanded of Reik, "Do you realize that you're going to look like a fool in front of your clients?"

"Don't you spend one minute worrying about that!" Reik snapped in reply. "I'm doing enough worrying about my clients for everybody. Don't you lose one night's sleep over it!"

At the same time that Reik resolutely resisted selling, he began to buy *New Yorker* stock because of what he calls "ultimate faith" in the value of the *New Yorker* franchise. At the same time, speculators began to enter the market, and the combined buying drove the price up. Traders not previously interested in *The New Yorker* logically guessed that Newhouse intended to acquire the company. In the last month of 1984, the price of *New Yorker* shares soared as high as $172 bid in the over-the-counter market. Only two months earlier, it had been at $135. The narrowing of the gap between the price he was offering and the market price can only have alarmed Newhouse. The higher the market price, the less incentive any holders had to deliver their shares to him at $180. That fact cannot have been lost on him. At the same time, he was stymied by Reik's refusal to subdivide his remaining stock, or to sell it, except into a tender offer. Newhouse hadn't even reached the 25 percent mark yet. He was stalled at 17 percent. Nor could Newhouse ignore what Sam Butler calls the Newhouse lawyers' own "paranoia" about violating the tender rules.

Withal, time was the enemy. Roy Disney, nephew of the late Walt Disney, entered the picture when he and a group of "investors" began to accumulate *New Yorker* stock, not because they wanted to own the company, but because they believed they would eventually get more for it when Newhouse extended his offer to other shareholders, or when another publisher came in to top Newhouse. Newhouse didn't need a price war. He had to act. Events accelerated his timetable.

In the new year, S. I. Newhouse again visited Peter Fleischmann at his apartment. This time, he told Fleischmann that he wanted to buy *The New Yorker*, not just pieces of it, but the whole thing. He was willing to extend an offer of $180 a share to all holders, including the Fleischmann family trusts. Peter Fleischmann did not tell him to go away. That in itself was not meaningful. Fleischmann often didn't *say* go away, even while thinking it. But this time, the *New Yorker* chairman stopped to consider. Perhaps he remembered the LIN debacle, Messinger's anger over not being informed of an offer. Maybe he believed the end was in sight anyway, as Milton Greenstein was convinced. And maybe it was too difficult to ignore $180 a share, either for yourself or for your shareholders, especially when you were convinced that Newhouse could buy the company anyway. Fleischmann consulted his advisers and fellow trustees, Milton Greenstein, his stepbrother, Gardner Botsford (who owned 5065 *New Yorker* shares), and his friend and lawyer, Ted Clark.

Five years earlier, maybe even one year earlier, Fleischmann might have reacted quite differently to the Newhouse offer. Time and events had battered him. Friends noticed that the prior year had taken its toll, that he was markedly more dispirited and frail. Stephen Fleischmann claims that his father was not even remotely upset at George Green's departure from *The New Yorker*, but close associates paint a different picture. They say it caused him great distress. Furthermore, Fleischmann confided to at least one person that he was unhappy with the job Bosee was doing as president. However, there was no apparent replacement inside the company. Certainly there were qualified applicants among those that the search firm had found. But talks with two of them had been reduced to haggling over money, and in any case, Fleischmann wasn't really comfortable with the idea of hiring an out-sider. He wanted to work with someone he knew.

The chairman's health was worse than ever, so in addition to grappling with the problem of finding a new president, he had to find his own successor. Related to that, he had to deal with the question of Stephen. Few, if any, of Fleischmann's executives believed that his son could run with the torch, if it was passed to him. Fleischmann himself had doubts. Many of Stephen's asso-ciates doubted that he wanted to be involved.

Fleischmann also felt pressure from the trustees to sell. They had fiduciary responsibilities. Notwithstanding their friendship with Peter Fleischmann, trust law dictated that they had to come up with some pretty convincing reasons why they *shouldn't* sell to Newhouse. Further, advisers reminded Fleischmann that in the event of his death, given the high price of the stock and the structure of the company, his heirs would have to pay astronom-ical estate taxes. They would probably be compelled to liquidate all or part of their stock to meet their financial obligations. There was no guarantee that they would not be forced to sell at distress prices, far below what Newhouse was offering. There would have been ways around that, had the company acted earlier. Now it was probably too late.

Peter Fleischmann was not old—he was sixty-three—but he did not have to be reminded of his own mortality. He had looked it square in the jaw many times. He had jousted with death on a battlefield in Belgium. He had survived an automobile crash, throat cancer, diverticulitis, and eye surgery. He had seen more operating rooms than some surgeons do. He had always beaten whatever befell him, to the amazement of legions of acquain-tances who couldn't see past the frail physique to what had to have been an indomitable will. He knew he couldn't beat it for-ever. He decided to sell.

The sale of The New Yorker was presented to the directors as a *fait accompli*. William Eiseman was at his home in Connecticut when a call came from Merrell Clark. The lawyer was in an office at *The New Yorker* with Walter Curley and Ken Bosee. Fleischmann was not with them. Clark told Eiseman that Fleischmann had decided to sell to Newhouse. Eiseman's opinion was not solicited. He was simply informed of the decision.

On February 12, just one week shy of the *New Yorker's* sixtieth anniversary, S. I. Newhouse, with the approval of Peter Fleischmann, filed with the SEC, and delivered to the board of The New Yorker Magazine, Inc., a letter of proposal for a cash merger under which he would pay $180 a share for the 83 percent of *The New Yorker* he did not already own. The letter began, "We are pleased to submit for your consideration...." In contrast to a tender offer, which is made directly to shareholders, a cash merger is submitted to a company's board, and once they have approved it, it is passed on to shareholders, a majority of whom must give their assent.

The Newhouse letter contained soothing assurances of a commitment to gentle handling of *The New Yorker*. It read: "We recognize that the unique quality of The New Yorker is the product of its personnel and of their operating practices and traditions, including the tradition of complete editorial independence...." Newhouse went on to say that if the offer was accepted, *The New Yorker* would be operated "on a stand-alone basis as a separate company."

On the same day on which the letter was dated, Peter Fleischmann called a special meeting of his board. In a four-hour session (attended also by Messinger's replacement, John L. Montgomery, a Smith Barney executive), Fleischmann reiterated his intention to sell. Not every director spoke up, but almost to a person, they opposed the sale. Walter Curley warned that once *The New Yorker* was acquired, it would lose its "mystique" and its specialness. If it fell into the hands of a very large publishing company, like Newhouse's, its character would be forever altered, "and *The New Yorker* would no longer exist," said Curley. Elaine Matteo, Ken Bosee, and Bob Young also opposed the sale, even though all three stood to make hundreds of thousands of dollars, thanks to the stock grant program. They would rather preserve the status quo. Bosee says, though, that much as he resisted the merger, $180 was compelling, especially since he and Fleischmann thought the company was worth $90 a share. (In a seeming contradiction, George Green says that he and Fleischmann often discussed what *The New Yorker* might sell for, and came up with the figure $200.) William Eiseman would have preferred to explore other buyers, but his business sense told him it was too late. Stephen Fleischmann said little, but he seemed quite happy at the turn of events. Some perceived what Messinger had noted months earlier: Stephen was relieved to be rid of an unwanted responsibility.

It was soon clear to the directors that Fleischmann would not be swayed—he had made up his mind. He did not want a fight. He would go with a whimper, not with a bang. Fleischmann made one concession: An investment bank could be retained to evaluate the fairness of the price. He did not insist on Smith Barney. Bosee and Matteo chose First Boston.

The *New Yorker* staff was in turmoil when the news reached it. On the eighteenth and nineteenth floors, stupefied editors and writers gathered in clumps to discuss their futures. On the business floors, staff members organized themselves into S.W.A.T. teams, devised methods of heading off the terrorist Newhouse. Five people—Pete Spelman, Elaine Matteo, Janet Muir, former retail ad director Louis Farrelly, and Luis Dominguez, head of the London sales office—mobilized into action, seeking out other buyers. Spelman, representing the delegation, visited Peter Fleischmann to plead with him not to sell to Newhouse. He said that he and his colleagues would raise the funds to buy the magazine themselves. They didn't *have* to sell to Newhouse. A sweet expression suffused the chairman's face. He told Spelman that he was "very flattered" by the offer. But it was too late, he said. He had already agreed.

In quest of a white knight, Janet Muir called Gordon Getty, the oil billionaire. Her mother's sister knew him slightly. Getty seemed a sensitive man—he composed music, even. He might be a latter-day Raoul Fleischmann, willing to put up money but not interfere. But Getty was embroiled in the litigation arising out of the sale of his family company, Getty Oil, to Texaco. When his family sold to Texaco, they allegedly reneged on an earlier agreement with Pennzoil. Getty wasn't willing to open himself up to more of the same kind of controversy.

William Shawn used his own money to retain a lawyer to explore ways to avert the sale. He hired Peter Ryan, a partner in the firm of Fried, Frank, Harris, Shriver & Jacobson.

Time passed.

On March 6, the board convened in a special session to hear and discuss First Boston's findings. The investment bank had compared the price being offered for *The New Yorker* with that being paid for other media companies and concluded that $180 a share was too low. They recommended that *The New Yorker* hold out for $200. The board agreed, and the word was passed to Newhouse. Newhouse did not haggle; he hit the bid. Newhouse met with the *New Yorker* directors and promised them that he would retain the board intact.

Newhouse agreed to pay a total of $142 million for the 83 percent of the stock he didn't already own. In addition, price protection clauses would raise to $28 million, from $26 million, the amount paid for the initial 17 percent. In total, Newhouse would pay $170 million for The New Yorker Magazine, Inc., and its subsidiaries.

Lawyers and investment bankers for Newhouse and *The New Yorker* drew up a plan of merger. Both sides took pains to develop language aimed at pacifying *New Yorker* employees. In addition to covenants stipulating that *The New Yorker* would be operated on a stand-alone basis, and not merged with Condé Nast, Advance stated that it "desires the continuation of the present directors, officers, editors, employees and contributors of the company and that there be no change in the company's organization." It also recognized "that the unique quality of The New Yorker is the product of its personnel and their operating practices and traditions, including the tradition of complete editorial independence: the editors having total control of the magazine's editorial character, policies, procedures and content.... Advance wishes to preserve this quality of The New Yorker through maintaining its personnel and traditions."

Elaine Matteo, for one, was unconvinced by the pretty words. She suggested to Ken Bosee that officers approach Newhouse and negotiate individual employment contracts. Bosee refused. He said the merger agreement covered it. The two argued about it at a lunch with Stu Jason. Matteo told Bosee that there was absolutely no guarantee that they would not be thrown out on the street. Bosee wouldn't budge.

They did extract from Newhouse a promise to maintain employee benefit plans, including profit sharing. Condé Nast offered no such plan to its employees, and the *New Yorker* executives worried that it would be an early casualty of the takeover.

The merger agreement also carried editorial warranties. Advance said it planned to maintain the *New Yorker*'s sixty-year tradition of complete editorial independence, that the editors would continue to control "editorial character and content...without intervention of any kind by the owners or publishers." Advance agreed to consult with the editor "on advertising-acceptance policy, on the magazine's own advertising, promotion and public relations, and on circulation policy."

And finally, the agreement grappled with the almighty ques-

271

tion of succession. Advance promised that "when a new editor-in-chief of The New Yorker is being considered, the final decision will be made by Advance, but it will consult with, and seek the advice and approval of, a group of staff members to be selected and to function in a manner then deemed to be appropriate by the senior editorial staff of The New Yorker."

William Shawn was consulted with regard to the sections regarding editorial independence and succession, and he took an active role in writing them.

On Friday, March 8, the board unanimously adopted the Plan of Merger. It now had to be submitted to the shareholders for approval, but practically speaking, the shareholders had no options. Bill Reik told reporters that he would probably vote his stock as the board voted, which is to say, in favor of selling. That meant that Newhouse now had well over 50 percent of the stock. There would not be much point in individual shareholders' refusing to sell. And besides, $200 was a damn good price. Most shareholders were thrilled.

The acquisition proved inconvenient in its timing for Ken Bosee because it coincided with his second acquisition. On March 5, he had agreed to buy Princeton Polychrome Press, a New Jersey printer of quality art prints, book jackets, and posters. Soon after it became apparent that Newhouse would be successful in his bid for The New Yorker, Bosee and Janet Muir made a scheduled trip to Princeton to meet with the company's employees and to close the deal. Bosee opened his address to the employees by noting that S. I. Newhouse was in the process of buying The New Yorker. Muir recalls the way that Bosee described the event: "You know the story about the middle-size fish that's going after the little fish in the middle of the ocean and he's going to gobble up the little fish? Then all of a sudden a *big shark* comes along and eats them *all* up."

Muir noticed that the faces of the Princeton employees took

on a "terrorized" look. She glanced at David Johnson, the president of Princeton Polychrome. The color had drained from his face. Suddenly the whole situation seemed absurd and funny and Muir had to restrain herself from bursting into laughter.

New Yorker employees were even more appalled. As news of the finality of it all spread, they reacted with anger, sadness, disbelief. They talked of leaving. Writer Calvin Trillin told the *Wall Street Journal:* "I don't know if depressed is the right word. I think edgy is closer. You don't know what to fear. You have an exceedingly benign headmaster and suddenly he leaves and another man comes from a school in California and nobody knows anything about him. You have to wonder if you're going to get away with staying out past the curfew or not."

Some of the writers' comments took on stamping-their-feet tones and displayed a naïveté about business. Writer Paul Brodeur said to the *New York Times:* "I think it's a deliberate affront to every artist, writer, and editorial staff member. It's a deliberate action." He seemed to imply that Peter Fleischmann had been out to get them, as if for some past offense.

In Notes and Comments, William Shawn himself penned these words: "We, the editorial people, knew by instinct that to be able to make The New Yorker the magazine we wanted it to be we had to separate ourselves from the business side of the venture.... In this atmosphere of freedom, we have never published anything in order to sell magazines, to cause a sensation, to be controversial, to be popular or fashionable, to be 'successful.'"

Those writers who had read the clauses in the merger agreement that guaranteed their independence were not mollified. At 4:00 P.M., on the May day they called "Black Friday," Mr. Shawn, with his lawyer, Peter Ryan, shuffled down the stairs from his nineteenth-floor office to the floor below. He stood on the first step. His staff gathered in front of him, huddled in the bulge in the hall that was their meeting place, like a flock before a shepherd in some biblical tale. The seventy-seven-year-old Shawn blinked back tears.

"The editorial staff was not a party to these negotiations," he said, his voice aquiver. "Nor were the views of the editorial staff solicited during these negotiations. We were not asked for our approval, and we did not give our approval." It was all he had to say. "When there are further developments," said Shawn, "I will meet with you again." Moses turned and climbed back up the mountain, his lawyer close by his side.

Shawn was not technically truthful when he said he had not been consulted. He *had* been consulted about the plan of the merger. He also had met personally with Newhouse, who had assured him he wouldn't interfere with the editorial department. But if not correct in letter, Shawn was accurate in spirit. Certainly the merger was not something editorial would have approved. They had no time to prepare for it. A hastily assembled twelve-person editorial council had been largely ignored. The revered wall that separated editorial from business, which in the past provided comfort, now had become their downfall. Shawn himself cannot have found comfort in newspaper reports that Newhouse had already narrowed down to two his choices of Shawn's replacement: Robert Gottlieb, editor in chief of Knopf, and Robert Silvers, editor of the *New York Review of Books*.

Many *New Yorker* readers were stirred and upset by the sale. The stalwarts who had remained true through the years didn't take *The New Yorker* lightly, they took it personally. One such was a Mrs. Winge, the mother of Robert Winge, the *New Yorker's* outside counsel. According to acquaintances of the lawyer, his mother called him at two in the morning after reading of Shawn's stirring oratory on the stairs.

"How could you let this happen?" she is said to have demanded. "You should be ashamed of yourself. Making a contract to sell *The New Yorker* and not even consulting Mr. Shawn!"

Winge was so upset by the call that he, in turn, phoned Shawn and chastised him for leaving the impression he hadn't been consulted.

In the publishing community, reaction to the sale was decidedly more sanguine. It was no secret in the industry that the *New Yorker*'s ad pages and circulation had both declined in 1984, even while revenues were up, thanks to higher ad rates. The trend continued as ads fell 207 pages in the first four months of 1985. The quality of circulation was questioned as well. A widely held perception was that the *New Yorker*'s older readers were dying off and not being replaced by new, younger ones. Perhaps, it was thought, Newhouse could provide some rejuvenation.

George Green told a reporter, "S. I. Newhouse could be the best thing to happen to *The New Yorker*."

Speculation was that Newhouse would tread softly, at first. And despite rumors to the contrary, most people guessed that he would allow Shawn to pick his own successor. He had to know that the political ramifications of doing otherwise would be great.

On April 19, Peter Fleischmann sent to each employee, at his or her home, a letter written on *New Yorker* stationery that bore the notation "Peter F. Fleischmann, Chairman of the Board." It read:

To the Staff:

Now that our board of Directors has approved Mr. Newhouse's proposal of a merger of The New Yorker Magazine, Inc., and Advance Publications, I thought I should express to you my personal thoughts.

I did not seek a change in the ownership of The New Yorker. When Mr. Newhouse first approached me, I tried to discourage him. I hoped that he would lose interest and go away. I did not want to give up the special relationship I have enjoyed as a result of my father's stock ownership and my own. I did not want any change.

But as time passed, I came to think that my feeling was unrealistic and that change was inevitable. I was, of course, influenced by the fact that Mr. Newhouse, if he so wished (though there was never a hint of such a desire on his part), could unilaterally accomplish what he sought; but beyond that, there was the inexorability of death and taxes. The day was bound to come when my death and the resulting estate taxes would require an uncontrolled sale and bring some new and unknown owner. If the change were unplanned and forced by circumstances, a smooth transition might be impossible, and permanent damage might be done to our fragile institution, which consists essentially of the interpersonal relationships among dedicated people of good will, ability, and creative genius. I decided that it was in the best interest of The New Yorker as an institution to have the change in ownership take place smoothly and agreeably on the basis of commitments that our people and our practices and traditions would be continued.

Mr. Newhouse has agreed to appropriate terms in these respects. During my meetings with him, he has volunteered his own wish to maintain our quality, our people, and our traditions. Mr. Newhouse has expressed to Mr. Shawn his desire "to be able thirty years from now to pick up a copy of The New Yorker and find it just what it is today and held in the same high esteem."

So, while there is a degree of personal sadness, I think this change is in the best interest of The New Yorker as an institution to which we are all dedicated.

I am happy to say that Mr. Newhouse has asked me to continue as Chairman and I have accepted. I will, therefore, be privileged to work with all of you in an uninterrupted effort to keep The New Yorker as successful as it can possibly be.

Sincerely and gratefully,

Peter F. Fleischmann

The final annual meeting of The New Yorker Magazine, Inc., public company, was called for May 7, 1985. It was, as always, scheduled to be held in the second-floor conference room of Morgan Guaranty Trust Company, Fifth Avenue and Forty-fourth Street, just out the *New Yorker's* back door. It was soon apparent that the room was too small.

In the past, the annual meetings had resembled the town meetings of some sleepy Southern burg. They were sparsely populated, but those who came cared. Reik remembers a woman who owned 200 shares telling him, years earlier, that she traveled every year from California to be present at this occasion. It was her statement in life, she said.

In the past, they fanned themselves idly with their proxy statements, counted Peter Fleischmann's cigarettes, asked few questions, with the exception, of course, of Charles Schwartz, the great debater. This day in 1985, management might have longed for Charles Schwartz's questions, but Charles Schwartz was not there. He had business to attend to in Chicago, and besides, he says, "By then it was all over."

Hundreds of people did come—some shareholders, some not, writers, artists, distressed employees. A guard stationed at Morgan Guaranty's front door told all comers that there was a change of location. He directed them down Forty-fourth Street, to a larger facility at the Bar Association building.

It was a turbulent, emotional affair. Neither Peter Fleischmann nor William Shawn attended. Ken Bosee presided. Messinger and Bill Reik arrived together. In front of them on the folding steel chairs sat two men who seemed awkwardly out of place: Newhouse executives. One was Steven T. Florio, thirty-six, whom Newhouse had already appointed to the vacant title of publisher of *The New Yorker*. Florio had been publisher through the stunning turnaround at *Gentleman's Quarterly* magazine. The other was Jonathan Newhouse, a cousin of S. I.'s and possible heir apparent to the empire, newly named a vice president of the *New Yorker* magazine company. They watched in silence.

The meeting began with the usual pro forma preliminaries, but it quickly deteriorated into "we-they" acrimony between financial and business interests and editors and writers. Sitting behind Reik and Messinger was Lillian Ross, the writer, then in her seventies, who was a close friend of Shawn's. Ross rose from her seat to denounce the sale as a travesty. She gave a stirring speech about the history of the magazine. It was an outrage that the *New Yorker*'s editors and writers and artists had not been consulted. They had made the magazine, she declared with barely restrained rage, yet they had been left out of the process. She hammered at the point so long that a shareholder, several rows behind, stood to offer an explanation. He said that she would have had a voice as well, and so, too, would the other writers and editors and artists, had they purchased stock at any time in the last ten or twenty or thirty years. He had done just that, as had many others in the room, and that's why they had the votes.

Ross pivoted and glared at him. "Who are you?!" she demanded.

Bill Reik turned in his seat to face Ross. "Who are you!?" he demanded in return. "That man is a shareholder. He has a right to speak!"

Writer Paul Brodeur also blasted management. A shareholder stood to counter his words, saying, "I speak for other shareholders when I say that management should be congratulated for an outstanding job." There was loud applause.

For all of their disdain of things financial, the writers and editorial staff exhibited a particular bitterness about the fact that they hadn't made any money on the deal. Mary D. Kierstead, a fiction editor, was greeted with applause when she said, "It is unjust that those in editorial who have worked with such dedication for this management get nothing out of this merger."

The editorial workers learned that top business officers were reaping rich rewards as a result of the merger, thanks to the stock incentive program. They were livid. Their reading of the proxy statement told them that Bosee, Spoto, Young, and Matteo had voted themselves large sums of stock in January when they knew that a sale was imminent. Many on the staff to this day voice outrage that the executives had awarded themselves golden parachutes. John Brooks, a *New Yorker* contributor who writes frequently on financial subjects, believes they plied themselves with stock because they knew about the takeover. Brooks is convinced that George Green masterminded the scheme. None of that is accurate. The stock award program was implemented in 1983. Grants went not just to top business executives, but to a total of twenty-six business employees. Under ordinary circumstances, it would have taken each of those employees many years—a lifetime, even—to earn out their shares, because only a small fraction of the number allotted per employee was actually divvied out each year. However, under a "corporate event" clause, the awardees became entitled to their entire grant when Newhouse acquired *The New Yorker*. George Green had forfeited his right to further awards of stock when he left the company one year earlier.

At the last annual meeting, angry editors demanded to know why *they* had not partaken of the bounty. All they had been offered were small portions of stock under the stock purchase plan. They had to *pay* for it. Why not the giant grants? Ken Bosee skirted the issue. He did not want to point the finger at Mr. Shawn. He avoided the truth so long that other executives began to lose patience. Why didn't he *tell* them? Why drag it out? Elaine Matteo became so frustrated she wanted to tear the microphone from Bosee's hands and tell them herself. The editors continued to hurl their questions at the podium, until at last Paul Brodeur demanded to know, "Was the editorial department even asked?"

Bosee finally gave the blunt reply. Management had tried on several occasions to give grants to editorial employees. William Shawn had refused to allow it. The blinding truth finally dawned on some. Many of the editors who would have been most likely to benefit became bitter at Shawn. But others, who likely would not have received grants, endorsed Shawn's refusal to name key employees. Some writers still insist that, as one puts it, "If anyone should have gotten money from the sale, it should have been Shawn." Another asks, "What did *those* people, the *business* people, have to do with the success of the magazine?" In blissful ignorance of things financial, many writers didn't understand the practical realities. They also didn't know that Shawn had once held what would have turned out to be valuable shares. He himself would have been a millionaire had he not sold 2500 shares in 1981, a move influenced by Milton Greenstein, who believed that the stock was overvalued. Those 2500 shares, after stock splits, became 12,500 shares. At the time of the merger, they were worth $2.5 million.

In turn, what the business-side architects of the grant program didn't understand was why, as Elaine Matteo expressed it, the editorial employees hadn't "bitched about the plan in 1983," when it was instituted. After all, the details of the plan were spelled out in the proxy each year.

(If employees had really concentrated on the relative values of who made what in the takeover, they might have been most furious to learn of the remuneration bestowed upon Bill Furth and Abe Blinder. Furth had eaten a deli lunch and made a phone call. Abe Blinder received the call. According to the proxy filed at the time of the acquisition, Newhouse paid Blinder $355,978 for finding the first batch of shares, then a bonus of 1 percent of the price for all additional shares, roughly another $140,000. Furth's compensation is not revealed in the proxy, but he has told acquaintances he received a large fee for his role in the sale.)

Some staff members at the annual meeting demanded reconsideration of the merger. Bosee patiently explained that it was too late. The deal was done. But the truth was too painful to grasp. *The New Yorker* was owned by Advance Publications. They worked for Samuel Irving Newhouse, Jr., now, not the Fleischmanns. It was straight out of Kafka. When the session finally petered to an end, the editorial staff filed listlessly out.

Immediately following the meeting, the board of *The New Yorker* met to elect two new directors, S. I. Newhouse and Steven Florio, both of whom attended the session. Newhouse was "low-key in demeanor," according to one director, "but it was clear that he was the boss." Another director says that Newhouse "looked at his feet and mumbled."

Afterwards, Newhouse, Florio, Ken Bosee, and Elaine Matteo shared a pleasant lunch at the Algonquin. Matteo remembers feeling optimistic about the future.

Ken Bosee was sure enough about his place in the empire to rent his Nantucket house out for the month of August. In a less busy year, he would have planned to use it himself.

Peter Fleischmann, though comfortable in the knowledge that he would stay on as chairman (and, friends report, gleeful at the $200-a-share price), was crushed at the staff's negative reaction to the *New Yorker* sale. Fleischmann was not a callous person. He was a sentimental man. He had always taken an interest in his employees; he had not set out to hurt them. According to Elaine Matteo, "Peter really believed that he was putting *The New Yorker* into loving hands."

19

The following morning, Ken Bosee invited all of the *New Yorker* employees to the sixteenth-floor conference room to meet the new owner and the new publisher. If one were looking for symbolism or irony, one might find both in the fact that this was the business conference room. Until that day, most writers and editors were unacquainted with the geography of the commercial side of *The New Yorker*.

The room was not large enough to accommodate the entire staff—virtually all of whom showed up—so two consecutive sessions were held, each hosted by Bosee. Peter Fleischmann did not attend. Bosee told the first assembly something they already knew: At a meeting the previous day, S. I. Newhouse and Steve Florio were elected directors of The New Yorker Magazine. Turning to Newhouse, Bosee said, "Let them get a look at you, S. I."

There was general nervous laughter, and Newhouse exclaimed, "If I wasn't intimidated by *The New Yorker* before, I am now!"

Newhouse opened his remarks by noting that the occasion

represented only his second speech of "a thirty-five-year-old career." The first, he said, was six months earlier, when the Magazine Publishers Association "dragooned me" into making one. He was on a panel that discussed the role of entrepreneurs in publishing.

"You all have been reading," Newhouse began this second speech, "about the one billion and two billion and three billion acquisitions occurring with increasing frequency as a changing of the guard among media owners. Within that area, the *New Yorker* transaction is relatively small. But what has surprised me and gratified me is that not one of these multibillion transactions has had the attention, created the interest, been as significant to people in the world out there as has been the *New Yorker* transaction. What that says to me is that *The New Yorker* is a magazine, is a concept, is an idea which is of extraordinary importance to the U.S. and to our audience, those who read us and those who don't. Even those who don't read us have an understanding of what the magazine is."

The new owner told his attentive audience that it was "self-evident that *The New Yorker* is *The New Yorker* and it is going to go on being *The New Yorker*. What changes will go on are those that are organic to *The New Yorker*." That, he said, was "common sense."

It was clear that Newhouse's intent was to steady the troops, quell anxieties about what might soon befall them. He said he realized there was still "considerable uncertainty...in the neighborhood of...what happened and what might have happened."

He mentioned Peter Fleischmann's letter to the staff, saying it "gracefully and attractively explained one of the unfortunate facts of life in the world," that it is "very difficult for businesses to pass from generation to generation. Government makes it extremely difficult to preserve business under private ownership or semiprivate as *The New Yorker* was." Newhouse noted, as Fleischmann had in his letter, that a transition to the next generation would make a sale "inevitable at some point."

"We came into the picture totally accidentally," Newhouse explained. He said that the purchase came about as a result of a "two-minute conversation with somebody from Wall Street at an auction." He was referring to Donald Marron. "What then happened took place over a period of time as we became used to each other."

"The fact is," Newhouse added, "that conversation could have been had with any number of other people. That it was with me I think was accidental, but it could have been with any one of fifty people involved with media ownership, any one of whom would have given his right arm to acquire the initial block of New Yorker stock that we acquired and that led eventually to my being here."

The last would have been news to Messinger and Reik, who had found no publishers willing to put up their money, let alone their limbs. As for the description of the impetus for the sale, it would have confused and angered Bill Reik. Newhouse gave Donald Marron credit for getting the ball rolling. He made no reference to the phone call he had received prior to that from Abe Blinder. If Marron had been the catalyst, why, then, did Blinder receive a large finder's fee?

Newhouse expressed his "self-serving" hope that the accident had "worked out best for The New Yorker." He said that many "serious journalistic products are forced to exist under a system of public ownership," but that they pay a price for it that has to do with forced performance and fiduciary responsibilities: "You have to perform or you're in trouble."

According to Newhouse, the New Yorker staff had, for "all of these years... been sheltered from that by an intelligent, enlightened management" whose "priorities [were] that of a private company. We as a private company have a different set of priorities."

It was easier to explain what Advance Publications was not, he continued, than what it was. It was not structured. They did not believe in budgets, elaborate reporting procedures, layered management "with armies of Harvard Business School people analyzing the results of management decisions and criticizing them to management and ownership." They had no home office. The organizational structure was simple, said Newhouse. "My brother and I share ownership and share responsibility. Each deals personally and directly with different parts of the organization." He and Donald, he said, were "sensitive to whatever we learn." It was not "an organization with a great deal of structure and form and ritual."

What could *The New Yorker* expect from Advance? "Well, I don't know," he said, and his audience laughed skittishly. "Each time we become familiar with a company that comes into our lives, it's like inventing the wheel all over again." But, he added, Advance was "very people-oriented... more sensitive to human values than to the bottom line" and "very much involved in the quality of what we publish." With that, he introduced the new publisher, Steve Florio. Newhouse explained that when he knew that *The New Yorker* was going to be "a reality," he decided to choose as publisher someone he had worked with before, and with whom he was comfortable. He had opted for Steve Florio, "the most dynamic young executive I've had at Condé Nast. He has a background of research, marketing, advertising. He has the intelligence to go into the other areas and enough familiarity with production and circulation so that he will not find himself at sea in these areas."

Florio, he added, had asked his—S. I.'s—young cousin Jonathan Newhouse to come on board as business manager. Jonathan had worked for more than five years at Condé Nast. Steve and Jonathan will be "our presence here," Newhouse explained. He said that in a very short time, the distinction between the new and the old "presences" would disappear, and that "it will be natural." He said that the new men would be "very much a part of your team."

Ken Bosee, standing to the side with a smile on his face, looked confident, but with no good reason. He might have wondered how he would fit in. He was president, but that title had carried with it the role of publisher. Could he and Florio perform their duties without bumping into one another? And what of Elaine Matteo? She was treasurer, but she had always thought she would be more appropriately dubbed general manager. What duties could Jonathan Newhouse, as business manager, assume that she wasn't handling already? Newhouse ended his remarks on a comic note. "I was quite disturbed," he said, "at a rumor that came across my desk today that at the board meeting, I had proposed that *The New Yorker* follow my own work schedule." He was referring to his famous 4:00 A.M. arrivals at the office, his weekend forays. "It really isn't true!" he exclaimed. His audience laughed merrily.

Now it was Steve Florio's turn. Florio, a New Yorker by birth, was a graduate of New York University. His first job in publishing was selling space for *Esquire.* In 1979 he moved to Condé Nast to become publisher of *Gentleman's Quarterly,* where he presided over a turnaround. Florio is a tall, burly man ("barrel-chested" is the description he prefers) with a bushy mustache. He was Mutt to the diminutive S. I. and Jonathan Newhouse's Jeffs. Florio's attempts at humor in front of the *New Yorker* audience fell flatter than Newhouse's. He began by saying that when Newhouse asked him to take the job of publisher of GQ and later offered him the same title at *The New Yorker,* he had thought to himself, "This guy Newhouse has got a hell of a training program for a young guy!"

The remark jolted many listeners. Former European sales head Luis Dominguez recalls being astounded at its "arrogance." Florio seemed to be saying that *The New Yorker* was one more rung on his climb to the top. There were many people in that room who would have considered the position the pinnacle of their careers.

Florio went on to say, "I am glad to hear I can sleep late from now on!"

Silence.

The new publisher told the employees that he had sat where

they were twice, when he lived to tell the tale of two changes of ownership at *Esquire* magazine. While he was there, the magazine was bought by Clay Felker, and that, he said, was a pleasant experience, even though "the noble experiment of *Esquire* fortnightly didn't work." Felker, who had previously lost control of *New York* magazine to Rupert Murdoch, had gone on to buy the once illustrious *Esquire* monthly and turn it into a biweekly. The new *Esquire* was not successful. It was sold to the 13-30 Corporation of Knoxville, Tennessee.

Founded by three young University of Tennessee graduates, Philip Moffit, Christopher Whittle, and Wilma Jordan, 13-30 had specialized in limited-circulation magazines aimed at college students. The *Esquire* purchase represented their plunge into big-time national publishing. Florio did not recall his 13-30 days kindly, because when Moffit and Whittle arrived, he said, they made it clear that "everybody that had been there for so many years had been doing it wrong. Everyone's professionalism was discounted." Anxiety had built, he continued, and those who weren't "bounced" searched for other jobs.

"Having that experience, both ways, taught me a big lesson," continued Florio. "S. I. and I have talked about this a lot. This is a great organization and I know it's a great organization and I am humbled, believe me, to have this job at this age." (Another jolt. Why the continued emphasis on age? Was he saying that it would not have been a great job at a *more advanced* age?) "I'm also challenged by it and I'll get into it. But rest assured that I will be learning a lot more from you for the first bit than you will be learning from me. I obviously respect this group.... You are a great team. You have had an incredible success here. And I hope that I can make a contribution here as well in the coming years."

He closed with more humor: "Incidentally, anybody from the Harvard Business School does not have to resign." More silence. Florio invited questions from the floor. An awkward silence followed. A voice said, "They're all shy." No one spoke up. There were countless questions, of course, but they went unspoken. The meeting ended.

In the second session, for the staff that didn't get into the first, Newhouse and Florio seemed more relaxed; their remarks were breezier. Ken Bosee opened by telling Newhouse that his talk didn't count as a "public appearance" because he was "talking to family now." Bosee told the staff that he was disappointed that there had been no questions at the previous meeting. He hoped there would be more this time, so that Newhouse didn't think he had "acquired a magazine of tongue-tied people."

Despite Bosee's familial assurances, Newhouse stuck to his script. He called this his "third public speech." Once again he extemporized about other media activity, how other stories were just "headlines for a day," but *The New Yorker* was special. He seemed to pick up Bosee's theme when he said that even those who didn't read *The New Yorker* "think of it a little bit like family." He explained that Advance had come into the picture accidentally as a result of a passing conversation he had had with "a Wall Street type." He went on to say that a serious magazine should not consider return on investment or profitability its first priority. If it does, he said, "someone's in big trouble, either *The New Yorker* or the person whose responsibility it is to perform." None of his properties had an annual budget, he noted. There were no layers of management. He told of the structure, of himself and his brother, and how they never expanded beyond the point where they could "handle things personally." Advance continued "to have something of the character of a small business," he said. They tried to keep up with modern techniques, but they didn't try to impose their preconceptions on "anyone that we're not involved with."

He promised the staff that they were not going to be "presented with some new way of working. It just isn't going to happen. Life will go on, *The New Yorker* will go on, and I hope you will all be as pleased with the relationship as you are now," he said.

He then described Steve Florio's "sterling career" at Condé Nast. He called Jonathan Newhouse "very very sound and very very smart and unprepossessing."

Florio came forward and began again with his "hell of a training program" remark. Apparently it wasn't a slip of the tongue the first time. He launched into the *Esquire* story, told how he had "sat where you are. Twice. [Gone through] the agony of waiting for new owners to show up. Twice. We all talked about what we were gonna do. Twice. It was awful. Twice." Silence.

He compared the different management styles of Clay Felker and the "bunch of guys from Knoxville" who acted as if "everything that had been done for forty years was wrong. Everything that we had thought of as good solid management practice wasn't."

He had learned, he said, "that the last thing you want to do is louse it up by coming with a broadsword approach to management. This is not my style at all."

Bosee again invited questions from the staff. This time some were forthcoming. Someone asked Newhouse why he wanted to own *The New Yorker*. He mentioned its "glorious" past and "glorious" future. What would happen to *Vanity Fair?* another employee wondered. There had been wide speculation in the industry and in the press that now that he owned *The New Yorker*, Newhouse would close *Vanity Fair*, which had yet to stumble to its feet. Ads and circulation were still declining.

"You mean you don't want Jerry Hall on the cover of *The New Yorker?*" Newhouse joked, referring to the blond Texas model—Mick Jagger's girlfriend—posed languidly in a towel on the cover of the *Vanity Fair* then on newsstands. *Vanity Fair* worried the *New Yorker* staff. The magazine had been revived as a means of capturing some of the *New Yorker*'s business. It had originally been billed as a serious journal, but more recently it was short on the esoteric and long on glitz and gossip. Would *The New Yorker* be similarly transmogrified?

Newhouse assured the staff that there would be no connection between *any* Condé Nast magazine and *The New Yorker*, "no intermingling of functions." He had heard the speculation about what the *New Yorker* purchase might mean to *Vanity Fair* and vice versa; people were "barking up the wrong tree." While noting that *Vanity Fair* as a publication had "quite a checkered career," Newhouse explained that it had recently become "hot" in circulation, and that its new editor, Tina Brown, had "found a voice for the magazine that is working." He was willing to be patient and professed "great expectations."

In response to a query about change at *The New Yorker*, Newhouse said that he would think "long and hard before altering any of the traditional practices of *The New Yorker*. It will not be done in any kind of casual way."

When the gathering broke up, the staff exited quietly. It was not Newhouse's fault that few of them found solace in his remarks. Some hoped that the new ownership would prove beneficial to *The New Yorker*. Others even welcomed the intrusion. A number of staff members, on both the business and editorial sides, had become impatient with lack of change, lack of movement, lack of growth. To many, *The New Yorker* had become a static thing. But even so, the Fleischmann family was the devil they knew, S. I. Newhouse the devil they didn't. Their worries were not confined to business and editorial considerations—although there were plenty of those. They applied, as well, to the character of the men they now would be working for.

Steve Florio, for all of his successes at Condé Nast, had acquired a reputation among some peers summed up by one former associate as: "Don't trust him." Many people felt that his ambitions were heartier than his scruples. When Florio left *GQ*, the staff threw a going-away party. In a skit with a "lying" theme,

Florio was depicted as Pinocchio. Every time someone asked him a question, he would lie and his nose would lengthen.

S. I. Newhouse was the unknown man. He occasionally prowled the halls at Condé Nast on his way to the office of some editor in chief, but the rank and file had little contact with him. One assistant editor recalls that she used to see him regularly in the elevator, where they would share a ride in silence. One morning, she was startled when Newhouse turned to her and asked, "Do you like your job?" "Why, yes!" she replied enthusiastically. Newhouse pivoted once more and faced the doors. The ride continued in silence.

His work habits are widely reported and thus were well known to the *New Yorker* staff. He is in his office by four in the morning. He often schedules meetings for 6:00 A.M. He eats lunch most days at the center booth at the Four Seasons. He goes home at 3:00 P.M. to read and exercise. He is not an avid socializer. His handsomer younger brother, Donald, is more affable and at ease with people.

Newhouse is not much different, in his office remoteness, from heads of other large corporations. Chains of command define a separation between the men at the top and the workers in the middle or at the bottom. But in Newhouse's case, the distance is lengthened by the publisher's reluctance to speak. There are no pep talks to the staff, not even a memo at Christmas. There are no personal interviews in papers to give hints about the man.

Newhouse rarely gave interviews to the press. In refusing to talk to *Fortune* editor Carol Loomis in 1987 he said, "My brother and I feel this goes against all our principles." It was an extraordinary statement coming from a man whose fortune had been built on the press and on people talking to *his* reporters. It revealed an odd set of principles.

The remark seems consistent with his personality. Many who know him offer, in describing him, the fact that he rarely looks anyone in the eye. It seems to make him uncomfortable. He is occasionally described as shy and introverted. He is also described as someone whose gaze strays over your shoulder when he is speaking to you at a cocktail party, as if to determine whether there is anyone more important in view. Newhouse lives with his second wife, Victoria, in their modern Upper East Side town house, though he lived in an apartment in the expensive and equally modern United Nations Plaza during a renovation of his house that took over a year. He has two sons and a daughter by his first wife. While he serves on the prestigious board of the Museum of Modern Art, he is not known as a generous philanthropist. Some employees who have worked closely with him say that he tends to be negative about others' ideas, and that once he has gotten an idea fixed in his mind, it is difficult to dislodge it with any argument, no matter how reasonable. But others counter that if he likes the job you are doing, he leaves you alone.

At the time the Newhouses bought *The New Yorker*, their company, Advance Publications, was the focus of two federal investigations. In the first, the Internal Revenue Service lodged against the Newhouse family the biggest estate tax claim in its history. The Feds contended that the Newhouse brothers underpaid the government by $609 million in taxes on the estate of their father, who had died in 1979. (S. I. Newhouse obviously knew whereof he spoke when discussing problems of estate taxes with the assembled *New Yorker* employees.) The Newhouses valued the estate at $90.9 million. The IRS said it was worth $1.23 billion. The IRS called the Newhouse return "frivolous" and sought to impose a fine of $305 million for alleged fraud in the case. The government charged that the underpayment was not an accident, or a misinterpretation, or even a case of reasonable men agreeing to disagree. They claim that the Newhouses consciously underpaid. The family termed the fraud charge "outrageous," but as of mid-1988, no settlement had been reached.

Perhaps more potentially mutilating to the Newhouse reputation at the time he bought *The New Yorker* was the federal investigation in Cleveland into claims that S. I. Newhouse conspired with Joseph E. Cole, publisher of the *Cleveland Press*, to close the daily, leaving the city, the twelfth largest newspaper market, wide open for monopoly by the Newhouse-owned *Cleveland Plain Dealer*. Newhouse and Cole, if indicted and convicted, would have faced jail terms of three years and fines of up to $100,000.

Joseph Cole had bought the paper for $1 million from E. W. Scripps in October 1981. He assured readers of his commitment to keeping Cleveland a two-paper town. But abruptly, without warning, he stopped the presses. The front page of the last issue, dated June 17, 1982, bore a photo of Cole's gray eminence next to an article entitled "'We gave it our best'—Joseph Cole." Cole revealed that he had sold the paper's subscription list to Newhouse, but for what amount, he wouldn't disclose. It was later revealed that Newhouse had paid $14.5 million for the list even though, according to U. S. District Judge Ann Aldrich, who presided over a related civil case against Cole, its value was "negligible or nonexistent." Newspaper industry analysts testified that the surviving paper in a formerly two-paper town rarely buys the subscription list of the defunct journal because most readers will automatically switch allegiances, since there is no longer a choice. Sources at the *Plain Dealer* told a *Business Week* reporter that they didn't even see the subscription list until two weeks after the *Press* went under. The experts said that by then, readers would already have gravitated to the *Plain Dealer*.

Newhouse also paid Cole $8 million for a subsidiary that published a shoppers' guide that Judge Aldrich called a "newly formed, debt-ridden entity" that had been created only months before with capital of $500. (By breaking up the payments that way, Advance avoided having to wait for Hart-Scott-Rodino clearance, required only when the sum paid exceeded $15 million.) In total, Cole received $22.5 million for properties he had paid $1 million for eight months earlier. That civil suit against Cole was dismissed for technical reasons, but Judge Aldrich encouraged the government to pursue the charges when she wrote: "The record is replete with facts from which a jury could conclude that Plain Dealer, Press Publishing, and Cole conspired together in restraint of trade...."

In the government case, an important witness was John R. Malone, a newspaper broker who, on behalf of a group of investors, tried to buy the *Press* with the intent of keeping it publishing. He claimed that when he tried to contact Cole, the publisher, knowing what he sought, avoided him. He finally reached him the day the paper was sold and offered $7 million for it. According to Malone, Cole said the subscription list was already sold. Malone countered that he didn't *care* about the subscription list, he wanted the *paper*. Cole said, "It's all gone, it's all sold," according to Malone.

A month after the *Press* closed, Malone and his group were at last granted a tour of the paper's plant. There they encountered devastation—equipment was dismantled, wires were ripped from walls, machinery was useless. Malone told *Business Week*: "It occurred to us that the plant was made absolutely inoperative so that there could be no continuing operations there. We finally came to the conclusion that there was no way we were going to be able to buy anything."

The obvious inference was that Newhouse was not interested in the *Press*'s subscription list, or in its shopper, but instead in paying vast sums to ensure that the paper would not publish again. The methods Newhouse was alleged to have employed were eerily similar to those reported to have been used by his late father. The same month of May that S. I. Newhouse stood before a wary audience in a conference room at *The New Yorker*, he sat for a week in a grand jury room in Cleveland, testifying in the case that could lead to his criminal indictment. It did not. In a move that stunned many of the reporters who covered the proceedings, the Justice Department announced in June 1987 that it had "insufficient evidence to proceed" with the case.

The *New Yorker* staff also could not help but note that there were major fundamental differences between the way Condé Nast operated and the way *The New Yorker* did. That wasn't surprising, and didn't put Condé Nast in exclusive company. *Everybody* in publishing operated differently from *The New Yorker*.

Advance Publications, for all of Newhouse's protestations, is a modern, efficient, practical company. Arguably, *The New Yorker* could stand to have a bit of the twentieth century rubbed off on it. But while many caring observers agreed that *The New Yorker* needed updating, both editorially and in business, almost nobody wanted to see the essential character changed. A close look at the way Advance and Condé Nast operated provided convincing reasons to believe that it would.

Many—if not most—of the Advance newspapers, while prosperous, are held in low editorial esteem. In an article published after Newhouse bought *The New Yorker*, the *Columbia Journalism Review* called them "a whole herd of bland newspapers, cash cows in a pasture, dutifully generating revenue for the next acquisition." Richard Meeker, a biographer of Newhouse, Jr., believes that the patriarch "began his life in newspapers with one goal—to accumulate capital... unaffected by the romance of journalism or by its element of public service...."

There is an unevenness to editorial product throughout the Newhouse enterprises, magazines included, which can probably be attributed to the company's willingness to tailor the editorial product to current trends and potential bottom line. Despite Newhouse assertions to the contrary, there often seems to be a "hurry up and perform" approach to individuals and publications. It is true that Newhouse gave Tina Brown and her incarnation of *Vanity Fair* time for the magazine to find itself, but nevertheless, in the first years of the publication's life, as noted, he fired two publishers and two editors before handing the reins to G. Douglas Johnston and Tina Brown. When the first editorial product didn't pan out, the formula was changed.

At *House & Garden*, as mentioned earlier, circulation was slashed, the price hiked, and the content transformed, all largely in the name of demographics and a stronger bottom line. The new formula seemed to work for a time, but then it stopped working. Advertising and sales flattened out. Later, in the fall of 1987, Newhouse replaced editor Louis Oliver Gropp with Anna Wintour, previously editor of British *Vogue*, in hopes of finding a *newer* new *House & Garden*. Newhouse handled the personnel transaction in what was becoming a characteristically insensitive way: Gropp was away on vacation when word got to him that he was no longer employed. The gossip in publishing was that Wintour called Newhouse and told him she had received an offer to be editor of *Elle*. (Another version has it as *Harper's Bazaar*.) Allegedly she told him that unless he found her a spot in New York *fast*, she would leave Condé Nast. Gropp was out and Wintour was in.

House & Garden became *HG*, and because of its new emphasis on clothes and socialites, industry wags took to calling it "House and Garment" and "Vanity Chair."

But the saga goes on. *HG*, under Wintour, was not a success. In July 1988, Wintour, thirty-eight, was reassigned. Newhouse made her editor of *Vogue*, thus rewarding her with one of the most coveted jobs in publishing. Again, the reshuffling was handled badly. Wintour replaced Grace Mirabella, who had spent thirty-seven years at *Vogue*, seventeen of them as editor. Mirabella learned she was to be fired from a friend who heard it reported by Liz Smith on WNBC-TV's "Live at Five" program. But this is getting ahead of the story. These events had not taken place when Newhouse bought *The New Yorker*.

When Newhouse bought the men's fashion monthly *Gentlemen's Quarterly* in 1981, the magazine labored under the perception that it was edited by and for gay men. Newhouse was determined to target it at a large, heterosexual audience. According to publishing sources, Newhouse instructed the editor to pose more women with the men in the fashion spreads. Female models began to appear more frequently, but most of them resembled young boys. The editor was fired and replaced by Arthur Cooper, a former *Penthouse* editor. With Cooper as editor and Steven Florio as advertising director, GQ proved a winner by every definition. It was well written, it ran interesting, timely stories and attractive fashion layouts (making liberal use of "real" women), and it became a circulation and advertising success. In the five years between 1979 and 1985, circulation rose from 250,000 to 700,000, and ad pages from 900 pages a year to 1930. The new GQ is a better magazine than the old, and thus a tribute to the Newhouse boys.

But the Newhouses cannot be said to be devoted to the notion of quality for its own sake. In magazines, as in newspapers, they have proved willing to *lower* their standards to better serve the bottom line. When the company transmogrified *Mademoiselle* magazine in the early eighties, quality was sacrificed and old readers were deserted. The editor of *Mademoiselle* from 1937 to 1971 was Betsy Talbot Blackwell, a "lady," under the old definition of the word, who took a white-gloves approach to fashion and beauty that was reflected in her magazine. She was succeeded by Edith Raymond Locke, a refugee, as a child, from Nazi Austria who rose through the ranks at *Mademoiselle* and went on to shepherd it through the new feminist era of the seventies and into the eighties as a fashionable yet aware monthly for educated women from eighteen to thirty-five.

Mademoiselle's thrust through the years was reflected in the fact that it boasted a separate department called "College and Careers." Among the monthly's more distinctive features was a yearly guest editor program. Participants, who had won a competition based on writing or artistic ability, worked in the magazine's office for a summer. (The guest editors' program was immortalized in the late writer Sylvia Plath's book *The Bell Jar*.)

Another of *Mademoiselle*'s attributes was fine fiction. Truman Capote and Joyce Carol Oates were just two of the writers who contributed short stories. *Mademoiselle* was often the first to publish writers who later found greater renown. The magazine encouraged young authors-to-be with an annual fiction contest.

Enter the eighties. In 1980, "Edie" Locke was summarily dismissed and replaced by Amy Levin (wife, incidentally, of *GQ*'s Arthur Cooper). The staff was overwhelmed by the immediate culture shock. Edie Locke wore fashionable yet classic Anne Klein clothing and armloads of jangling silver jewelry. Amy Levin appeared in a jumpsuit, wearing silver nail polish, frizzed-out hair, and colorful plastic shoes with ankle socks. Levin's mission was soon evident. The average age of the magazine's reader was notched down considerably, as were her educational stats. Condé Nast had studied its circulation figures and ad rates, compared them with those of the thriving *Cosmopolitan* magazine, and found them wanting. *Cosmo* was luring more readers via secretaries' desks, not students'. Secretaries spent more. *Mademoiselle* went after them.

Photos of career girls on the climb were soon replaced by ones of models perched on toilets, their panties resting around their ankles. A new binding and different paper gave *Mademoiselle* a more accessible—some might say cheaper—look. And then there were the articles. Colleges and careers were not what the new *Mademoiselle* was about. One former editor recalls a meeting at which an agitated Amy Levin brandished a copy of *Esquire* that carried an article on vibrators, and demanded to know why none of her staff ever came up with ideas like that. Months later, the cover of *Mademoiselle* heralded an article called "Vibrators: Today's Love Toy." Thank heavens Betsy Talbot Blackwell hadn't lived to see it.

For a time the formula worked. It sold ads and lured in readers. They were not old readers, naturally. *Mademoiselle* editors explained to their writers that their reader was younger than *Glamour*'s (in the past it had been exactly the other way around) and that she was less educated.

In 1985, the numbers began to slacken. The publishing rumor mills churned out stories that a worried S. I. Newhouse told Levin to tone it down a bit. For a time, vibrator stories disappeared, though "Fifty Ways to Leave Your Lover"–type how-to's continued to abound. But if indeed Newhouse had urged such a reversal, the results of his dictum seemed short-lived. The March 1988 issue carried an article called "Beyond Promiscuous: The Secret Life of a Sex Addict ('Her friends know her as shy. What they don't know is that she can't face the world without a steady supply of sex')" and another called "You Can Love These Guys... or Turn the Page." It began:

> "So what are we talking about here...sperm or semen?"
> "Both."
> "Oh, sperm and semen?"
> "Or spunk and spooey?"
> One has only to see them to love them.
> "Spooey or spoody?"
> Pad o'Guys! Imagine them running through the maidens of Hollywood till there remains not a lady left fit for carnal copulation!

Clearly, sensationalism is still prized at Condé Nast if it gets results on the bottom line. A controversial 1986 fashion layout in *Vogue* depicted a woman entwined with her lover while her baby, in the same room, cried, and her husband looked on from the doorway.

In late 1987, Condé Nast seemed to make an effort to make

its British magazine *Tatler* more visible to an American audience. On the cover of the October 1987 issue, one of the first to be splashed across newsstands, was a model wearing a large bow hat and long black gloves, and nothing else from the waist up. One arm artfully covered her right breast. Her left nipple was prominently displayed. It could easily have passed for the cover of *Penthouse*.

A second vital difference between *The New Yorker* and Condé Nast was that at Condé Nast, the wall between editorial and advertising was made not of steel but of something more akin to silk tulle. *Glamour* readers who wonder why the lipstick the model wears on the cover never appears the same color on their own lips might be surprised to learn that it's not just because the model is gorgeous but because the shade is not what it is reported to be. The makeup artist attending to that month's cover girl will pull from his or her kit whatever looks good. The beauty department then attributes the product, in the magazine text, to an advertiser who has bought a lot of pages that month, or one whose business the ad department hopes to land. The credits enter the realm of the absurd when they mention the perfume the model is wearing. Condé Nast is far from alone in doling out such credits. It is standard practice among fashion magazines. But it would be unthinkable for a *New Yorker* writer to tout a product as a favor to a client. In fact, ornery writers often did the opposite—dumped on a major advertiser.

For all of the criticisms that have been leveled at *The New Yorker* over the years, it has rarely been said of it that it displayed anything less than total integrity. When it *was* said, a media event was made of it. That such lapses drew so much attention was testament to how rarely they occurred.

20

The day after Newhouse and Florio delivered their message to the troops, Janet Muir resigned to join *Esquire* magazine, owned by the 13-30 Corporation, which Florio had spoken so ill of. Muir's job at *The New Yorker*, before the sale to Newhouse, was to analyze possible new investments. She doubted that Newhouse would require her services for that. The way she saw it, her job was now redundant. On several occasions, she asked Bosee to ask Newhouse if there was a place for her in the organization. When weeks had gone by with no report from Bosee, Muir quit.

After she resigned, Newhouse phoned her and said, "Ken told me about you. We should have talked, but I hear you've resigned so let's leave it at that."

Muir replied that she would be happy to leave it at that, but that she would like to brief somebody at Advance on the status of the *New Yorker*'s investments. She was the person who had most closely tracked them. Newhouse said, "Come right over." Muir walked the few blocks to the Condé Nast building and met with Newhouse, "a very nice, very lovely man." Muir was a confident young woman, then thirty-two, *The New Yorker*'s preeminent yuppie on the fast track. She did not feel intimidated by S. I. Newhouse, and while she had desperately wished, months earlier, that he wouldn't buy *The New Yorker*, she communicated no such sentiment to him now. She sketched the history and prospects of *Cook's*, *Horticulture*, Princeton Polychrome, Drever, and the other properties. Newhouse seemed quite interested. Muir returned to her office and packed up her things. She found it a wrenching experience. "Nowhere else is like working for *The New Yorker*," she says.

Newhouse moved quickly to dispose of the *New Yorker* investments. Jonathan Newhouse called David Johnson, the president of Princeton Polychrome, and made him an offer to break the new contract with *The New Yorker*. Johnson readily agreed. Elliot Wadsworth, the editor of *Horticulture*, phoned Newhouse and told him he wanted to buy the magazine. An agreement was soon cut. *Cook's* was put up for sale. It took a while, but eventually, it sold to a Swedish company at a large profit. Teleram, through no fault of Newhouse or Florio, went bankrupt six weeks after Advance bought *The New Yorker*.

The *New Yorker*'s stake in Drever, the Colorado furniture maker, was put on the block. There were no immediate takers. Raven, the publisher of medical textbooks, sold quickly, to a Dutch concern, for $12 million. The *New Yorker*'s 38 percent of Raven was worth $4.6 million in the transaction. "It was a good divestiture," says Florio, with interesting emphasis. Some might have called it a good investment, since *The New Yorker* had paid just $1 million three years earlier. The profit, of course, went to Advance. The only property Newhouse decided to keep was Boulder Enterprise, the Colorado printing forms company.

After Janet Muir left *The New Yorker*, Steve Florio called her and invited her to lunch at the Four Seasons. He tried to persuade her to return to the fold. At the restaurant, they ran into S. I. Newhouse, who, when finished dining at his accustomed booth in the Grill Room, stopped by their table to say hello.

"I'm just trying to get her back," Florio told Newhouse jocularly. Florio plied Muir with assurances that *The New Yorker* would be making some investments of its own; she could work on those. "It didn't make sense to me," says Muir, who declined. And indeed, *The New Yorker* did not again make any investments.

Ken Bosee departed under less amicable circumstances. An executive still at *The New Yorker* tells a story about a man who was hired by Condé Nast and assumed his post, only to learn that there was a fellow whom he had not previously met who bore a title that would have made him the newcomer's boss. The recent hire went to his ultimate boss and said, "Who's he? Do I have to report to him?" The hireling was told, "Don't worry about it. He's been here for a hundred years. He's not a factor." The clear message was that the man was no longer useful, but was allowed to hang around. It could be called a kind approach on Newhouse's part, but kindness is often in the eyes of the receiver.

"If Ken Bosee and Peter Fleischmann had been content to come in late every day, read the paper, go to lunch, read the paper again, and go home," says *New Yorker* comptroller Stu Jason, "they could have had their jobs as long as they wanted." It took Bosee only a couple of weeks to discover that he couldn't be content with that sort of daily routine.

Within days of Florio's arrival, it became clear to Bosee that he was now president in title only. He had been silently stripped of most of his duties, which were now being carried out by Florio. That Florio was in charge was evident in the extreme. Florio had access to Newhouse that didn't exist for Bosee. For several weeks after the merger, at four-thirty every morning, a Newhouse limousine would pick Florio and Jonathan Newhouse up at their

305

homes on Long Island, then drive them through the Midtown Tunnel into Manhattan and deposit them at 350 Madison Avenue for a daily 6:00 A.M. meeting with the boss. Bosee never met with Newhouse.

Bosee had a loftier title than Florio, but Florio didn't intend to report to him. On several occasions, Florio reversed decisions made by Bosee without first consulting the president. It bothered Bosee. He says that there was no one event that irked him, but instead "multiple events." He decided to complain to Newhouse after learning that a video promotion he had put a lot of time and effort into had been canceled by Florio. Bosee got the news through the grapevine at an advertising meeting in Florida.

Bosee trekked over to 350 Madison to pay a call on S. I. "If I'm president of *The New Yorker*," he said to the Advance chairman, "I ought to know what's going on."

"In effect," says Bosee, "S. I. told me that I wasn't *going* to know what's going on. So in effect I was out." Bosee "resigned" June 1, three weeks after Newhouse had become the official owner of *The New Yorker*.

Peter Fleischmann threw a farewell party for the departing president at his apartment. Steve Florio didn't attend, but Jonathan and S. I. Newhouse both did. Bosee was in a festive mood and seemed happy. He had owned a lot of stock, so the *New Yorker* sale provided him with a soft financial cushion on which to retire. He ended his career at the company with the exalted title of president. That would look good on any retirement résumé. He received the benefits that were due him, one year's severance pay and one year's use of a *New Yorker* car. But Bosee nevertheless felt cast aside, and he wondered why Newhouse couldn't have waited the six months until his scheduled retirement to dispose of him.

Newhouse circulated among the party guests asking probing questions of members of *The New Yorker* ad sales staff, "as if he was appraising everyone," recalls a partygoer. Ad director Bob Young remembers the evening best for a haunting line that passed from Jonathan Newhouse's lips. Referring to himself, his cousin S. I., and Florio, the younger Newhouse told Young: "There's nothing wrong with *The New Yorker* that *we* can't fix."

Two weeks later, on June 17, S. I. Newhouse named publisher Steven Florio to the additional post of president of *The New Yorker*. Jonathan Newhouse was named executive vice president, the title that had been created for Florio only one month earlier. The Newhouse cousin retained the title of business manager.

Over the next several weeks, the bodies began dropping on Forty-third Street. It had been mere months since S. I. Newhouse had put his name to a merger agreement that contained, among others, these pledges: "Advance states... that it desires the continuation of the present directors, officers, editors, employees and contributors... and that there be no change in the Company's organization as a result of the Merger.... Advance wishes to preserve [the] quality of The New Yorker through maintaining its personnel and its traditions."

It had been only weeks since Florio had stood in front of the *New Yorker* staff and assured them that "the last thing" he wanted to do was "louse it up by coming with a broadsword approach to management. This is not my style at all." He did not take a broadsword approach. He chose another metaphor when he told a reporter, "I just blew it out of here with a fire hose."

Florio fired twenty-five advertising people within a year. That number represented most of the old staff. In October 1985, he ousted ad chief Bob Young and replaced him with Mike Trainor, whom he brought in from *Esquire*. Within six months, in March 1986, he canned Trainor and put in his place veteran *New Yorker* adman Owen Hochreiter. Hochreiter had earned the enmity of many of his old colleagues with what some saw as his friendship-

and-history-be-damned politics. After the sale to Newhouse, Hochreiter, according to former associates, immediately began to criticize the old regime to the new one. When he became ad director, he presided over the firing of people who had once toiled beside him. But Hochreiter, too, would feel the cold edge of the blade—or the cold sting of the fire hose, to borrow Florio's terminology. Florio fired him the Friday before Christmas, 1986.

In a conversation with me, Florio seemed almost gleeful in his descriptions of the ousters. He did not make diplomatic remarks like "They were all good people but these things are bound to happen." Instead, he said that the story of The New Yorker "in a nutshell" was "We fired everybody, hired new people."

Florio said that when he arrived at The New Yorker, he didn't realize how bad it would be, and therefore he didn't expect to make so many "personnel changes." He described a turning point: "I literally had someone in my office who was making $100,000 a year. I asked him what he did. He said, 'Everybody knows what I do.' I said, 'Humor me, I'm new around here. What do you do?' He said, 'I network.' I said, 'Do you have a territory?' He said, 'Not really.' I said, 'Do you have your own accounts?' He said, 'Not really.' He came in here at ten. He left and played squash."

He was fired, of course.

Newhouse himself dispensed with the directors, even though he had promised to retain the board intact. They had believed him when he said it, which made them feel pretty naïve and silly afterwards. "All amiability fell off as soon as the deal was done," says Walter Curley.

Two other departures are best mentioned here.

The day that Steve Florio moved in at The New Yorker, Peter Fleischmann, a few doors down the hall, became, to his profound sadness, a man in isolation. Employees jostling to be accepted by the new regime disassociated themselves from the old one. Peter Fleischmann was overnight a pariah. It was harsh enough that his title of chairman became an empty one. Florio consulted him no more often than he did Bosee. But it was worse that many of Fleischmann's former associates dropped out of his life. There were few visitors to his office, with the exceptions of Elaine Matteo, ad director Bob Young (before he himself was excused from duty), Stu Jason, and Sam Spoto, he of Sam's Club, that relic of the good old days. But for them, Fleischmann sat alone in his office on the days he came in.

In mid-January 1986, reacting not to direct pressure from the Newhouse interests but to the pressure that comes from feeling useless, Peter F. Fleischmann announced that he intended to resign as chairman of *The New Yorker*. Two weeks later he was gone.

The end came for Elaine Matteo four months later. Matteo had always been a plugger, a person who believed you could get what you wanted if you tried hard enough. Those traits helped her ascend from a secretary's desk to the treasurer's post. They aided her in adapting to the new management.

Florio, when he became publisher and then president, allowed a certain insecurity to permeate the air. (It would have been hard to avoid, given the number of dismissals.) He employed a sports vocabulary to describe the test of success at the new *New Yorker*. In late 1985 he told employees, "Anyone who makes it to the sales meeting in February is on my team," meaning, if you lasted until then, you were in. Matteo lasted that long and went to the annual sales outing, held in Boca Raton, Florida. Matteo hadn't felt overly anxious, anyway. She had been working diligently—effectively, she thought. Just a few months earlier, in October, she had been rewarded with a vice presidency. S. I. Newhouse himself wrote her a letter of commendation. In late April 1986, Steve Florio called Matteo to his office to tell her what a great job she had been doing, how valuable an employee she was. She left feeling pleased and even a little secure. Two weeks later, Florio fired her.

Matteo did not believe that Florio intended to fire her when he praised her. Instead, it was apparent to her that she had been fired so that Jonathan Newhouse could obtain more room in which to maneuver. Florio told Matteo, "You and Jonathan are tripping all over each other, and his last name is Newhouse."

Matteo spent the next several days after her dismissal sorting through papers and finishing odd bits of business. Steve Florio dropped by frequently to see how she was doing. Jonathan Newhouse ignored her. One afternoon, Matteo entered the elevator as Newhouse exited. He looked pointedly away.

Matteo, like a number of other employees, was granted a one-year settlement, contingent on her signing a so-called "good-boy" agreement promising to say nothing negative about the Newhouses, Advance, or any of its employees for the next twelve months.

The first person Matteo went to with news of her firing was William Shawn. Shawn wept when she told him. Matteo will not reveal the content of their discussion, except to say that Shawn was wonderfully warm and caring. Another person says that Shawn commented that Matteo had been the last line of resistance. Now, there was only one person left from the old order: him. He wondered when his turn would come.

Steve Florio's style was quite different from that of either Ken Bosee or George Green. Some co-workers had previously complained that Green was too brash and aggressive. They hadn't seen anything yet. Florio was big in every sense—a big, bulky man, a big spender, a big tipper, and a big talker. His ways were showy. The license plates on his BMW read "MAGAZINE."

A couple of weeks after Florio arrived at The New Yorker, an anonymous staffer deposited on his desk a cartoon depicting two

Harvard Club–type oldsters peering at a door on which is written, "Publisher, New Yorker." One man says to the other, "My God, Buffy, he's Italian." Florio perceived the "gift" as an ethnic slur. Its intent, he says, was to remind him that his "parents" (*sic*) hadn't come over on the *Mayflower*. Florio claims he was not offended, though, and had the cartoon framed and hung on his office wall. He often mentions it in conversation.

Cartoons that seemed to poke gentle fun at the new owner and manager began to appear in the pages of *The New Yorker* not long after the sale. One that ran in July 1985 showed a bunch of stodgy-looking businessmen gathered around a conference table. One is extending his arms toward another, more reluctant-seeming one, and saying, "Now that the merger is completed, Stahlmeyer, how's about a hug?" The editorial department could afford in the very beginning to take the merger lightly. The Huns were not yet at the gates of the eighteenth and nineteenth floors.

Mr. Shawn and S. I. Newhouse didn't do any hugging, but they did frequently have lunch together. Many observers read meaning into the fact that the lunches took place at Newhouse's choice spot, the Four Seasons, and not at Shawn's more discreet haunt, the Algonquin. Newhouse called Shawn "Bill" and Shawn called him "S. I." Shawn accorded Florio no such rights to familiarity. Florio tried early in his tenure to get on a first-name basis with Shawn. He said to the editor, "Why don't you call me Steve and I'll call you Bill." Shawn replied: "You were Mr. Florio to me yesterday, you are Mr. Florio to me today, and you will be Mr. Florio tomorrow." Later in the same session, Shawn bade the president, "Good day, Mr. Florio."

Florio has told acquaintances that Shawn objected when Florio complimented him on a particular story that ran in the magazine. Shawn said that if Florio assumed he had the right to single out a piece for praise, he would assume the same privilege when he *didn't* like something. So, said Shawn, he would just as soon Florio kept his comments to himself. Ken Bosee says that he often commended Shawn on stories well done, and that the editor never objected, but instead accepted the praise graciously.

With the Newhouse acquisition of *The New Yorker*, William Shawn's ability to influence business affairs was eradicated. Steve Florio says, "It's a new game here and our editors know that. I have certain freedoms George Green didn't have. Peter Fleischmann was indecisive. Mr. Shawn had the run of the place. Mr. Shawn oversaw and approved everything. If he didn't like an ad, the ad didn't run. That has changed dramatically."

If Florio knew that a particular ad would cause the editor distress, he showed it to him first. Early on, Florio accepted the ad for Calvin Klein's Obsession perfume that featured an indeterminate number of naked bodies, male and female, intertwined and squeezed into the photo frame. Florio showed Shawn the ad, not to obtain his approval—he knew he wouldn't get it—but instead to prepare him. Said Florio of the process: "I explain that the greatest insurance he has of freedom is a strong commercial base. The great danger is when you have a property that's struggling." Shawn was not appeased.

Not only did Florio accept ads that Shawn deemed too racy, but he also broke with a number of other *New Yorker* traditions, read: laws. He accepted horizontal half-page ads that broke up the magazine's long-standing graphic adherence to vertical columns only; he allowed the placement of insert cards which readers could tear out and send back to the direct-response advertiser (the first ran for L. L. Bean); and he made what seemed like a life's mission out of devising, selling, and running advertorials, the one-theme, many-page advertisements that masquerade as real copy.

Florio ran five advertorials in his first year and a half at *The New Yorker*. Many readers chuckled knowingly at a cartoon that ran in the fall of 1986. It showed a country road, with a farm-house on the left and a road sign on the right that read: "Special Advertising Section ½ Mile." The cartoon was humorous, but the editorial department, in fact, was not amused.

The editors and writers had begun ruminating since as early as the earliest acquisition rumor about how they would react if Newhouse started encroaching on their territory. When he actually took over, they began to "percolate," as one writer puts it. They could not feign indifference, but they agreed to hold themselves to an attitude that was resigned, as long as "S. I. stayed on his side of the weekly line," says a writer. A core group of writers and editors devised a specific list of what they would *not* tolerate. If Newhouse imposed any of those specifics on the magazine, they would quit *en masse*.

"It was a joke," says a writer. At the top of the list were half-page horizontal ads. If those ran, they would all walk out. Then along came half-page horizontal ads. The writers and editors met and reruminated. What would they do now? Okay, they would draw a *new* line. If Florio ran a gatefold cover, as the trade press was reporting he would, they'd quit. The front cover must be indented to allow for a gatefold, an ad which swings out from behind it. As such, then, editorial—namely, the cover art—is being abridged by an ad.

It took Florio a while longer to get to the gatefold, but eventually he did. The writers stayed.

"A lot of them have families," says an editor. "Where would they go?"

The *New Yorker* writers are not blind to the fact that their kind of journalism has disappeared from the world at large. There are no other outlets for 60,000-word stories.

The writers also found the advertorials an abomination, but Florio ran them fast and furiously. The writers decided they would leave when advertorials were inserted in the middle of a story.

Soon, Florio allowed an ad section on the America's Cup to cut a swath right through the middle of a story. He added insult to injury by allowing ever-longer ad sections to intrude. One forty-page section that ran in the fall of 1987 sliced an article in half. The reader was forced to wade through the forty pages to figure out where the story continued. There was no hint at the bottom of the editorial page. The writers stayed.

Editorial also objected to "Our Selection of Books," a section which looked like a book review section but actually featured publishers' and book retailers' paid ads. "Who is this 'Our'?" Shawn inquired, rhetorically, of one of his editors. But what could they do? They stayed, and once again revised their list. They would all quit the day most now viewed as inevitable, when Newhouse fired Shawn. That day, said a writer, "would be sad, sad, sad and *ugly*."

Florio frequently said that Newhouse brought him in to "save" *The New Yorker*. Florio was willing to rock the foundations to carry out his mission. His was not an evolutionary approach; he set out to remake the business completely. He spearheaded a $2 million direct-mail circulation drive, the first at *The New Yorker* since 1971. Invitations to subscribe were mailed to four million potential readers whose names were culled from "affluent" mailing lists purchased by the magazine. Florio did not alter a standing policy and allow readers to subscribe for a limited number of weeks—say, twelve—as *Time* magazine and others do, but some of the ads imparted a cost-conscious attitude. Ads for *The New Yorker* popped up in *Vogue*, *GQ*, *Vanity Fair*, and *House & Garden*. They carried a small cut-it-out order form carrying the slogan: "And it's all just 62 cents an issue!" Convincing people that they were getting a bargain had never been a priority at *The New Yorker*. Eventually Florio broke with tradition and actually began discounting the magazine to subscribers, as well as extending "bill me later"–type credits.

Florio also approached the magazine's advertising agency—

Lord, Geller, Federico & Einstein (later fired then rehired by Florio, and, unrelated to that, now split into two warring firms—but that's another story)—and told them to pull out all the stops, forget about money, forget anything anyone had ever told them about how to promote *The New Yorker*. They should just go ahead and plan their dream campaign. Four months and $2.5 million later, on September 26, 1985, the *New Yorker's* television advertising blitz was launched, not where anyone would expect to see it—say, following a "Live from Lincoln Center" broadcast—but during shows like "Miami Vice" and "Cagney and Lacey." This was the hip *new New Yorker*.

The ads presented video scenes from *New Yorker* stories. The first was an excerpt from Calvin Trillin's profile of Art Kirk, a Nebraska farmer who barricaded himself in his house and shot at—and was killed by—the police who had come to evict him following a foreclosure on his farm. The next one, on a more upbeat note, focused on the life and times of a North Carolina revenue agent on the prowl for bootleggers. It was based on a piece by Alec Wilkinson. Another ad illustrated a short story by Frederic Barthelme. Florio, in a conversation with this writer, described that one this way:

"A WASP guy comes from the Northeast, goes to L.A., becomes infatuated with a car. He drives around in a 1953 apple-red Mercury. He becomes infatuated with hot young Spanish women, a Hispanic girl walking down the street. Really *hot*."

When the ad appeared, according to Florio, people exclaimed to him, "I didn't know *that* was in *The New Yorker*." The trouble was, it wasn't, really. The promotions were original and eye-catching, lauded in the field, *noticed*. They were precedent-making because for the first time, the magazine touted individual stories, made them into "key" stories, to use a term Shawn might eschew. But did they really provide an accurate picture of what *The New Yorker was*, week after week? It seemed not. *The New Yorker* was advertising one magazine and delivering another.

Imagine a nineteen-year-old college student sprawled, on a Friday night, in front of "Miami Vice." Crockett's girlfriend has just died because she was carrying cocaine through Customs in a balloon in her stomach, Tubbs is being tortured in a chicken shack, and a woman murders her lover because fathers aren't supposed to do to their daughters the dirty things that he was doing to her. Fade and cut to an ad starring a "hot" Hispanic woman tripping mysteriously down a flight of stairs. "Yes, *The New Yorker*," runs the voice-over. So the college kid buys *The New Yorker* and what does he find? A hundred pages by Ved Mehta on childhood in an Indian village, a three-part series on the menace of asbestos, and a short story by Ann Beattie on life in suburbia. It is not what he expected. In the past, *New Yorker* executives had looked for what they called a "natural" circulation. In modern times, they did not believe, as Harold Ross had, that you were doing something wrong if too many people liked you. But they *did* want potential readers to seek out *The New Yorker* for the right and true reasons.

Competitors questioned whether Florio moved too fast in trying to remake *The New Yorker*. "You don't toss around a Ming vase," said George Green.

There was also a rising tide of opinion in publishing that Newhouse and Florio were minding the wrong store, that many of the business problems were brought on by the magazine's editorial deficiencies. If you gave readers a magazine they wanted to read, ran the argument, business success would follow. *New Yorker* critics trotted out all of the familiar charges: The stories were too long, the subject matter was dull, the cartoons weren't funny. After the Newhouse sale, though not related to it except in that it intensified interest in the magazine, the criticisms seemed to reach a crescendo. In both conversations and print, critics blasted *The New Yorker*.

They weren't just making the same old points, they said. *The*

New Yorker really *had* gone downhill. In late 1985, Richard Brookhiser, writing in the *National Review*, presented two pieces of *New Yorker* political reporting. Here is the first:

> [The candidate] wore a jacket, shirt, and tie, a pattern of statesmanlike conventionality on a night when everybody off the platform was coatless and tieless. The tie itself was a quiet pattern of ink blots against an olive and pearl background.... "We got a wonderful climate," he said, and paused to wipe the sweat from his face with a handkerchief soaked in Coca-Cola, which he poured from a bottle out of a bucket of ice handed to him by one of the lesser candidates on his ticket. The bugs soaring up at the edge of the lighted area and converging on the floodlights formed a haze as thick as a beaded curtain.

The second specimen was this:

> Little Rock, Arkansas. The chartered DC-9 in which we have been travelling—carrying 13 Mondale staff members as well as the candidate, 33 reporters, and 11 still photographers, members of television crews, and television producers—arrived here early this evening. Mondale also has Zell Miller, the Lieutenant Governor of Georgia, and Ned McWherter, the Speaker of the House of Tennessee, travelling with him, and he introduces them at his various stops.

Few readers could quibble with Brookhiser's assessment that the first example was far superior—*New Yorker* political writing at its best. Brookhiser remarked that "Facts on File" could have stated the second one better.

The first paragraph was written by A. J. Liebling, covering

the Louisiana gubernatorial race in 1960. The second was penned by Elizabeth Drew in 1985.

More than ever, *New Yorker* readers complained that the magazine seemed to be offering up research for the sake of research, and throwing it at them willy-nilly. It was as if writers took the attitude that they had to cram everything they had learned into a story, instead of carefully culling it for the reader. It was copy that cried out for a firm blue pencil.

An article that ran in three parts in May of 1986 was much discussed, not for the reasons that, say, "Silent Spring" was, but because it bombarded the reader with so many extraneous—and worse, uninteresting—facts that it seemed as if the magazine was parodying itself.

Susan Sheehan, a superb Pulitzer Prize–winning writer, reported on the army's attempts to identify the recently discovered remains of military personnel who died in a plane crash in New Guinea in 1944. What follows is a segment of the piece that discussed dental records:

Once again, he began with Robert Allred, whose dental record was complete and contradicted X-1's in many ways. Allred had one filling on No. 6, No. 8, and No. 9, and two fillings on No. 10, No. 12, and No. 15; these six teeth were virgins in the man on X-1. Alfred had one filling, an O-AM, in No. 14, whereas the man on X-1 had two, an OL-AM and an O-AM. Alfred's record also showed that he had had six teeth extracted—all four wisdom teeth and No. 7 and No. 13. Furue did not place much value on the discrepancy between Allred's No. 14 and X-1's No. 14: it was conceivable that the man on X-1 had had an OL-AM filling after Allred's last dental examination. Allred's teeth No. 6, No. 7, No. 8, No. 9, No. 10, No. 12, No. 13, and No. 15 could not, however, have been X-

1's. Teeth that have been filled can never again be virgins, and teeth that have been extracted do not reappear.
Furue's experience had taught him that except in the case
of wisdom teeth dentists were quite accurate in recording
extractions unless a tooth—say, No. 19—had decayed and
been pulled, No. 18 had drifted into the position of the
lost tooth, and a dentist had subsequently marked No. 18
as having been extracted instead of No. 19.

An interesting point was no doubt made there, but it was
hard to retrieve from under the mountain of verbiage. The
fault lay with the writer, but perhaps more with the editor—
William Shawn. Shawn approved every single word that ran in
The New Yorker.

Shawn, of course, could not be expected to agree that the
New Yorker stories were too long and wordy. He told the advertising staff, when he met with them in 1983, that he was against
the "general tendency" in magazines "to make everything short
and quick and tight." He said, "It's our feeling" (one assumes
that to be an editorial "our") "that every piece that we run is run
at its ideal length." He said that "ideal" could mean anything
from 5,000 words to 50,000 or more. He emphasized that the
stories didn't necessarily run at the length at which they were
written, but instead at the length "that something has to be in
order to deal with the subject adequately, intelligently, thoroughly," so that it has "real substance."

Shawn elaborated: "We don't want pieces to just *appear* to
be about something, we want really to cover the subject. We want
to offer the pieces at their best, and this is what we think is the
pieces at their best."

As for the dearth of humor, Shawn himself regretted it. An
advertising man asked the editor why there weren't more funny
stories in *The New Yorker.* Shawn said it was because no one was

writing them. The exception to the rule was Woody Allen, he said, whose short stories occasionally appeared in the magazine, and the mention of whose name could cause Shawn's face to glow. Shawn was sad that Allen did not have more time to devote to fiction. (Elaine Matteo once sat next to Shawn at a retirement party for a production worker. She found it difficult to talk to the editor until she hit upon a subject of mutual interest: Woody Allen. From there it was easy sailing.)

Through the early to the mid-1980s, dissent in Shawn's own department was mounting. Bitter feelings lingered in some editors as a result of the Jonathan Schell episode. Further, no one was convinced that Shawn had truly put to rest the idea of Schell as successor. Schell's "The Fate of the Earth," a horrific verbal portrait of the aftermath of nuclear war, had been published in 1982 in *The New Yorker* and then in book form. William Shawn seemed in awe of Fate. He said that it might "some day be looked back upon as a crucial event in the history of human thought." Others were less sure. Critics complained about its extreme verbosity, and took exception to an attitude they perceived on Schell's part that he was the first to discover that nuclear war was a drag. They called it pretentious and bullying. Yet the articles seemed to bring Schell and Shawn even closer together. Shawn visited with Schell every afternoon in his office. Colleagues said they began to walk and talk alike. Shawn once again assigned Schell some editing duties, and that was viewed by some as a prelude to another attempt to anoint the younger man.

More than one of Shawn's staff and a number of interested outsiders have likened his psychological hold on some writers to the case of the Reverend Jim Jones, who led his followers to mass fruit-punch suicide in the jungles of Guyana. The comparison is hyperbolic, but the point is this: One man served as leader—as doctor, lawyer, mother, brother. Shawn was an autocrat, a benevolent despot who was occasionally not so benevolent. The editors and writers had learned, at the last annual meeting, that Shawn had twice denied them the opportunity to receive grants of stock.

Even some who wouldn't have benefited felt cheated by what they saw as Shawn's stinginess. Says one bitter staff member: "Shawn kept [the writers and artists] deliberately poor. Shawn kept control by impoverishing" them. Many years earlier, writers at *The New Yorker* had talked about joining the Newspaper Guild. Shawn, who would have been the first to champion the rights of textile workers in the South to unionize, was initially against it, because he didn't want to upset the fragile mechanism of the magazine. Later, for the same reason, he supported it; he didn't want unrest to break the fragile mechanism. It was Milton Green who dissuaded the creative force. Brendan Gill in his book *Here at The New Yorker* wrote of the writers: "They preferred lodging their hopes in Ol' Massa to fighting for their freedom. They were being dealt with as if they were untaught and unteachable children, and they appeared to enjoy it." Only by the mid-eighties, some were enjoying it less.

Finally, writers were discouraged by the constant criticisms of the magazine, and a few even admitted to siding with critics. There had been fresh cause for embarrassment in June of 1984 when Alastair Reid, a *New Yorker* writer since 1951, admitted to routinely fabricating facts in his nonfiction pieces.

Also embarrassing was Renata Adler's 1986 dissection of the Westmoreland versus CBS and Sharon versus Time Inc. libel trials. Critics found serious fault with Adler's impenetrable prose and her presentation of "the facts," and considered the pieces' damning conclusions about CBS and *Time* flawed. Steve Florio says that the Renata Adler pieces caused writers to "begin talking in the halls again," but most of what they had to say was negative. William Shawn defended Adler and her pieces. Some of his editors considered his loyalty well intended but misguided.

Some critics' comments on *New Yorker* writers and books became scathing and even pointed and vicious. Raymond Sokolov, in a July 1986 piece in the *Wall Street Journal*, wrote: "At age 80, [Shawn] has become a laughingstock, devoting his once-distinguished, once-amusing magazine to n-part screeds on staple grains and vanished airplanes, indulging an old man's whim for young women writers of dubious (literary) virtue." The occasion for the attack was a review of *Slaves of New York*, a collection of short stories by Tama Janowitz, a young *New Yorker* fiction writer who drew her settings and characters from the downtown Manhattan clubs and art scene. Needless to say, the review was not favorable. Sokolov's remarks were prompted by anger he seemed to feel about the state of *The New Yorker:* "It is the only strong force for potential good left on our literary landscape. The rest is publicity or trend. But The New Yorker can still bring the general reader together with the serious writer, or could if it wanted. The worrisome thing is that the influence built up over decades is ebbing in the uncertain atmosphere of the Shawnian twilight."

Despite the external carping, all comments emanating from "upstairs" at Advance Publications about Shawn and the editorial efforts were positive. Both Newhouse and Florio publicly championed the product. Newhouse even singled Shawn out for praise in the fourth public address of his career.

In early 1986, the Magazine Publishers Association bestowed upon Newhouse its Henry Johnson Fisher Award, presented each year to a publisher or editor who has displayed outstanding career achievement. On January 15, at a gala black-tie dinner in a packed ballroom at the Waldorf-Astoria, Newhouse stood before his fellow publishers and reminisced about thirty-five years in publishing. "What comes to mind," he said, "are the friends and associates with whom I have shared the successes and failures that are the stuff of our lives."

Specific among those were "three journalists." The first and "most consequential" was his father, "a giant, a man of colossal intelligence, drive and achievement who built his business solidly on the basis of quality, integrity and professionalism." The second was Alexander Liberman, who was editorial director of all Condé Nast magazines, as well as a renowned sculptor. Newhouse said, "After all our years together, I haven't lost my awe of the man as I watch him work."

The third influential person was William Shawn, "a recent acquaintance."

Newhouse said: "When luck was with us last year and we were able to acquire *The New Yorker*, I became one of the few people with access to its very private and very formidable editor in chief, William Shawn. Around his shop Mr. Shawn is known as Mr. Shawn.

"He has been described as the least-known best-known man in America and I believe it. One of his writers, Harold Brodkey, calls him a combination of Napoleon and St. Francis of Assisi... and I believe that too.

"Meeting Mr. Shawn is an event one doesn't forget. Precise, eloquent, never wasting a word or a minute, this extraordinary man is what *The New Yorker* itself is all about."

21

Despite the turmoil in editorial, in the early days of the new administration, Newhouse and Florio devoted their attention to business. It was on the numbers that Florio would be judged.

A grade-school textbook on the magazine publishing business might describe the industry as a big machine—an airplane, perhaps—and explain that there are two engines that drive the motor: circulation and advertising. They are the two prime sources of revenue, separate but at times inextricable. The right kind of circulation brings in the right kinds of ads. At *The New Yorker*, once upon a time, the right kinds of ads even helped attract the right kind of reader.

Steve Florio set his tools to tinkering on both engines. Within six months of taking over, Florio got circulation up from 500,000, the level at which it had been hovering persistently for more than half a decade, to 540,000. In mid-1986 he predicted gains to the area of 575,000 by late that year. (It reached 550,000.) The "rate base," the circulation figure which magazines use to sell to advertisers, was raised by 9 percent to 525,000, the largest-ever hike in that figure. Florio called the increases "wonderful."

Skeptics wondered why, if the numbers were so wonderful, did Florio, in the late spring of 1986, fire the circulation director, Douglas Florenzie? "If numbers were so great," said a competitor, "why do you fire the guy who's responsible for them?" The obvious answer was that it was Florio who came up with all the innovative—by *New Yorker* standards—approaches to generating new circulation.

But competitors and advertisers alike examined the figure more closely. Who *were* these new readers? And how much did it cost to find them? Since *The New Yorker* now belonged to a private company, it was not required to spell out costs or report profits. Clearly, though, the circulation campaign, including the ads, the direct-mail advertising, and the late-night TV solicitations, came very dear. Add to the total costs those associated with Florio's new "bill-me-later" extensions of credit to subscribers.

More important than the circulation number was the renewal rate—the percentage of readers who resubscribed within six months of the expiration of their subscription. Racy ads and an aggressive direct-mail approach brought new readers in, but could the magazine's editorial product hold them? Traditionally, *The New Yorker* had a rate so lofty—around 75 to 80 percent—as to be the envy of nearly everyone else in publishing. (More than 30 percent of the renewals came from Christmas gift-givers. People tended to continue to give *The New Yorker* to the same friend or relative year after year.) Early results indicated that 75 percent of the people who were subscribers in June 1985 had resubscribed by June 1986. But the June 1985 readers had been in place well before Florio started his campaign. More meaningful were the June 1987 numbers. The rate fell to 72.7 percent. If the renewal rate has hit the skids, the magazine will have to continue to pour large sums of money into circulation efforts in order to bring in new readers to replace the ones who fell by the wayside.

By late 1986, there was wide speculation in publishing that

because the *New Yorker's* costs had soared so—one estimate put promotion and circulation spending at $3 million a year—the magazine was barely breaking even. Some guessed that it actually lost as much as $5 million in 1986—a contention that Florio vehemently denied.

Nor could *The New Yorker* look toward advertising to bolster its income. When Florio took office, he gave an interview to Stuart J. Elliott of *Advertising Age* in which he predicted that the *New Yorker* ad pages—which had declined about 3 percent in 1984, Bosee's year as president, to 3539—would bottom out at over 3100 in 1985. In 1986, he declared they would gain "hundreds of pages." Instead, they declined in 1985 to 2997 pages, and while it was the lowest yearly total since 1945, it didn't constitute a bottom. In 1986, pages went into a free-fall. Not only did they not add hundreds of new pages, they *lost* that many. The final figure for 1986 was 2683 pages, for a decline of 10.5 percent. As late as the summer of 1986, Florio had been estimating that ad pages for the full year would come in at 2900 to 3100, calling 2900 "our worst scenario." The final figure, then, was 200-plus pages worse than Florio's "worst." Revenues fell 12 percent to $46.3 million, despite a hike in the ad rates in the fall. Even in the crucial pre-Christmas selling season of 1986, the magazine was painfully thin. ("It broke my heart to see those issues," Elaine Matteo says.) Florio couldn't seem to stanch the bleeding.

S. I. Newhouse, in one of his rare appearances in print, admitted to an *Advertising Age* reporter that *The New Yorker* had "more complicated and interesting problems than I usually run into." As a result, he said, it was "the most interesting business situation I've ever had an opportunity to work with."

Newhouse said, "Advertising is slow"—*Ad Age* called that "a euphemism"—and added, "There's no reason for us to have expected an instantaneous communication of our confidence in the magazine, no reason why it suddenly should be shared by the advertising community. It will take the time it's going to take; it's certainly going to happen.... We have begun to solve the reader problem. We hope to solve the advertiser problem quite quickly, and know we will solve it eventually."

Florio had predicted an immediate rush of success in ads. When later asked by *Ad Age* to comment on that, he said, "I believed it. I believed it and I was wrong. I just could not resist stepping up to the plate and pointing to the bleachers." In a somewhat contradictory vein, Florio told this writer, a couple of months after that, "if you had told me a year and a half ago that we would see ads and circulation up to what they are now, I would have thought about that." Asked if he meant he didn't expect such gains he said, "Right."

The magazine trade is a talky one—it has a supersonic grapevine. Of particular fascination, as the *New Yorker* problems worsened, were Florio's escalating attacks on his predecessors. Instead of just attending to the business at hand, Florio, and even Newhouse, seemed to find satisfaction in telling everyone how bad it had been before. The attacks soon disintegrated into a dogfight-by-newsprint between Florio and George Green.

Florio told a couple of reporters that the former management's sales effort was so sluggish that they didn't even hold yearly sales meetings. Actually, they had held them since well before Florio was born. Florio announced to one interviewer that George Green told *Business Week* that in his ten years as president of *The New Yorker*, he had rarely read the magazine. Green didn't say it and *Business Week* hadn't printed it. S. I. Newhouse took off his gloves in *Ad Age* in June 1986 when he said, "The ad community reacted against" *The New Yorker* under previous management "because, I think, there was no sense of confidence in the product on the part of the people who were running *The New Yorker*."

Florio contends that he was on the receiving end of the first strike—that Green criticized him and the job he was doing to other publishers and advertisers. After Florio hit print with his attacks, Green started giving interviews in which he expressed doubts about the way *The New Yorker* was being run. He said that a magazine that was once special had become, under new management, "I'm sorry to say, just one of the crowd."

Nor did Florio view Green as the only enemy. His defensiveness seemed at times almost paranoid. He told a *Los Angeles Times* reporter, "A lot of people out there are waiting for me to fall on my butt. But I won't fail at this."

Luis Dominguez, the London-based head of *The New Yorker*'s European sales, left the magazine to join George Green at Hearst. Even after he had left, European advertisers frequently asked him what was happening at *The New Yorker*. He replied that he didn't really know, since he was no longer there. He did, though, send a couple of the questioners a copy of the June 1986 *Ad Age* article. (Steve Florio told this writer that the *Ad Age* stories were "pretty accurate.") Within weeks, the news had traveled across the Atlantic and a stinging letter from Florio arrived on Dominguez's desk. Florio wrote that he had heard Dominguez had been slandering him and demanded that it stop.

In the summer of 1986, George Green and Steve Florio encountered one another at the Radcliffe publishing course in Cambridge, where both men were scheduled to appear. Green strolled into a waiting room to find Florio and a *Newsweek* reporter. Green and Florio exchanged a cordial, but not friendly, greeting, and made small talk. After Green left the room, Florio suddenly flung himself into a chair, doubled over, and grabbed his head between his hands. He had been struck by a sudden and blinding migraine headache and couldn't go on. It may very well have been a coincidence. Migraines are notoriously random in their appearance.

Newhouse bought *The New Yorker* in a year, 1985, that was

a difficult one for all magazines. Such diverse titles as *Business Week*, *People*, and *Sports Illustrated* all lost ad pages. No one was sure why advertisers cut back, though all of the usual explanations were offered—fear of a stalling economy, more competition, a growing tendency by advertisers to direct their messages toward retailers, not consumers, and lack of new products in the market. *The New Yorker* was susceptible to all of those conditions. But nevertheless, *The New Yorker*'s 15 percent decline in pages in 1985 compared with minus 3 percent in the industry as a whole. Its decline of 10.5 percent in 1986 compared with minus 1.4 for the industry. *The New Yorker* seemed to have special problems. Some media buyers lauded the new, more aggressive selling approach of the *New Yorker* sales staff. Many of them remembered the old arrogant days of the sixties. But others perceived a change for the worse in the company they would be keeping if they advertised in *The New Yorker*. Leonard Lauder, president of Estée Lauder cosmetics, a previously and potentially important *New Yorker* advertiser, told people that he thought *The New Yorker* had tarnished its image by accepting the ads it ran. Lauder had strong opinions on what was proper and in keeping with the character of *The New Yorker*. He once asked Ken Bosee if *The New Yorker* intended to accept "scent strip" advertising. Bosee told him they had tried it once and met with such reader disapproval that they would not try again.

"Good," said Lauder. "I don't think you should. If you ever decide to, let me know because we will be the first to run one. But I don't think you should."

Some *New Yorker* advertisers complained that the tender care they had received at the hands of the advertising department was often lacking under the new regime. Steve Florio developed a reputation for not showing up at meetings he had promised to attend. When an advertiser expects the president of the company and the president stands him up, it's bad for business. Also bad for business were guarantees not honored. When the advertising department decided to prepare an advertorial on New York City, one of the first advertisers it rounded up was the Philip Morris Corporate Museum. It was also one of the last. The sales force had trouble selling the section, and when it appeared, in September 1986, it was an embarrassingly undernourished version of an advertorial. It probably should have been dropped. Not only wasn't it, but nobody at *The New Yorker* told Philip Morris that the section would not live up to promises and expectations. Joseph Corr of Corr and Till, Philip Morris's ad agency (and former publisher of *Vanity Fair*), calls the section "three pages of nothing" written by "a four-year-old." The advertorial did not offer the sort of "class" environment Philip Morris had sought for its museum.

In early 1987, a media planner for Chubb Insurance assembled an advertising package that included several magazines, but not *The New Yorker*. Newhouse personally called the head of Chubb and complained, saying, "You ought to use us. We use Chubb Insurance." The story circulated in the industry as a case of Advance heavy-handedness (A Chubb spokesman says Chubb did not find the call inappropriate.) Perhaps worse, it gave people the idea that *The New Yorker* was getting desperate.

22

On Monday, January 12, 1987, almost a year to the day after S. I. Newhouse gave a speech that hailed William Shawn as "what *The New Yorker* itself is all about," Shawn was fired. Newhouse himself executed the deed. Simultaneous with his announcement that Shawn would be leaving was the report that Shawn's successor would be Robert A. Gottlieb, fifty-five, the president of Alfred A. Knopf, a book publisher owned by Advance. Gottlieb had been a rumored choice as a replacement for Shawn since the day Newhouse bought *The New Yorker*. The dismissal was front-page news throughout the country and even the world.

During his by then nearly two-year-old term as owner, Newhouse had continued to insist that Shawn could stay on as long as he liked. As recently before the firing as September 1986, Steve Florio told this writer, "Shawn will be here as long as he wants to be." He also said, "absolutely his successor will come from within. The culture almost demands it." Newhouse made similar remarks in interviews. Florio and Newhouse may have believed their words when they uttered them. Perhaps the demands of commerce—namely, the magazine's sinking fortunes—caused Newhouse to change his mind.

The writers, editors, and artists at *The New Yorker* were catapulted into a fit of fury by the dismissal. It wasn't that they didn't agree it was time for Shawn to go. Some, as noted, had thought it was time twenty years earlier. They objected, instead, that Shawn was not allowed to choose his successor and that the new editor was an "outsider." They were equally upset at the manner in which Shawn was treated. Newhouse, says a writer, "displayed complete contempt for the rhythms of the magazine." The writers were worried, he adds, about "the kind of treatment that implies and portends for the future."

According to sources on the editorial staff, here is what happened.

In November 1986, William Shawn told S. I. Newhouse that he had at last chosen a man to succeed him, Charles "Chip" McGrath, the managing editor in charge of fiction. Shawn explained that McGrath would be moving from his twentieth-floor office to one near Shawn's on the nineteenth floor so that the two men could work closely together. By some accounts, Shawn did not put a date on his own departure. He wanted to stay around long enough to break the new editor in. Heaven knew how long that would be. But by other accounts, Shawn told Newhouse that he expected McGrath to assume most of his duties by March 1.

Newhouse may have doubted that the changeover would ever really occur, at least in Shawn's lifetime. Shawn had been crying wolf for decades. In any case, Newhouse is said by writers to have told Shawn that he was quite pleased with the news, and that McGrath was an acceptable choice to him. The selection of McGrath was greeted with almost unanimous enthusiasm among the staff, because he was well liked, and because the selection meant that "a long period of anguish for everyone," says an editor, had finally ended. However, not long after Shawn spoke to

Newhouse, S. I. had dinner with McGrath and, unknown to the staff, found him wanting.

In January 1987, McGrath did indeed begin to make the move to the lower floor, and some staff members believed that is what provoked Newhouse's precipitous action.

On Monday, January 12, Newhouse visited Shawn in his office and told him, according to staff sources, that he had changed his mind. He did not feel that McGrath was capable of assuming the editorship of *The New Yorker*. Newhouse himself later told the *New York Times*, "My job was to select a man who I think can carry on in the tradition of *The New Yorker* established by Ross and Shawn, two brilliant editors. If I had found that man within the magazine, that would have been great, but I didn't feel that man existed within the *New Yorker* family and I did not compromise."

Newhouse then presented Shawn with a prepared memo to be distributed that day under Newhouse's signature. It read, "Recently Mr. Shawn informed me that he will retire on March 1." It went on to laud the brilliance of Shawn, and to announce the appointment of Gottlieb. Newhouse also had prepared a letter to the *New Yorker* staff in which he said that Shawn was the foremost editor of "his time," but now comes the finest editor of "*our* time."

According to Newhouse, Shawn accepted the news calmly. Newhouse told a reporter that Shawn "said he was very flattered by what I said about him [in the memo], he said he was sorry I was not able to pick somebody from *The New Yorker*, and he felt it would have been better had I picked somebody from the inside." Newhouse added that the decision to retire was Shawn's: "He set the date. He brought up the question to me about eight weeks ago."

Shawn, of course, had broached the subject in a very different context, and he had not so much set a date for his own retirement as he had guessed that McGrath would be doing most of his work by March 1.

Sources close to Shawn say that in the meeting on the day the staff came to call "black Monday," Shawn tried to persuade Newhouse to change his mind. He urged him to talk to some of the other editors, to find out from them how unsettling to the magazine the imposition of an outsider would be. After all, in the merger agreement signed by Newhouse, these words had appeared: "Advance... agrees... that when a new editor-in-chief of The New Yorker is being considered, the final decision will be made by Advance, but it will consult with, and seek the advice and approval of, a group of staff members to be selected and to function in a manner then deemed to be appropriate by the senior editorial staff of The New Yorker." (That clause notwithstanding, it is ironic that Shawn wanted Newhouse to talk to others. The editor had refused, over the preceding years, when Ken Bosee, and George Green before him, suggested he seek the editors' opinions on the stock incentive program management wanted to implement for key editorial employees.)

Newhouse refused to consult other editors. He said that an insider would either try to run the magazine exactly as Shawn had, or push too hard to establish a new identity and put his own brand on the publication. Either would be unfortunate. Newhouse had made up his mind. His choice was Gottlieb.

Also, according to staff, Newhouse told Shawn that he was going to send his announcement to the *New York Times* that day. The writers called the Newhouse memo, in the words of one, "a piece of shit." They could not help but notice that it contained misspelled words and used "ridiculous language."

Later in the day, a bereaved William Shawn penned this letter to his staff:

Dear colleagues, dear friends:
My feelings at this perplexed moment are too strong for farewells. I will miss you terribly, but I can be grateful to

have had your companionship for part of my journey through the years. Whatever our individual roles at *The New Yorker*, whether on the 18th, 19th, or 20th floor, we have built something quite wonderful together. Love has been the controlling emotion, and love is the essential word. We have done our work with honesty and love. The New Yorker, as a reader once said, has been the gentlest of magazines. Perhaps it has also been the greatest, but that matters far less. What matters most is that you and I, working together, taking strength from the inspiration that our first editor, Harold Ross, gave us, have tried constantly to find and say what is true. I must speak of love once more. I love all of you, and will love you as long as I live.

    William Shawn

Above the typewritten signature he signed his name. The signature is small, clear, and modest.

It was a letter written with emotion and perhaps even calculated to inspire the same in others; it achieved that. Two points seem particularly noteworthy. First, all credit for building "something quite wonderful together" went to the eighteenth, nineteenth, and twentieth floors—the editorial floors—and none to business. Second, Shawn called *The New Yorker*, the "gentlest of magazines." In that, he was speaking more of Ross's *New Yorker* than his own. His *New Yorker* was often gentle, but, with its devotion to controversy and politics, it was often harsh as well.

The following day, all morning, writers, editors, and artists streamed into the offices, looking frayed, speaking angrily, crying. They traded rumors and facts, drifted about in unarranged, confused, milling patterns. Only William Shawn, among editors and writers, seemed capable that morning of pursuing business as usual. Tuesday was cartoon meeting day. Artist William Hamilton dropped by to see if Shawn could use a cartoon he had drawn. Shawn said he could, but objected to the fact that a hairdresser depicted in the drawing was holding his comb to his mouth. "Can you move it two inches away from his mouth?" Shawn wondered. The traumatic events had not blurred his sharp eye for detail.

In contrast to the chaos in editorial that morning, a couple of floors below, in the sixteenth-floor conference room, far calmer members of the business departments sat in orderly fashion at a 9:30 meeting and listened to Steve Florio describe the changes.

Florio was characteristically upbeat. He emphasized not the fact that Shawn had been fired—it was still being called a "retirement"—but the wonderful things that everyone could expect from Bob Gottlieb. He said, "Gottlieb is the equivalent in book publishing of what Shawn is in magazine publishing."

Florio joked that his life with Gottlieb was not going to be easy because the new editor had already informed him, "I'm not going to be working for you." When the two first met, a couple of weeks earlier, Gottlieb had made it clear to Florio, "You're not interviewing me." But Florio declared that there would no longer be an absolute wall between business and editorial, that they would coexist in greater, more flexible and giving harmony than in the past. Florio made a reference to advertisers' being told what was to run six to eight weeks in advance so that they could decide whether to buy ad space near a particular story. There is disagreement among Florio's listeners as to whether he said that was how it was *going* to be or that was how he *wished* it would be.

At two o'clock that afternoon, editorial workers assembled in a rally of sorts that writers describe as "spontaneous" in the bulge in the hall at the bottom of the stairs on the eighteenth floor.

The staff "invited" Shawn to address them. Editors are careful to mention that Shawn did not "instigate" the gathering. However, one writer who spoke to Shawn on the phone early that afternoon recalls that he said he was going to a meeting and that some sort of letter of protest would be written.

Shawn walked to his accustomed spot on the step and answered questions about what had happened. Most of his listeners were moved by what they heard.

"Shawn is the most extraordinarily precise speaker," says one of the writers who attended the rally. "He never lets the other shoe drop. He outlines a constellation of facts in the sky with such crystalline precision that he doesn't have to connect the dots. Everyone else does. He bent over backward to give Newhouse the benefit of the doubt."

A more distant observer, or maybe just more cynical, might add that Shawn was much too intelligent a man, and far too skilled with language, *not* to have been able to measure the probable effect of each and every one of his words, both spoken and unspoken.

The Boston Tea Party cannot have been planned with more revolutionary spirit than existed that day. (Perhaps a better analogy is the French Revolution, since the *New Yorker* rebels dubbed themselves the *"sans-culottes."*) But the throng at *The New Yorker* was no more cohesive in opinion than had been the motley crowd that assembled two hundred years earlier. "What shall we do?" was the pivotal question in the estimated crowd of 150 to 200 staffers, writers, and artists. They agreed on the question, but not on the answer. Most of the writers opposed the selection of Gottlieb, but some did not. Brendan Gill later said that Jesus Christ could have come into their midst and he would have been rejected because he was not an insider.

One writer, Renata Adler, called for reason. "Let's all calm down," someone recalls her saying. She went on to defend Gottlieb as a great editor. Gottlieb edited Adler's books at Knopf, as he did those of Janet Malcolm and Jonathan Schell. Others cast venomous glances in Adler's direction. They remembered Adler's libel stories, which some had considered not only impenetrable but also spurious. They recalled that through the storm of criticism that rained down, Shawn had consistently and arduously defended both Adler and the magazine. The rebels thought Adler was a turncoat.

According to one writer, another of Gottlieb's authors was as set against the choice as Adler was *for* it, arguing that Gottlieb was "absolutely the wrong person" for the job. Someone started circulating a story about how Knopf published one *New Yorker* writer's book with a last page missing. The author pointed out the omission to Gottlieb, who told him it was too late. Only after a long fight did Gottlieb agree to republish with the page intact. Or so went the story.

Word of the business meeting that morning had traveled up to editorial. Writers bitterly resented the fact that details about an editor were filtering to them from members of the business staff. They took it as a bad omen. It was reported to the writers that Florio had said that from now on there would be "one magazine" at *The New Yorker*, not two, meaning a closing of the gap between business and editorial. The writers hated that idea. They also heard that Florio said that under Gottlieb, there would be shorter articles, funny articles, funnier cartoons, and flashier covers. They heard that advertisers would be given six weeks' notice of everything scheduled to run so they could place ads against stories.

"Who's going to want to advertise against a story about torture in Brazil?" moaned one writer.

It was the redoubtable literary dowager Lillian Ross who came up with the idea of writing a letter. To whom? Newhouse? No, not him, it wouldn't help. Gottlieb? Yes. And send it first to whom? Gottlieb? Newhouse? The *New York Times?* Why not send one each to Gottlieb and Newhouse by messenger and then send a copy to the press tonight? But, oh dear, no, that wouldn't be polite. It was too "Newhouse" a thing to do. Maybe we should wait for a reply.

Seven members of the staff retreated to an office and set about composing the letter. They were fiction editor Roger Angell, writers Philip Hamburger, Janet Malcolm, Mark Singer, and Calvin Trillin, and Talk of the Town writers Lawrence Weschler and Bill McKibben. When they had finished penning their plea, they sent it through to copyediting. It was not shown to William Shawn. "It was probably the first piece of copy in thirty years that wasn't sent to Shawn," says one of the composers. The letter asked Gottlieb to refuse the post.

"Dear Mr. Gottlieb," it read. "At a spontaneous meeting this afternoon on one of the editorial floors of this magazine, there was a powerful and apparently unanimous expression of sadness and outrage over the manner in which a new editor has been imposed on us. . . . It is our strange and powerfully held conviction that only an editor who has been a longstanding member of the staff will have a reasonable chance of assuring our continuity, cohesion and independence."

The writers took pains to assure Gottlieb that there was nothing personal in what they were asking, but nevertheless, they urged him to "withdraw your acceptance of the post that has been offered to you." They signed the letter, "Sincerely and hopefully."

A small battalion of writers took to the phones to call their counterparts who were not there in person, asking them if they would agree to lend their names to the petition. The letter, when released, was considered noteworthy in its own right, but even more so because among the signers was J. D. Salinger. The Howard Hughes of letters had emerged from his warren—telephonically, anyway—long enough to give his assent. Some writers did not sign, among them Brendan Gill, Renata Adler, Pauline Kael, John Updike, and John Newhouse. Gill had been vocal about his dissatisfactions with editorial management. Adler was a champion of Gottlieb. John Newhouse feared that the letter would backfire, that it would only serve to make the staff look "foolish."

According to sources on the staff, editors and writers asked Shawn to call S. I. Newhouse and request a meeting with both Newhouse and Gottlieb to hand them the letter personally. Shawn placed the call and, according to sources close to him, was greeted by a livid Newhouse. Newhouse, they claim, said, "You will *not* meet with Gottlieb! You will meet with *me!*"

At seven o'clock that night, Shawn and Newhouse met at the Algonquin. (Newhouse did not insist on the high-profile Four Seasons for that encounter.) "How could you let this happen?" sources say Newhouse demanded of Shawn.

Shawn is said to have replied: "I've been telling you this would happen."

According to writers, Newhouse said, "Your job was to keep this from happening!"

William Shawn replied: "That is not my job. I am a servant of my staff."

Newhouse is said to have told Shawn that he had come to "save" *The New Yorker* and this was the thanks he got.

On Wednesday, Shawn and Gottlieb met for lunch, again at the Algonquin, and Gottlieb handed Shawn his written reply. He said that he was in sympathy with the writers' feelings, but that "I do intend to take up this job."

Gottlieb was scheduled to begin work March 1, but the date was pushed up to February 15. Some writers believe that the change in date was intended by Newhouse to be a "punishment" to Shawn. They claim, in fact, that Gottlieb and Newhouse engaged in a kind of "good cop/bad cop" routine. That Newhouse, furious with Shawn, threatened to force him to vacate the premises on Monday, January 19, one week from the day of his dismissal. They claim that Gottlieb entered as the voice of reason, saying, "Oh, no, S. I., let him stay until February 15." Perhaps Newhouse didn't have punishment in mind, but instead just getting it over with.

The debate that followed became, for weeks, an almost daily obsession in the press. As John Newhouse had predicted, the staff's reactions, and particularly the letter to Gottlieb, were denounced in the press. Other writers came forward to say that it was about time someone shook up *The New Yorker*. The most common description aimed at the protesters was that they were "crybabies." The *Washington Post* headlined one of its stories: "Shawn (Yawn) Gone: Unlike New Yorker Sentences, an Editor Can't Go On Forever."

The staff countered that outsiders could not understand the peculiar and precious culture at *The New Yorker*. William Shawn stayed until Friday, February 13, to help Gottlieb ease into his job and to help the staff in the transition. A dozen staffers pooled funds and took out a full-page ad in the entertainment trade paper *Variety* reading, "Thank You William Shawn." It went on to laud his "thirty-five wonderful years" as editor and to wish him all future success "with deepest affection."

Jonathan Schell quit almost immediately. In a press release, he deplored the "shameful, brutal, summary dismissal" of Shawn. Soon after, Bill McKibben quit. He and Schell planned to start a magazine together. Later on a fiction editor, Gwyneth Cravens, also left. But the vast majority of editors and writers stayed on to make their peace with Robert Gottlieb.

There was the Gottlieb garb to get used to. He rarely wore ties. He favored casual shirts, sweaters, and sneakers. He was frequently compared, in dress and appearance, to Woody Allen. There was the staff to become acquainted with. Accompanying Gottlieb were Martha Kaplan, who had been a Knopf editor for seventeen years; Adam Gopnick, an editor formerly of GQ, lately of Knopf; and Mary Maguire, Gottlieb's assistant at Knopf.

Gottlieb himself garnered mixed reviews. He was born on Manhattan's Upper East Side, graduated from Columbia University, and spent two years at Cambridge University. He started his career at Simon & Schuster in 1955, rising from editorial assistant that year to editor in chief ten years later. In his Simon & Schuster years, he worked with such notable *New Yorker* writers as S. J. Perelman, James Thurber, and Lillian Ross. One of his oft-cited accomplishments in publishing was inventing the title for Joseph Heller's *Catch-22*. Gottlieb moved to Knopf as editor in chief in 1968, and was named president in 1973. He is married to an actress, Maria Tucci, the daughter of Niccolo Tucci, a *New Yorker* writer in the 1950s. They have two children.

Two words frequently used to characterize Gottlieb are "arrogant" and "gifted." An editor recalls taking a seat at a dais she would share with Gottlieb and six other editors for a panel discussion. There were no nameplates in front of the seats, yet Gottlieb approached her and said, "I'm sorry, you're in my seat."

"What makes it your seat?" she asked him.

"It's in the middle," he replied.

Yet friends characterize Gottlieb as a warm, generous, and, obviously, intelligent person. In the great tradition of *The New Yorker*, he has quirks. His hobbies include working needlepoint and collecting ladies' plastic pocketbooks. He is also a fanatical fan of the ballet.

Robert Gottlieb declined to talk to me. He told an acquaintance who interceded on my behalf: "Please, *please* don't make me give another interview."

Gottlieb did not prove the horror that some envisioned. He made headway toward organizing the place. He went through Shawn's large inventory and put an end to all of the long-standing speculation about what would run and what would not. He honored financial agreements that Shawn had made. He began to evolve the payments system away from contracts and toward salaries. He still gave writers generous amounts of time and money to go to faraway places to report stories.

Under Gottlieb, there were hints of a return to Russian ideals. Covers got colorful and humorous again. Stories got *somewhat* shorter.

But the jury of his staff and readers is still out. Gottlieb was called upon to navigate the tricky pass between too much change (which might alienate loyal subscribers) and too little. At the time of his two-year anniversary as editor, in early 1989, Gottlieb's *New Yorker* seemed to be not much different from Shawn's. What changes were evident were not universally approved. In Gottlieb's tenure, the four-letter words Ross and Shawn so assiduously rejected, including ones Shawn deemed obscene, became commonplace in *The New Yorker*. Gottlieb's devotion to Kitsch exhibited itself in the pages of the magazine when he ran a piece by Jane and Michael Stern, who had written a book for him at Knopf on Elvis Presley, about a convention of Scottish terrier fanatics. He showed signs of letting ideology run more rampant through the pages than had Shawn and, needless to say, Ross, when he devoted the entire four pages of Talk of the Town to a piece by Renata Adler opposing the Supreme Court nomination of Robert H. Bork. And *still* there persisted that old complaint: despite some tightening, stories were *too long*.

Staffers gave Gottlieb credit for being approachable, and for being open to discussion on editing changes.

But the old business versus editorial conflicts are not likely to fade anytime soon. Throughout the whole of 1987 and 1988, and into 1989, *The New Yorker* continued to struggle for ads. It was hard *not* to come to the conclusion that despite all of their boasts that they had come to save the magazine, Florio and Newhouse really didn't have a clue how to do it.

The results give rise to inevitable questions and eventually the inevitable rumors. The questions: Can a magazine devoted to serious thought and sophisticated humor, with a high regard for the intellectual grasp of its readers, find its way in a publishing world increasingly devoted to short takes and celebrity gossip? Can it prove itself relevant? Strike a balance between editorial excellence and the pressures of commerce?

The rumors: that S. I. Newhouse had begun to cast about for replacements for both Robert Gottlieb and Stephen Florio.

One thing seems certain. S. I. Newhouse will not close *The New Yorker*. He doesn't have to. He has the luxury of time and money to try to reverse the rapid decline.

In 1925, *The New Yorker* was saved from almost certian extinction by the editorial brilliance of Harold Ross. S. I. Newhouse, businessman, has a similar challenge before him.

Epilogue

Peter Fleischmann has, since he left *The New Yorker*, continued to be plagued with health problems that have sent him on a number of occasions to the hospital. His recoveries continue to astound. Friends say he was anguished over Shawn's dismissal. He stays in contact with Elaine Matteo, Ken Bosee, Sam Spoto, and a few others. He did not speak to George Green for two years after Green quit *The New Yorker*, but the two have now made amends and occasionally have lunch together at the Sky Club.

George Green, well into his service at Hearst, continued to carry the familiar blue *New Yorker* duffel bag to the office each day. He seemed reluctant to give it up. Later, though, he switched to a satchel touting *Town & Country*. Late in 1986, he signed a new three-year contract with Hearst. Also in 1986, he married Wilma Jordan, a founder of the 13-30 Corp., which Steve Florio disliked so much.

Ken Bosee became a partner in a firm involved in renting and selling videotapes through vending machines. He later retired.

Elaine Matteo, following her dismissal from *The New Yorker*, spent two years traveling and thinking. She has begun to look for a new job. It won't be in publishing, she says.

Stephen Fleischmann was offered a job at Condé Nast by S. I. Newhouse. Newhouse, while demonstrably not opposed to nepotism, did not feel that Stephen should remain at *The New Yorker*. However, Stephen and executives at Condé Nast could not agree on a job for the young man, so he left the company altogether.

Another young family member, Jonathan Newhouse, left *The New Yorker* when he was reassigned within Condé Nast. He became publisher of *Details* magazine, and later was sent to London to head up European operations.

Philip Messinger, on New Year's Eve, 1986, was married, for the third time, to a stockbroker, Leticia Celenza. They divide their time between a co-op in Manhattan and a condominium in Palm Beach. (He frequently sees chauffeurs holding aloft a "Newhouse" sign in the Palm Beach airport.) Messinger has begun managing other people's money again. He has not spoken to Peter Fleischmann, Ken Bosee, or Elaine Matteo since the day he left the board. He occasionally has dinner with George Green, but he and Bill Reik fell out over a financial disagreement.

William Reik is still an investment manager at Paine Webber Mitchell Hutchins. Well after the *New Yorker* deal was done, he and his boss, Donald Marron, continued to hold roaring arguments behind closed doors. Unintentional eavesdroppers believe they argued on the subject of what fee Reik should get for bringing in the *New Yorker* deal. Eventually they came to terms and the shouting stopped. Reik still longs to own *The New Yorker*. He spends a fair amount of time wondering if he can get George Green back.

S. I. Newhouse works on, but occasionally takes a moment to engage in frivolity. A *New Yorker* free-lancer sat next to Newhouse at a dinner. Midway through the meal, Newhouse turned to him and said, "Do you think Mr. Shawn is getting it on with Lillian Ross?" Ironically, Newhouse himself has recently become the target of similar idle speculation. Rumors that he was having an affair with new *Vogue* editor Anna Wintour were so rife in publishing in the summer of 1988 that Wintour felt compelled to deny them in front of the *Vogue* staff.

William Shawn was distraught at his dismissal, and profoundly saddened at no longer being a part of *The New Yorker*. It was his life. Shawn, shortly after leaving *The New Yorker*, began to work as an editor for Farrar, Straus & Giroux, a publishing house noted for the high quality of its books. Among his authors there was Lillian Ross. *Publishers Weekly* asked FS&G's president, Roger W. Straus, if he expected Shawn to bring in other writers from *The New Yorker*. Straus replied, "I assume they won't be coming from *Screw*."

A *New Yorker* writer who spoke with Shawn said that the editor did not sound much like the man he once knew. He seemed, he said, diminished.

Index

351